FAULKNER'S PEOPLE, A COMPLETE
PS 3511 A86Z87

A04428641001

DATE DUE

NO 2'90		
FE 1991		

D0820595

faulkner's People

UNIVERSITY OF CALIFORNIA PRESS

Berkeley and Los Angeles, 1963

faulkner's people

A COMPLETE GUIDE AND INDEX

TO CHARACTERS IN THE FICTION

OF WILLIAM FAULKNER

BY ROBERT W. KIRK

with MARVIN KLOTZ

Riverside City College Library
Riverside, California

PS 3511 A86Z87
Kirk, Robert Warner.
Faulkner's people, a
complete guide and index to
characters in the fiction o
William Faulkner.

UNIVERSITY OF CALIFORNIA PRESS
BERKELEY AND LOS ANGELES

CAMBRIDGE UNIVERSITY PRESS
LONDON, ENGLAND

© 1963 BY THE REGENTS OF THE UNIVERSITY OF CALIFORNIA
LIBRARY OF CONGRESS CATALOG CARD NO.: 63–19476
PRINTED IN THE UNITED STATES OF AMERICA

To Bruce R. McElderry, Jr.

ISSETIBBEHA'S

TALLAHATCHIE RIVER

Fishing Camp where Wash Jones killed Sutpen, later bought and restored by Major Cassius de Spain

CHICKASAW

John Sartoris' Railroad

To Memphis Junction

McCallum's, where young Bayard Sartoris went when his grandfather's heart failed in the car wreck

GRANT

Sutpen's Hundred 12 mi.

Sartoris Plantation E. Gin. 4 mi.

PINE

Church which Thomas Sutpen rode fast to

Where old Bayard Sartoris died in young Bayard's car

John Sartoris' statue & Effigy where he can watch his railroad, and cemetery where they buried Addie Bundren at last

Reverend Hightower's, where Christmas was killed

Belle Mitchell's
Holston House
Benbow's
Jail where Goodwin was lynched

Miss Joanna Burden's, where Christmas killed Miss Burden, & where Lena Grove's child was born

Courthouse where Temple Drake testified, and Confederate Monument which Benjy had to pass on his LEFT side

Old Bayard Sartoris' bank, which Byron Snopes robbed, which Flem Snopes later became president of

Sawmill where Byron Bunch first saw Lena Grove

HILLS

Miss Rosa Coldfield's

Compson's, where they sold the pasture to the Golf Club so Quentin could go to Harvard

To Mottstown, where Jason Compson lost his niece's trail, and where Anse Bundren and his boys had to go in order to reach Jefferson

Suratt's

PINE

Armstid's

HILLS

Tull's

Varner's store, where Flem Snopes got his start

Bridge which washed away so Anse Bundren and his son's could not cross it with Addie's body

FRENCHMAN'S

YOKNAPATAWPHA

RIVER

BEND

Old Frenchman Place, which Flem Snopes unloaded on Henry Armstid and Suratt, and where Popeye killed Tommy

Bundren's

JEFFERSON, YOKNAPATAWPHA CO., Mississippi
Area, 2400 Square Miles ~ Population, Whites, 6298; Negroes, 9313
WILLIAM FAULKNER, Sole Owner & Proprietor

[Courtesy Random House, Inc. © 1951]

The map of Jefferson, Yoknapatawpha County, reproduced in the 1951 Modern Library edition of *Absalom, Absalom!*

INTRODUCTION

THE GUIDE includes approximately 1,200 named persons found in 19 novels and 94 short stories and sketches (21 of which, often in an extensively revised form, have been incorporated in the novels). About 175 of these persons are participants, or are mentioned, in more than one of Faulkner's fictional works. In addition to setting forth a brief description, chiefly as to function, of every named character in each story in which he (or she) is found, the Guide lists every page on which each character's name appears, whether the character is there taking part in the action or is merely referred to. All variations of the names, including nicknames, are listed, but no more than once to a page, regardless of how many versions of a given character's name appear on one page. For example, if Narcissa, Narcissa Benbow, Miss Benbow, Mrs. Bayard Sartoris, and Narcy all appear on, say, page 283 of *Sartoris,* one listing only is made for her on that particular page.

Personal titles alone are not listed even though their designation is clear. To qualify for inclusion in the Guide they must be accompanied by family names, given names, or some variation of one of these. For example, Colonel or Cunnel or Lawyer is excluded from the Guide; Colonel John or Lawyer Stevens is, of course, included. The same distinction applies to designations of family relationship: Uncle and Aunt are not listed. Uncle Maury and Aunt Jenny are. (In this connection it should be borne in mind that in general the entries have been arranged according to the customary rules of indexing: when two or more persons have the same surname, those with the least identification precede those with more complete identification; titles such as Aunt, Uncle, and Colonel are disregarded when the full name or initials are given; and names beginning with "Mc" are listed as if the prefix were spelled "Mac.")

There are six exceptions to this rule: the principal character in *Pylon* has no name other than that of "the Reporter"; hence he is so listed, under R. The same arrangement applies to "the Convict" in *The Old Man,* listed under C, as well as to "the Cajan" in the same story, and to "the Runner" in *A Fable,* listed under R. The fifth exception is Mrs.

Rosa Millard, of *The Unvanquished*, who is called Granny countless times. Only rarely do we get any part of her real name. She becomes Granny to the reader and she is therefore listed under this name as well as under her legal name. Finally, in *The Reivers* Lucius Priest, Sr. is most important as plain Grandfather; therefore, references to him by that name are also listed.

The listing also includes possessive forms of a personal name. "Horace's sister," for example, is listed under the name Horace. Listing of the possessive also extends to such a situation as the designation of a home or a store or a farm. In such instances it was necessary to take a peculiar liberty. If, for example, the author says, "It is near the Mac-Callum place" or "We were ten miles from MacCallum's," Virginius MacCallum, Sr., the nominal head of the family, qualifies for a listing; such a reference is not interpreted to include any of his six sons. Like-wise "Varner's" or "Varner's store" means, for our purpose, "Will Varner's," not "Jody Varner's," even though the son is just as active about the store and the farm as is his father.

Still another difficulty presents itself in relation to the identity of characters. Since in a single story there are often two persons with iden-tical names (in *Sartoris* there are three John Sartorises and four Bayard Sartorises), the casual reader may be confused, even baffled, in trying to decide which John or which Bayard is being referred to. Faulkner is of no immediate help here because he will not slow up his narrative to put the reader straight. Yet the necessary evidence is almost invariably near at hand; and the reader can usually work out the answer, even if doing so often requires considerable effort. Part of the purpose of this Guide is, of course, to solve these problems and set the puzzling names under the proper headings.

A much more difficult problem grows out of Faulkner's use of "his-torical" and "fictional" characters. Robert E. Lee, Jeb Stuart, Nathan Bedford Forrest, and a host of other historical characters, military and nonmilitary, appear from time to time in this Southern writer's pages. In certain instances they interact somewhat convincingly with fictional people. For example, the brother of Miss Jenny, Bayard Sartoris, is killed on a raiding party with Jeb Stuart. Miss Jenny, in her narration of this escapade, speaks of General Stuart with a personal affection, a tenderness: " 'Poor man,' she says, 'I danced a valse with him in Balti-more in '58,' and her voice was proud and still as banners in the dust" (*Sartoris*, p. 40). And Andrew Jackson is described in the history of the Compson family (see *The Sound and the Fury*, p. 3) in such a vivid way as to almost make it possible for him to leap over into the empire of Faulkner's incomparable fictional folk. In the historical interchapters of *Requiem for a Nun* many real and unreal people (both types largely nonmilitary here) interact. Mr. Vardaman, a famous Mississippi political figure, is mentioned in many of Faulkner's novels; and we may be sure that the youngest Bundren boy in *As I Lay Dying* has been named after this old lion-maned, picture-book Southern Congressman. But these people are allusions, not characters, and really come alive only through their impingement on Faulkner's creations; hence they are not listed in the Guide.

Still another group of characters may or may not be historical. These are the persons who are at least partly legendary. Notable among these are the Indians in such short stories as "A Justice" and "Red Leaves": Issetibbeha, Moketubbe, Ikkemotubbe, Mohataha, Herman Basket, Louis Berry. Real or unreal, however, these people are woven so completely into the Yoknapatawpha texture as to forfeit whatever historical identity they may have in favor of a greater role; and this list includes such white men as Chevalier Soeur-Blonde de Vitry, who is closely associated with the Indians. All of these people, therefore, are included in the Guide.

True, these distinctions are not scientific ones, and an occasional name that should not be listed may find its way into the Guide; but such names will be few and are relatively unimportant, for no actual historical character is of any real significance in Faulkner's stories. Faulkner uses his historical people mainly for atmosphere. The whole problem of whether these borderline characters are historical, semihistorical, or entirely fictional might well be the subject of a separate study.

One of the most persistent challenges to be met in preparing the Guide was that of tense. Few writers are more aware of the past, even as they write of the present, than is Faulkner. To preserve a firm sense of perspective we have endeavored to state in the past tense all action that occurred prior to the actual events set forth in the stories. The present tense is normally reserved for current actions only.

Faulkner's practice with regard to his "carryover" characters and incidents makes it clear that he allowed himself to be governed by present needs rather than by any slavish devotion to consistency. Many of his inconsistencies are extremely important, for they involve central shifts in the very nature of characters and relationships; notice, for in-

stance, the development from the merely gossipy country salesman
Suratt of *Sartoris* and *As I Lay Dying* to the wily Ratliff of *The Hamlet*
and the humane and philosophical Ratliff of *The Town* and *The Mansion*. Further, mark the switch in the presentation of Mink Snopes and
Jack Houston in *The Mansion* from the original version in *The Hamlet*.
In the earlier novel Mink is a vicious murderer, Houston a sympathetic,
tragic figure. In the later novel Mink commands our sympathy and
Houston is described as an acidulous and vindictive man. Even Flem
Snopes, the giant among the Snopeses, a monster of avarice in *The Hamlet*, is in *The Mansion* presented as a man who has at least a few appealing qualities. Lucas Beauchamp is in part a humorous character in *Go
Down, Moses*, but in *Intruder in the Dust*, written six years later, he
says in answer to an insult: "I ain't a Edmonds. I don't belong to these
new folks. I belongs to the old lot. I'm a McCaslin." In the later novel
Lucas is characterized with strong and quiet dignity. Eula Varner
Snopes, a voluptuous vegetable in *The Hamlet*, commits suicide by the
end of *The Town* to protect her daughter. Even some relatively minor
inconsistencies reveal that Faulkner, without much thought, one suspects, bowed to the aesthetic demands of the moment rather than to
the demands of consistency. For instance, in *Absalom, Absalom!* Sutpen's mansion, we are told, is constructed of brick. At the end, it is
of wood and highly inflammable. In "The Bear," from *Go Down,
Moses*, Ike McCaslin speaks about the peculiar responsibilities of land
ownership: "He [God; the Arbiter] saw the land already accursed even
as Ikkemotubbe and Ikkemotubbe's father, old Issetibbeha, and old
Issetibbeha's fathers too held it. . . ." Now, in all the other sections
of *Go Down, Moses* Ikkemotubbe is Issetibbeha's nephew, not his son
(though different relationships prevail in the early story "Red Leaves").
But the expediencies of the moment in "The Bear"—a passage speaking
of the heritage of fathers to their sons, of the passing of land through
the generations—required a father-and-son relationship, so Faulkner
complied with the requirements of aesthetics rather than the demands
of consistency. A more significant inconsistency involving the same
story emerges when one compares the account of Cass Edmonds' succession to the McCaslin land as related in "The Fire and the Hearth"
with the account in "The Bear." In the former story Cass has enough
of the blood of old Carothers McCaslin "to take the land from the true
heir simply because he wanted it and knew he could use it better and
was strong enough, ruthless enough. . . ." In part four of "The Bear"

Faulkner, responding to a more sophisticated notion of the responsibilities of land ownership, has Ike willingly relinquish, even force, his patrimony on his cousin Cass, who is reluctant to accept it. Again, in *Go Down, Moses* Sam Fathers' paternity is inconsistent with the account given in the early story "A Justice," in which he is the son of a no-account Indian named Crawfishford; in *Go Down, Moses* he is the son of the chieftain Ikkemotubbe and he carries himself with pride.

The most frequent inconsistency occurs in the attribution and spelling of names. Such inconsistencies doubtless reflect Faulkner's local prejudices or carelessness rather than any significant aesthetic decision. Most of the inconsistencies due to changed relationships are similarly without aesthetic relevance. A list of the inconsistencies in Faulkner's work is provided in the Appendix.

A short summary of the longer narratives might prove useful to those who need such basic information but lack the time or the desire to read or reread a given story. However, most of Faulkner's novels cannot be summarized briefly without losing a great deal of their meaning. The surest way to get at the core of a Faulkner story quickly is to read the accounts of the principal characters indicated in the Guide by **boldface type**.

We are indebted to Random House, Inc., the copyright owner, for permission to reproduce the map of Yoknapatawpha County from *Absalom, Absalom!* (Copyright © 1951) and to reprint in full Faulkner's own appendix to the Modern Library edition of *The Sound and the Fury* (Copyright © 1946).

The Guide as it now appears owes a debt to Mrs. Mason Altiery, whose unpublished Master's thesis (University of Hawaii, 1955) provided some useful hints on form and approach. To Professor Bruce R. McElderry, Jr., of the University of Southern California, who suggested the project, and whose advice helped immeasurably to make the work possible, special acknowledgment is due.

TO THE READER

THE GUIDE itself is constructed as follows: The novels are listed by title in order of their publication, and under each title all of the named characters who appear or are mentioned in that work are listed alphabetically, together with a notation of every page on which their names occur. In addition there appears after the name of each character a brief account of his actions that are significant to the story and, whenever it seems important, a short description of that character's salient personality features. As an aid to the reader, the name under which a character is listed in the Guide is often supplied within brackets when a nickname, maiden name, or other variant is used in the sketches. The major characters in each novel are indicated by boldface type. Immediately following the section devoted to the novels appear the named characters in all the short stories and sketches, which are also treated in order of publication. Carryover characters who are handled inconsistently by Faulkner are marked with an asterisk and treated further in the Appendix. Finally there appears an alphabetically arranged Master Index of all of Faulkner's named fictional characters which lists every work in which their names occur.

The editions of the novels used in this work were all copies of the first editions except for the four following Modern Library editions, all printed from the original plates: *Sanctuary, The Sound and the Fury* and *As I Lay Dying* (published together in one volume), and *Absalom, Absalom!*

One book of short stories, *Go Down, Moses,* was also printed in the Modern Library series from the original plates and was therefore used for the present work.

Some of the short stories presented a special problem inasmuch as many of them have been revised at least once since they were published. Since it would have been impractical to represent all versions in this work, we have confined ourselves to final revisions only. In this connection we have taken a special liberty with respect to the *Collected Stories of William Faulkner* and *New Orleans Sketches*. Since *Collected Stories* includes all of the final versions of the stories found in two earlier collections, *These Thirteen* and *Dr. Martino,* as well as seventeen stories that do not appear in these volumes, we have used it rather than the two earlier collections. Our decision here was based on considerations of convenience: the availability of the later collection and the greater number of final revisions under one cover. Except for those three short stories which are incorporated, extensively revised, in the novels of Faulkner ("Centaur in Brass," "Mule in the Yard" [both in *The Town*], and "Wash" [in *Absalom, Absalom!*]; these are treated as part of the novel in the Guide), only one story originally included in *Collected Stories* has a subsequent revision. This is "A Bear Hunt," which appears in its latest form in *Big Woods.* We have used *New Orleans Sketches,* likewise, for reasons of convenience. It is the only published volume that includes all sixteen of the sketches originally printed in the New Orleans *Times-Picayune* between February and September, 1925, plus the eleven short sketches under the title "New Orleans" which appeared in *Double Dealer,* VII (January–February 1925), 102–107 ("Frankie and Johnny" is the only one of the eleven short *Double Dealer* sketches which has named characters).

Specific bibliographical information concerning the editions used in preparing the Guide (together with other editions, American and British, with the same pagination) is given facing the beginning of the Novels section (page 2) and at the beginning of the Short Stories section (pp. 230–231). For a thorough descriptive bibliography of Faulkner's writings see James B. Meriwether, "William Faulkner: A Check List," *The Princeton University Library Chronicle,* XVIII, 3 (Spring 1957), 136–158, and James B. Meriwether, *The Literary Career of William Faulkner* (Princeton, N.J.: Princeton University Press, 1961).

CONTENTS

* See headnotes to pages 256 and 295 and the bibliographical details on pages 230–231.

The Novels

EDITIONS USED IN THE PREPARATION OF THE GUIDE

Soldier's Pay. New York: Boni and Liveright, 1926. *319 pp.*

Mosquitoes. New York: Boni and Liveright, 1927. *349 pp.*

Sartoris. New York: Harcourt, Brace, 1929. *380 pp.* The 1932 Chatto and Windus (London) edition and the same publisher's 1933 Centaur Library edition and 1954 "Uniform" edition have the same pagination.

The Sound and the Fury (with *As I Lay Dying*). With a new appendix as a foreword by the author. New York: Modern Library, 1946. *532 pp.* The Vintage Books paperback edition of *The Sound and the Fury* has the same pagination.

As I Lay Dying (with *The Sound and the Fury*). New York: Modern Library, 1946. *532 pp.*

Sanctuary. With an introduction by the author. New York: Modern Library, 1932. *380 pp.* The 1931 Cape and Smith (New York) edition has the same pagination.

Light in August. Norfolk, Conn.: New Directions (Modern Readers Series), 1947. *480 pp.* The 1932 Smith and Haas (New York) edition has the same pagination. The 1933 Chatto and Windus (London) edition and the same publisher's 1934 Phoenix Library edition and 1952 "Uniform" edition have the same pagination also.

Pylon. New York: Smith and Haas, 1935. *315 pp.*

Absalom, Absalom! Introduction by Harvey Breit. New York: Modern Library, 1951. *378 pp.* The 1936 Random House (New York) edition has the same pagination.

The Unvanquished. New York: Random House, 1938. *293 pp.*

The Wild Palms (with *The Old Man* in alternating chapters). New York: Random House, 1939. *339 pp.*

The Old Man. See *The Wild Palms.*

The Hamlet. New York: Random House, 1940. *421 pp.*

Intruder in the Dust. New York: Random House, 1948. *247 pp.* The 1949 Chatto and Windus (London) edition has the same pagination.

Knight's Gambit. New York: Random House, 1949. *246 pp.*

Requiem for a Nun. (A novel in the form of a three-act play.) New York: Random House, 1951. *286 pp.*

A Fable. New York: Random House, 1954. *437 pp.*

The Town. New York: Random House, 1957. *371 pp.* The Vintage Books paperback edition has the same pagination.

The Mansion. New York: Random House, 1959. *436 pp.*

The Reivers. New York: Random House, 1962. *305 pp.*

SOLDIERS' PAY (1926)

Baird, Dr. Eye specialist from Atlanta who examines Donald Mahon's eyes and, at Margaret Powers' [*see* Mahon] suggestion, humanely keeps from the rector the knowledge that Donald is going blind.
156

Bleyth, Captain. A (British) Royal Air Force pilot whom Cadet Lowe knew.
9

Burney, Mr. Man whose occupation is sawing boards and nailing them together again; he takes all of his ideas from his wife.
180

Burney, Mrs. His wife, who flaunts the mourning she wears for her dead soldier son, whom she knew to be worthless when alive, and who glories in being spoken to by important women of the town.
179, 181–185, 257, 258, 261–263

Burney, Dewey. Their son. Under indictment for stealing 50 pounds of sugar, he was released to join the army under Captain Green. Hysterical with fear when in combat, he killed Richard Powers, his lieutenant, and was later killed himself, a hero insofar as his home town ever knows.
181–183, 185, 262, 263

Coleman, Mrs. Friend of Mrs. Saunders.
233

Dough, James. Nephew of Mrs. Wardle. He lost a leg and had an arm maimed during two years' service with a French escadrille. He is a spectator at Mrs. Worthington's dance.
189–191, 193–195, 201

Ed. Policeman who attempts to arrest Gilligan and Lowe for being drunk and rowdy on the train.
21

Emmy. Young girl who left her drunken father to live at the home of Rector Mahon. She and young Donald Mahon became lovers before he went to war, and she is distressed when he returns so seriously wounded that he does not recognize her. Still loyal, however, she nurses him even after his marriage to Margaret Powers [Mahon]. She is relentlessly pursued by Jones and in a confused moment after Donald's death gives in to him.
65, 66, 68–71, 73–75, 78, 79, 90, 92, 93, 109, 110, 116, 120–129, 133, 134, 166, 167, 250–253, 263, 270–274, 282–284, 286, 287, 289–291, 296, 297, 300, 313, 315–317

Farr, Cecily Saunders. Daughter of Robert and Minnie Saunders. She is a weak and selfish, but attractive young girl, who loves male attention but cannot keep her engagement to Donald Mahon when she sees how badly wounded he is. Although she is adored by George Farr, whose mistress she has become, she continues to flirt with other men. At length she marries George, seemingly as a way out of her generally confused state.
66, 70, 73, 74, 80–83, 85–90, 92–99, 101, 111, 113–115, 117–119, 129, 130, 133, 135–141, 143–145, 148, 152, 168, 182, 190, 192, 193, 198, 200, 207, 208, 210, 214, 215, 217–219, 225, 230–233, 244–246, 249–251, 255–257, 259–268, 270, 271, 273, 275–277, 280, 281, 290, 306

Farr, George. Young man desperately in love with Cecily Saunders. He finally gets her to marry him after they have had an affair.
77, 84–86, 88, 89, 96, 132, 135, 138, 140, 142, 143, 145, 146–148, 152, 195, 211–218, 220, 225, 228, 230, 233, 235, 239–244, 261–263, 268–270, 281, 306

Gary, Doctor. Man mentioned as one of Cecily's [Farr] suitors. He is a dandified practitioner with offensive manners, who examines Donald Mahon.
99, 166, 167, 193, 198, 199, 200, 212, 285

Gilligan, Joe (Yaphank). An ex-enlisted man who meets Donald
Mahon on the train, escorts him home, and tends him until Mahon
dies. He falls in love with Margaret Powers [Mahon], but hope-
lessly, because he will not take her without marriage. She, believing a marriage would be unlucky for both of them, refuses his
proposal.

7–12, 14–35, 37–49, 51, 52, 55, 82, 103–110, 115, 123, 135,
136, 138, 149, 150, 152–154, 156–162, 163–172, 182–184, 187,
196–202, 205–208, 211, 246, 249–252, 254, 255, 263, 270, 271,
273, 278, 279, 282–292, 295, 301–308, 310–319

Green, Captain. Businessman who got his commission because he organized a Charleston Company; he was a friend of Madden, whom he
made a sergeant. Green was killed in World War I.

173, 177, 179, 185

Henderson, Mrs. Meddlesome old woman on the train, who insists that
Donald Mahon needs better attention than he is getting from
Gilligan and Lowe.

31

Henry. Negro porter on the train en route to Buffalo. At the request of
his train conductor, he tells the chief conductor to wire the Buffalo police to arrest Gilligan and Lowe on arrival.

15, 16

Jones, Januarius. Lately a fellow of Latin in a small college. He is a
fat, lecherous young man who brazenly pursues Cecily Saunders
[Farr] and, after losing her to George Farr, tirelessly chases Emmy.

56–60, 62–77, 79–85, 89–94, 133–138, 202–209, 217–221,
223–225, 228, 230–232, 239–244, 247–254, 257, 283, 284, 286–
291, 295, 297, 302, 304, 313–315

Lowe, Julian. A very young flying cadet, disappointed because the war
ended before he saw action. He falls in love with Margaret Powers
[Mahon], who mothers him. After they part he writes boyish love
letters to her which become increasingly impersonal.

7–20, 22–35, 37, 38, 45–55, 103, 104, 153, 187, 278, 280,
285, 315

Lufbery. An American mentioned by Lowe as having been with the French military until the U.S. entered the war.
33

Madden, Rufus. Sergeant in Green's company, who saw Dewey Burney shoot Richard Powers yet never mentions it.
173–177, 179, 181, 186, 191, 193, 194, 200–202, 205–211, 262

Mahon, Donald. The rector's son. Shot down in Flanders while a lieutenant in the RAF, he is dying from a head wound which leaves him helpless. He is unable to remember the past, and finally becomes blind. Some time after he returns to his father's home he is married to Margaret Powers, who cares for him until he dies shortly after he recalls to memory the events of the day he was wounded.
30, 33–35, 37, 38, 44–49, 55, 67, 68, 76, 77, 81, 84, 85, 87, 89, 94, 97, 99–101, 103, 107–110, 112–115, 117, 118, 120, 121, 123–127, 129, 130, 133, 135–139, 141, 149, 151–153, 156, 165–167, 169–172, 181–184, 187, 197, 198, 200–203, 206, 207, 219, 221, 228, 245, 255–257, 260, 262–266, 268, 270–274, 276, 278, 279, 282, 285, 286, 291, 292, 295–297, 301, 316

Mahon, Margaret Powers. A war widow whose marriage to Richard Powers consisted of a three-day honeymoon. After Powers went overseas she wrote him a letter explaining that their marriage was a result merely of wartime hysteria. Dying before he received the letter, Powers believed in her love until the last, and to her this in some way seemed to be infidelity on her part. This experience left her empty and incapable of loving anyone. At this juncture she meets the dying Mahon boy on the train and, seeing something to live for, she goes to the Mahon home with Donald and Gilligan, where she helps tend the invalid and finally marries him when Cecily Saunders [Farr] proves too selfish to do so. After Donald's death she is willing to be the object of Gilligan's love but refuses to marry him, believing that such a union would be unlucky for them both, since both her previous husbands had died.
34, 35, 38, 48, 49, 51, 52, 81–84, 94, 103, 105, 108–110, 114, 116, 117, 121–125, 127–129, 136, 137, 140, 150, 152, 153, 156,

162, 166–172, 181, 186, 187, 196–198, 201–203, 205–207, 209, 210, 244–247, 250, 251, 254, 255, 257, 258, 262–267, 271, 273–275, 277–279, 282, 284–289, 291, 295, 296, 301, 305, 306, 308

Mahon, Rector (Uncle Joe). Donald's father, a clergyman who thinks his only son has been killed in action. When Donald does come home gravely wounded but alive, the old man plans for the boy's future only to lose him to death, as it were, a second time.

65, 69–73, 75, 76, 78, 81–85, 87, 94, 121, 129, 136, 160, 168, 217, 252, 257, 258, 261, 263, 267, 268, 273, 275, 276, 278, 281, 301

Maurier, Harrison. Man from Atlanta mentioned as one of Cecily Saunders' [Farr] suitors.

99

Miller, Mrs. Dressmaker with whom Emmy lived and for whom she worked when she first left home.

128

Mitchell, Mrs. Charleston resident.

182

Nelson, Aunt Callie. Old Negro woman who formerly worked for the Mahons and helped raise the child Donald. When Donald returns she comes with Loosh Nelson to visit him.

170, 259

Nelson, Loosh. Aunt Callie's grandson, who worked for the Mahons before joining the army. Still wearing his private's uniform, he comes to visit Donald Mahon.

170, 171, 296

Powers, Richard (Dick). A lieutenant who went overseas three days after his marriage. He was killed by one of his own men, Dewey Burney, before he ever received his wife's letter telling him their marriage was a mistake.

36, 39, 44, 45, 162, 163, 176, 178, 179, 181–184, 210, 211, 262, 279

Price. Owner of a store from which Mrs. Worthington is seen driving.
   184

Rivers, Lee. Unpopular young man who has spent a year at Princeton,
   where he acquired the culture he exhibits at Mrs. Worthington's
   dance. An impeccable dresser and good dancer, he is persistent in
   his efforts to dance with Cecily Saunders [Farr].
   190–195, 203, 204, 208, 209

Saunders, Minnie. Wife of Robert, Sr. She browbeats her husband in
   an effort to make him tell Rector Mahon that Cecily Saunders
   [Farr] cannot marry Donald Mahon.
   *95, 96, 98, 99, 103, 113–116, 133, 139, 140, 181, 183, 218,
   219, 228–233, 255, 259–261, 263, 267*

Saunders, Robert (Bob). Son of Robert, Sr., and Minnie. A tactless,
   vindictive youth. He is morbidly curious about Donald Mahon's
   scarred face and brings his friends to see it. Because he thinks that
   Gilligan and Margaret Powers [Mahon] are spying on him when
   they see him swimming nude, he, in turn, spies on them. He sees
   them embrace and, as he overhears them talk of Donald, concludes
   that Margaret is trying to steal his sister's "feller." Seeing a chance
   for revenge, he loses no time in reporting to his sister all that he
   has seen and heard. After Donald's funeral, however, Bob seems a
   different boy as he weeps in the arms of the Saunders' Negro
   serving-woman.
   *95–97, 100–103, 120, 130, 142, 148–152, 159–161, 164, 165,
   168, 218–220, 230, 231, 295, 298*

Saunders, Robert, Sr. A weak man, much influenced by his wife. He
   wants to do the honorable thing, however, and acting on Margaret
   Powers' [Mahon] advice, he coerces his daughter Cecily [Farr]
   into keeping her engagement to Donald Mahon, for a time at least.
   *97–99, 103, 111–119, 133, 139, 140, 218, 219, 239, 252, 254–
   256, 267*

Schluss. Salesman of ladies' underwear. He is one of two men on the
   train whom the conductor asks to keep an eye on the drunken
   Gilligan and Lowe. Soon Schluss becomes quite intoxicated himself

by way of being agreeable to Gilligan and is mistakenly picked up
by Buffalo police who have been called to arrest Gilligan and Lowe.
16–20, 22

Tobe. Negro servant of the Saunders family.
97, 99, 100, 102, 133, 138, 238

Wardle, Mrs. Resident of Charleston.
181, 189, 192, 210

White, Hank. A name the "sodden" drunk on the train mutters in his
stupor. This may or may not be the name of the man who tries to
climb out of the train window after his suitcase, which Gilligan
has tossed out.
16, 18, 19

Willard. Owner of a small house and a good fruit orchard near the
home of Rector Mahon.
318

Worthington, Mrs. A wealthy widow who believes in women's rights
as long as she can dictate them. She takes Donald Mahon for automobile rides and, because he loves music, invites him to the big
dance she gives. She suffers from gout and a flouted will.
181–184, 187, 257, 282

Ayers, Major. Britisher who, believing all Americans are constipated, is trying to put a laxative on the market. He is a regular member of Fairchild's drinking group aboard the yacht and asks Jenny Steinbauer to go with him to Mandeville.

61–63, 66–69, 71–73, 79–82, 85–88, 92, 97–99, 114, 132, 155, 173, 208, 210, 217–220, 222–224, 245, 253, 258, 259, 261, 275, 277–279, 281, 282, 284, 285, 288–293, 303, 304

Broussard. Owner of a restaurant in New Orleans.

33, 38

Ed. Captain of Mrs. Maurier's yacht, the *Nausikaa.*

195

Fairchild, Dawson. Novelist who presides over most of the philosophical discussions on Mrs. Maurier's yacht and who is responsible for much of the chaos aboard it. Fairchild maliciously advises Mr. Talliaferro, who believes him to be an expert on love, to be forceful with women, a method with which he knows one such as Talliaferro will have little success.

27, 33–44, 49–52, 55, 57, 61–73, 79–81, 84–88, 92, 97–99, 103, 104, 110, 112–118, 120, 122, 123, 126, 127, 130–132, 136, 138, 151, 155, 181–186, 191–199, 201, 207–211, 217–222, 227–231, 234–242, 245–249, 250–257, 259–268, 274–277, 281, 283–285, 288–293, 301–305, 307–313, 317–323, 325–329, 331, 335, 336, 338–341, 348, 349

Faulkner. A shabby, dark man, who, by his own admission, is a professional liar. He once complimented Jenny Steinbauer on her digestion and told her that if the straps of her dress ever broke she would devastate the country.

145

Frost, Mark. A poet who produces "an occasional cerebral and obscure poem." Opposed to physical activity of any sort, he spends much of his time lying down smoking numberless cigarettes. After the yacht trip he calls on Miss Jameson and unknowingly disappoints her when he rushes from her home to catch his streetcar even while she is in her bedroom, "putting on something more comfortable."

    52, 54, 63, 70, 84, 91, 92, 93, 95, 102, 103, 132, 138, 151, 155, 182, 183, 185, 186, 189, 192–199, 209, 210, 217–220, 227, 228, 230–234, 237, 239, 241, 243, 246, 255, 256, 258–259, 262, 264, 275, 276, 313, 327, 329, 331–334

Ginotta. Father of Joe and Pete. He loves his old restaurant and fears the prosperity that comes with his son's new order of things. Not long after Joe modernizes the family restaurant, the old man dies at an advanced age.

    296, 297

Ginotta, Mrs. Wife of Ginotta. She is deaf and hardly talks at all. After her husband's death she putters around in the kitchen of the new restaurant preparing Italian dishes for her family.

    296, 297

Ginotta, Joe. Ginotta's oldest son, who persuades his father to modernize their old restaurant. He becomes the manager after his father's death and does well selling whisky illegally.

    296–298, 300, 301

Ginotta, Pete. Younger son of the Ginottas, who makes deliveries for his brother Joe. Patricia Robyn invites him and his sweetheart Jenny Steinbauer to go on the *Nausikaa.*

    55–61, 70, 73–75, 80, 81, 83, 94, 104, 105, 107–109, 129, 133, 134, 138, 141–148, 150, 151, 153, 155, 175–177, 192–195, 201, 236–239, 244, 253, 254, 274, 276, 277, 283–288, 294–296, 299–302

Gordon. A sculptor dedicated to his calling. Aloof, arrogant, honest, he has little time for those who play at art. He consents to come aboard the yacht because he is strangely drawn by the open, almost boyish, charm of Patricia Robyn. For a time Gordon is thought to have drowned; but he, believing Fairchild to have suffered this fate, is found searching for him. After the trip he makes a bust of Mrs. Maurier that "explains" her nature.

18–24, 26–30, 42–44, 47, 49–51, 55, 62, 69–72, 80, 82, 92–95, 97, 104, 132, 151–155, 183, 195, 196, 207, 211, 217, 222, 254, 255, 259, 265–268, 283–285, 313, 318, 321–323, 325, 327–329, 335–338

Hooper. A businessman who preaches God and the peppy, planned life. While lunching with Fairchild to see the bohemian side of life, he is disappointed to learn that Talliaferro is not a Rotarian. Rushing away, ostensibly to catch a train, he takes a taxi to a hotel three blocks away, where he dozes for an hour over the next day's newspapers.

34, 38, 40

Jackson, Al. A character in one of Fairchild's wild tales, who began as a fisherd with his father and now has the largest fish ranch in the world. He wears congress boots even while bathing because he has webbed feet.

66, 86–88, 276

Jackson, Claude. Al's brother. He turns into a half-shark while herding his father's fish-sheep. Later he chases blonde women swimmers at bathing beaches along the Gulf Coast.

87, 279–281

Jackson, "Old man." Father of Al and Claude and descendant of Andrew Jackson. According to Fairchild, the old man becomes a fish rancher when the sheep on his swampy ranch gradually turn into fish. It is old man Jackson who gives his son Al a start toward becoming a fisherd.

277–280

Jameson, Dorothy. A painter of portraits who prefers still life. Though she has taken a lover in Greenwich Village, she is still a virgin. She tries hard to get a man, even to the point of being overly considerate of men, but they always manage to elude her.

27, 55, 60, 62, 63, 69, 70, 84, 91, 95, 96, 101, 102, 105, 108, 110, 111, 132–134, 141, 151, 153, 155, 169, 181, 182, 185, 186, 216, 237, 259, 260, 275, 284, 286, 331–333

Kauffman, Julius. Brother of Eva Wiseman. The "Semitic man," he stands outside the circle of artists and "pokes sense" at them. He is the constant companion of the erratic Fairchild, whom he usually bests in their nearly endless discussions on practically all subjects.

44, 49–51, 62, 63, 65–69, 71, 86, 110, 114, 132, 154, 155, 184, 195, 198, 199, 220, 228, 237, 241, 248, 254, 275, 276, 281, 283, 289, 290, 293, 322, 331

Kauffman, Julius. Grandfather of the younger Julius. He helped Maurier make a fortune on questionable land deals during the Civil War.

324, 327

Maurier. Onetime overseer, who amassed a fortune during the Civil War, and because of his wealth, won an unwilling Patricia from the boy she loved. Maurier is by now long dead.

323–326

Maurier, Mrs. Patricia. Wealthy widow, owner of the *Nausikaa,* a would-be dilettante never quite aware of what is happening around her. She finally reveals the secret of her tragic life: she had given up the boy she loved in her youth in order to marry the rich Maurier.

12, 16–18, 20–31, 45, 50, 54–66, 68–72, 79, 83–88, 91–95, 104, 109, 110, 122, 132–134, 138, 151, 152, 154–156, 163, 181

Reichmann. Businessman whose financial backing Major Ayers hopes to secure so that he may put his laxative on the American market.

304

Robyn, Henry (Hank). Father of Patricia and Theodore.

124, 125, 191, 256–258, 288

Robyn, Patricia. Mrs. Maurier's niece, attractive, honest, but surprisingly unsophisticated. While the yacht is aground she secretly sets out for Mandeville with the ship's steward. Exhausted and much the worse for wear after having been lost for a time, they finally return to the *Nausikaa* in a hired launch.

16, 17, 21, 28, 29, 56, 58, 59, 69, 81, 97, 103, 137, 203, 216, 217, 256, 257, 276, 313, 314

Robyn, Theodore (Josh; Gus). Patricia's twin, who secretly takes a part of the ship's machinery to make a tobacco pipe, thus causing the steering gear to break down and the yacht to go aground.

46, 57, 60, 61, 77, 94, 110, 111, 125, 136, 143, 150, 157, 212, 217, 251, 255, 256, 313, 315–317

Roy. Thelma's gentleman friend.
144–147

Steinbauer, Genevieve (Jenny). Blonde whom Patricia Robyn invites aboard the *Nausikaa*. Jenny, though untidy and apparently brainless, has physical attractions which prove devastating to the males, and seemingly to some of the females, on Mrs. Maurier's yacht.

56–61, 66, 69, 73–75, 79–81, 83, 86, 87, 94, 104, 108, 126–130, 132, 133, 136–145, 147–151, 153, 168, 175–178, 188–190, 193–204, 207, 218, 222–227, 232, 237–239, 243, 244, 249, 251, 255, 271, 281–284, 287, 288, 290, 294, 295, 344

Talliaferro, Ernest. Man who has changed his name from "Tarver." A sort of aide to Mrs. Maurier, he is the butt of much humor. Carefully brought up to ignore all natural impulses, he is, at thirty-eight, quite ignorant on the subject of women; consequently, he seeks the advice of Fairchild, who has much fun at his expense.

9–44 (as Tarver, pp. 31, 33), 55, 57, 60–66, 69–72, 78, 79–81, 83–89, 91, 93, 95–99, 104, 111–113, 126–132, 141, 143, 144, 151, 152, 178, 184, 188–190, 193–201, 207, 208, 217, 218, 225, 232, 237–239, 249, 258–260, 266, 269, 283–285, 288–290, 292, 305–313, 341–346

Thelma. A friend whom Jenny Steinbauer mentions to Patricia Robyn.
144–147

Walter. Mrs. Maurier's Negro servant, a quiet but efficient worker.
46, 58

Walter. One of the crew of the tugboat that pulls the grounded *Nausikaa* into deep water.
262, 264, 265

West, David. Young steward on the *Nausikaa,* who loves Patricia Robyn with a doglike devotion and runs away with her toward Mandeville on an adventure that fails. When they return he quits his job and disappears.
122, 124–126, 135, 156–159, 161, 165, 166, 170–172, 174, 177–181, 187, 188, 190, 191, 201, 202, 205, 211–216, 235, 236

Wiseman, Mrs. Eva Kauffman. Sister of the younger Julius Kauffman. She has published a book of poetry entitled *Satyricon in Starlight,* which Major Ayers calls "the syphilis book." Having left her husband, she is without escort aboard the yacht and is well liked by most of the men: they cannot but admire her good sense.
27, 44, 55, 57, 60–62, 64–67, 69, 70, 84–88, 91–97, 103, 109, 110, 132, 138, 151–156, 169, 178, 181–185, 193–203, 217, 220, 225–227, 237–239, 241, 245–251, 254, 255, 260, 264, 268, 269, 274–276, 284

SARTORIS (1929)

(See the genealogical chart of the Sartoris family on page 318.)

Abe. Negro who works for the elder Dr. Peabody. He shot the dog that young "Loosh" Peabody operated on.
293, 378

Alford, Dr. Serious young physician interested in Narcissa Sartoris. He treats old Bayard Sartoris' wen and takes him to a specialist in Memphis.
94, 95, 99–101, 153, 180, 215, 216, 229, 238–241, 262

Beard, Mrs. Will's wife and Virgil's mother.
106

Beard, Virgil. Son of Will. He is the boy who writes Byron Snopes's letters to Narcissa. He is apparently simple-minded in most matters, but he is shrewd in collecting his fee, an air gun, from Byron. (*See* Butler, Joe.)
106, 107, 112, 228, 229, 264

Beard, Will C. Virgil's father. He owns a grist mill in Jefferson.
107, 168, 228

Benbow, Belle Mitchell. Woman who, according to Narcissa Benbow Sartoris, has a "backstairs" nature. She has an affair with Horace Benbow while still married to Harry Mitchell, whom she later divorces to marry Horace.
29, 30, 176, 178, 180, 182–197, 256, 257, 259, 262, 353, 370

Benbow, "Little" Belle Mitchell. Daughter of Harry and Belle. She is often made to feel unwanted by her mother.
190, 195–197, 353

Benbow, Francis. Probably grandfather of Horace and Narcissa [Sartoris]. In '71 he brought a lantana from Barbados and planted it on the front lawn of the Benbow home.
169, 170

* **Benbow, Horace (Horry).** Sensitive brother of Narcissa [Sartoris], and a lawyer in the family tradition. After duty overseas as an officer in the YMCA, he returns still infatuated with Belle Mitchell, a married woman. After Belle's divorce, Horace marries her, although Narcissa disapproves of the match. The newly married couple, with Belle's daughter, then move to a nearby town.
3, 32, 53, 54, 70, 72, 73, 153, 154, 161–165, 167–171, 173–199, 201, 202, 217, 254–259, 262, 290, 292, 294, 299–303, 351, 353, 358, 378

Benbow, Julia. Will's genteel wife, mother of Narcissa [Sartoris] and Horace. She died when Narcissa was seven.
174, 179

Benbow, Will. Father of Narcissa [Sartoris] and Horace. He died shortly after Horace's return from Oxford University, where Horace had been studying law.
170, 174, 179, 180

Bird, Uncle. Negro member of deputation calling on Simon Strother about the church money, for which Simon, as treasurer, is responsible.
270

Brandt, Dr. Specialist in Memphis to whom old Bayard Sartoris is taken.
240

Buck. Marshal in Jefferson. To please Miss Jenny [Du Pre] he takes young Bayard Sartoris into custody on the night of the serenade because Bayard has that day been injured in a fall while riding a wild stallion. While under "arrest," Bayard sleeps in Buck's bed.
158–160

Butler, Joe. Fictitious addressee's name used by Byron Snopes on the letter that he has Virgil Beard write for him to send to Narcissa

Benbow Sartoris. Byron thus prevents Virgil from knowing for whom the letter is intended.
109

Comyn. A man referred to by Monaghan in recalling experiences of World War I. Comyn was "a big Irish devil" who, with Monaghan and other servicemen, figured in a café brawl in Paris.
362

Deacon. Proprietor of a grocery-café in Jefferson. He likes to drink with Bayard Sartoris and Rafe MacCallum because they have good whisky.
125, 128, 145

* Du Pre, Virginia (Jenny; Aunt Jenny; Miss Jenny). Sister of Colonel John Sartoris. She is in charge of her nephew Bayard's household. She is one of Faulkner's indomitable Southern women. Two years a wife and seven years a widow at thirty, she lives to see all of her beloved Sartoris men die by violence, yet remains unbroken.
7, 8, 10, 11, 17, 18, 20, 24, 25, 28–34, 36–41, 44–46, 48–61, 64, 66–73, 75–78, 81, 83–85, 87–89, 93–101, 103–105, 113, 114, 123, 135, 140, 144, 152, 155, 159, 167, 168, 199, 200, 201, 202, 204, 205, 212, 213, 216–218, 222, 229–231, 236, 238–243, 247, 248, 256, 259–262, 270–273, 275–277, 281, 288, 290–295, 297–299, 349, 354–359, 364, 366–373, 376–380

Elnora or *Elnore.* Mulatto servant in the home of old Bayard Sartoris. She is the daughter of Simon Strother.
8, 19, 24, 38, 39, 41, 42, 61–64, 81, 82, 113, 215, 229, 236–238, 246, 248, 371–373, 380

Eunice. The Benbow's cook.
299, 300

Falls, Will. An old man of ninety-three. He walks into Jefferson from his home at the county poor farm to visit his friend, old Bayard Sartoris, whose wen he treats with a homemade remedy. He spends much of his time recounting the exploits of Colonel John Sartoris.

*1, 2, 20, 22, 79–81, 83, 91, 100, 101, 103, 104, 218–224, 226–
229, 234–237, 241, 291, 378*

Frankie. Young girl, who, as a guest at Belle Mitchell's [Benbow],
plays tennis with Horace Benbow.
183, 185, 186, 189, 190, 192

Graham, Eustace. The lawyer in Deacon's Café who introduces young
Bayard Sartoris to Mr. Gratton. He is a cripple.
129

Gratton. Man introduced to young Bayard Sartoris in Deacon's Café
as one who had been on the British front. Bayard ignores the
introduction and nearly precipitates a fight.
128

Harris, Meloney. Young mulatto woman who leaves the employ of
Belle Mitchell [Benbow] to set up a beauty parlor. It is in her
cabin that old Simon Strother is found with his head crushed.
27, 183, 184, 370

Henry, Uncle. Negro, probably, behind whose house young Bayard
Sartoris' 'possum hunt begins. One of Uncle Henry's dogs is used
in the hunt.
282, 283, 285

Houston. Negro waiter in Deacon's Café.
123, 124, 126

Hub. Youth who supplies Suratt and young Bayard Sartoris with
homemade liquor after Bayard's accident with the horse. Later he
goes serenading with Bayard's party.
138–140, 142, 143, 145–149, 157–159

Isom. Son of Elnora and grandson of Simon Strother. He does odd jobs
about the Sartoris place
*8, 35, 50–52, 56–59, 61–66, 77, 78, 81, 82, 84, 87, 88, 112,
113, 115, 199, 200, 218, 236–238, 244, 247, 277, 281–285, 287–
289, 296, 358, 371–374, 376*

* *Joby*. Possibly Simon Strother's paternal grandfather. *See* Strother, Joby.

Joe. Tennis player at Mitchell's.
190

John Henry. Negro youth who sees young Bayard Sartoris unconscious in his wrecked car as it sits in the creek. John Henry, with the aid of his cautious father, lifts Bayard out of the wreck and drives him into town in a farm wagon.
207–211

Jones (Doctor). Puttering old Negro janitor at the Sartoris Bank.
219

Louvinia. Probably Joby's wife. *See* Strother, Louvinia.

MacCallum, Henry. Second son of Virginius, Sr. He makes the whisky and superintends the kitchen.
123, 124, 309–314, 316–318, 325, 329–332, 337, 338

MacCallum, Jackson. Oldest son of Virginius.
315, 325–332, 334–336

MacCallum, Lee. Introspective son who sings at Sunday church services and who loves to go for lonely walks in the woods.
311, 312, 325, 330, 333, 334, 336

MacCallum, Raphael Semmes (Rafe). Twin of Stuart. Rafe loves horses. It is he who gets drunk with young Bayard Sartoris on the day the stallion throws Bayard.
121–135, 309–315, 317, 318, 320, 325–330, 333–336, 339

MacCallum, Stuart. Rafe's twin, a good farmer and trader.
315, 318, 325, 332, 334, 336

MacCallum, Virginius, Jr. (Buddy). Youngest son of Virginius, Sr., by a second marriage. He shamed his father by joining the "Yankee" army in World War I.

124, 308, 309, 313, 314, 316–322, 324–326, 329, 330–335, 337, 338

* *MacCallum, Virginius, Sr.* Strong-willed old farmer. A widower, he lives a few miles outside of Jefferson with his six grown sons. For a short time after old Bayard Sartoris' death, the MacCallums, unaware of the tragedy, are hosts to young Bayard Sartoris.
214, 309–312, 317, 326, 328, 329, 332, 333, 336, 337, 339, 346

Mandy. Negro cook of the MacCallums.
310, 313–316, 325, 326, 332, 337

Marders, Mrs. Frequent visitor at the home of Belle Mitchell [Benbow]. She understands Belle's nature and often comments knowingly on her hostess's activities.
183–190, 192, 197, 202

Mitch. Jefferson freight agent. He goes serenading with young Bayard Sartoris and Hub and the Negro musicians.
145, 146, 148, 149, 157–159

Mitchell, Harry. Good-natured man of some means. Though he is likable, he is ugly and somewhat dull; and his wife Belle [Benbow] holds him in contempt. After she divorces Harry, young Bayard Sartoris sees him in a Chicago tavern drinking with a woman who is trying to steal his stickpin.
29, 30, 180, 183, 185–197, 202, 256, 257, 353, 363, 364

Monaghan. Aviator who was with young Bayard Sartoris in World War I. They meet again in Chicago.
362

Moore, Brother. Member of the delegation of Negroes who call on Simon Strother to get an accounting of the money for the church fund with which Simon has been entrusted.
272, 273, 275

Myrtle. Receptionist for Dr. Alford.
94

Peabody, Dr. Lucius (young Loosh). Son of old Dr. Peabody. A skillful surgeon, he now lives in New York but often visits his father in Jefferson.
376–378

* *Peabody, Dr. Lucius Quintus (Loosh)*. Old friend of the Sartoris family (he had been regimental surgeon with Colonel John Sartoris). Humorous and wise, he sees through petty conventions. He is eighty-seven years old and weighs 310 pounds.
97–105, 123, 135, 138, 140, 144, 152, 215, 220, 229, 241, 290–296, 367–370, 376–378

Plöeckner. German aviator, one of Richthofen's best pupils. He shot Johnny Sartoris down in World War I.
46

Rachel. The Mitchell's Negro cook. Believing Belle Mitchell [Benbow] to be ruthless and selfish, she sympathizes with Harry Mitchell.
27, 28, 187, 189, 191, 193, 195, 196

* *Redlaw*. One-time partner of Colonel John Sartoris in building a railroad. Later he killed the Colonel.
23, 376

Reno. Negro clarinetist who goes on young Bayard Sartoris' serenading party.
149, 158

Res. Cashier in old Bayard Sartoris' bank.
227, 264

Richard (Dick). One of the Negro boys at MacCallum's.
315–317

Richthofen. German aviator, instructor of Plöeckner.
46

Rogers. Café owner in Jefferson.
158

Samson. Farmer who lives near the MacCallums. His bridge is mentioned.

125

Sartoris, Bayard. Infant son of young Bayard and Caroline, his first wife. Caroline named the baby "nine months before it was born and told everybody about it." The mother and the son died when Bayard was still a flyer in World War I.

55

Sartoris, Bayard. Foolhardy brother of Colonel John. He was killed in the Civil War while on a raid with Jeb Stuart. Aunt Jenny [Du Pre] proudly says of him that he raised the devil like a gentleman.

9, 10, 13, 16–18, 47, 230

Sartoris, Bayard (old). Banker son of Colonel John and nominal head of a large household, the management of which, even to the superintending of his personal life, he blusteringly surrenders to Miss Jenny [Du Pre], his aunt. His attempt to preserve tradition is symbolized by the carriage in which he is driven, each working day, to his office at the bank. But he loses his struggle with change and modernity, since he dies of heart failure in his grandson's auto, a victim of his grandson's reckless driving which old Bayard had hoped to modify by riding with him.

1–8, 11, 19, 20, 23, 24, 29, 30, 34–41, 43–47, 51, 56, 61, 68, 69, 71–73, 77–88, 91–101, 103–106, 167, 168, 172, 199, 200, 204, 205, 208, 215, 216, 218–224, 227–229, 231–241, 264, 270– 276, 281, 282, 291–294, 297, 303, 305, 354, 355, 357, 370, 374, 375

Sartoris, Bayard (young). Grandson of old Bayard. He mourns the loss in World War I of his twin brother Johnny, for whose death he sometimes needlessly blames himself. He also feels responsible for his grandfather's death, although he did not know of the old man's heart ailment when the two took their last ride together. Finally he marries Narcissa Benbow, then ends his violent life testing a faulty airplane.

4, 33, 34, 37, 43–48, 53–57, 60, 72, 75–78, 83, 86, 87, 103, 113–123, 125–143, 145–147, 149, 150, 152, 158–160, 167, 168,

199, 202, 204, 206–213, 215–218, 229–231, 238, 241, 242, 244–
248, 258–263, 270, 277–279, 281–295, 297, 303–321, 324–327,
329, 330, 333, 336–350, 353–357, 359–365, 373

Sartoris, Benbow. The son of young Bayard and Narcissa Benbow,
Bayard's second wife. He was born the day his father was killed.
380

Sartoris, Caroline White. Young Bayard's first wife, who married him
and died when he was still a flyer in World War I.
54, 55, 93

Sartoris, John (Johnny). Young Bayard's twin. An aviator killed in
action in World War I.
5, 31, 45, 47, 54, 56, 60, 71–74, 93, 121, 125, 127, 167, 214,
215, 252, 277, 288, 289, 311, 314, 321, 332, 349, 354–357, 358,
374

Sartoris, John, II. Son of old Bayard and father of the twins. He died of
yellow fever and an old Spanish bullet wound in 1901.
59, 90, 374

Sartoris, Colonel John. Officer in the Civil War. Violence did not end
for him with the cessation of hostilities. In postwar years he killed
several men, risked his life to build a railroad, won a hard, bitter
fight to get elected to the state legislature. Finally, tired of blood-
shed and violence, he faced, unarmed, his former partner Redlaw,
who shot him to death. Though he has long been dead when
Sartoris begins, his spirit is still a potent influence in the Sartoris
household.
1, 2, 6, 8, 10, 11, 18, 21, 23, 40, 43, 59, 92, 98, 112–114, 295,
304, 367, 373, 375

Sartoris, Lucy Cranston. Wife of John Sartoris II and mother of the
twins, Johnny and Bayard.
74

Sartoris, Narcissa Benbow (Narcy). Possessive sister of Horace
Benbow. In all other relationships she plays the role of a sweet,

innocent Southern maiden. From the first she is in love with young Bayard, and finally she succeeds in marrying him. She gives birth to a boy at about the time her husband is killed in an airplane accident.

29–31, 52, 56, 60, 66, 67, 69–72, 74–77, 105, 151–153, 155, 156, 161, 162, 164, 165, 168, 170, 174–182, 184, 197, 198, 200, 201, 202, 205, 212, 216, 217, 231, 238, 245, 246, 255, 259–262, 270, 276–279, 281–299, 302, 303, 354–357, 359, 366, 371, 372, 376, 379, 380

Sibleigh. Aviator in World War I. He is mentioned by young Bayard Sartoris in recounting a war incident.

44

Smith, Mrs. Switchboard operator for the specialist, Dr. Brandt, to whom Dr. Alford takes old Bayard Sartoris.

239

* *Snopes, Byron.* Bookkeeper in old Bayard Sartoris' bank. With the aid of Virgil Beard, he writes obscene letters to Narcissa [Sartoris]. One night he retrieves these letters and also steals one of Narcissa's undergarments after breaking into the deserted Benbow house and lying on her bed. The same night he absconds with money from the bank.

80, 87, 106–111, 228, 229, 264, 265

Snopes, Flem. The first Snopes to move to Jefferson. Starting as proprietor of a restaurant, he works his quiet way up to the vice-presidency of the Sartoris Bank, meanwhile sponsoring the others of his tribe who begin infiltrating Jefferson.

172

* *Snopes, Montgomery Ward.* Draft-evader. By keeping a plug of tobacco under his left armpit for several hours before his physical examination (to speed up his heartbeat), he gets himself rejected for military service because of his apparently weak heart. Later he departs with Horace Benbow to an overseas post with the YMCA.

172, 173

Sol. Negro porter at the Jefferson railway station who aids Horace.
165

Straud, Dr. Doctor mentioned by young "Loosh" Peabody as a man who has been experimenting with electricity on animals.
378

Strother, Caspey. Simon's son, Negro, who served with the U.S. Army overseas and thus got ideas about racial equality not consistent with his role at home. After his return, however, he gradually comes to accept the *status quo.*
52, 59, 61–67, 81–83, 199, 203, 236–238, 281–289, 371

Strother, Euphrony. Wife of Simon.
290

Strother (?), Joby. Negro servant of John Sartoris. He was possibly Simon's grandfather.
11, 39

Strother (?), Louvinia. (Probably Joby's wife.) Old Negro servant of Colonel John Sartoris. She helped the Colonel escape from the Yankees by having his boots and pistols ready for him at the right instant.
20, 21

* *Strother, Simon.* Joby's grandson. He is an old Negro servant of the Sartorises. Though Colonel John Sartoris has been dead more than forty years, Simon still talks to him. He is found murdered in the cabin of Meloney Harris, attractive young mulatto to whom he gives church money entrusted to him.
2–6, 24–28, 32, 34, 36–40, 42, 44, 46, 50–52, 60–66, 77, 78, 82–84, 86–88, 112–119, 199, 212–216, 218, 229, 231–234, 236–238, 241–247, 249, 270–276, 290–294, 296, 349, 354, 355, 366–370, 372, 373

Sue. Girl mentioned by Hub. (She is probably his sister.)
142

* *Suratt, V. K.* Itinerant salesman of sewing machines. After young Bayard Sartoris has had an accident riding a wild stallion, Suratt takes him in his car to get whisky from Hub. Many drinks later Suratt drops Bayard at a restaurant.
    135–144, 213

Tobe. Negro man, the only person who can handle the wild stallion that injures young Bayard Sartoris.
    131

Wagner, Hal. Fictitious name used by Byron Snopes in a letter to Narcissa Benbow Sartoris. (*See* Butler, Joe.)
    110, 111

Watts. Owner of a hardware store in Jefferson.
    109, 111

Winterbottom, Mrs. Woman in whose boardinghouse Colonel John Sartoris killed two carpetbaggers for their efforts to promote Negro suffrage.
    235, 236

Wyatt, Aunt Sally. Old maid who stays with Narcissa Benbow [Sartoris] while Horace Benbow is away at war and for a time afterward, making herself very much at home.
    68, 70–72, 74, 75, 151–154, 165, 168, 170, 172–176, 179–181

Wyatt, Miss Sophia. One of Aunt Sally's two maiden sisters, who treat Aunt Sally as if she were still a child.
    181

THE SOUND AND THE FURY (1929)

(Faulkner himself provided a series of biographical sketches of the Compson family and their retainers as an appendix to *The Portable Faulkner* [New York: Viking, 1946] which he later revised as a "foreword" to the 1946 Modern Library edition of *The Sound and the Fury*. The later version of the appendix is reproduced in full on pages 38–49 of the Guide by the courtesy of the copyright owner, Random House, Inc. Characters discussed in Faulkner's appendix are marked here with a dagger.)

Ames, Dalton. Caddy Compson's seducer, whom Quentin Compson threatens to kill if he does not leave town. Ames, unaffected by the threat, shows some concern for Caddy's welfare, but when he says all girls are bitches, Quentin tries to hit him. Ames imprisons both of Quentin's hands in one of his own and with the other demonstrates his marksmanship with a pistol, which he then gives to Quentin, suggesting that Quentin will need it if he is to carry out his threat. Again Quentin strikes at Ames, who this time fells Quentin, and then offers Quentin his horse, which Quentin refuses. (Important references to Ames occur on pages 177–180.)
99, 111, 124, 182

Anse. Marshal of a Cambridge suburb, who takes Quentin Compson in custody on the charge of abducting a little Italian girl.
149, 158–163

Bascomb, Maury. Brother of Mrs. Caroline Bascomb Compson. Jobless, he lives with and off the Compsons, drinking the elder Jason Compson's whisky and borrowing money from anyone he can, even from Dilsey Gibson. Though he mouths high ideals, he fools only his sister, who does not perceive his hypocrisy. Retribution catches up with him in at least one instance when his romance with Mrs. Patterson is discovered, and he receives a beating at the hands of her husband.
24, 25, 27, 28, 31–33, 62, 63, 120, 122, 193, 194, 214, 215, 218–222, 224, 240, 242, 278

Beard. The owner of the lot in Jefferson where the carnival is held.
206

Bland, Mrs. Wealthy class-conscious mother of Gerald. An effusive
woman, she brags constantly about her son's exploits.
109, 110, 120, 125, 159, 160, 164–166, 184, 186, 190

Bland, Gerald. Harvard classmate of Quentin Compson and pride of his
wealthy mother. He rows in flannels and stiff hat in the manner
of Oxford students. When, at his mother's picnic, he makes coarse
remarks about girls, and Quentin, confusing him with Dalton
Ames, fights him, he beats Quentin badly.
109, 110, 120, 124–126, 139, 159, 160, 162, 164–167, 184

Burgess. Neighbor of the Compsons. He knocks Benjy Compson out
with a fence rail when Benjy frightens his daughter and some
other little girls.
280

Burgess, Mrs. Wife of Burgess.
71

Charlie. Employee of the carnival with whom Miss Quentin Compson
runs away after she has taken from the younger Jason Compson's
room money that is rightfully hers as well as some that belongs to
Jason.
66, 67

Clay, Sis Beulah. Negro woman at whose funeral, according to Frony,
"they moaned two days."
52

* † Compson, Benjamin (Benjy). Idiot son of Jason, Sr., and
Caroline. His name was originally Maury (after his uncle), but his
mother had it changed to Benjamin. Benjy loves his sister Candace
(Caddy), who "smelled like trees," is inconsolable when she gives
herself to Dalton Ames, and never gets over her leaving home.
He spends his days about the golf links adjacent to his home,

listening to the golfers cry "Caddy!" (The first section of *The Sound and the Fury* is narrated through him.)

24–30, 39–42, 51, 53, 56, 58–61, 63, 65–67, 70, 71, 75, 77, 79–89, 93, 94, 101, 107, 109, 113, 121, 122, 125, 134, 142, 143, 148, 168–170, 174–176, 178, 188–190, 192, 193, 195, 199, 214, 215, 222, 224, 239, 253, 260, 268–270, 272, 273, 278, 285–287, 289–294, 300–305, 307, 309, 311, 313, 314, 316, 317, 329–336

† Compson, Candace (Caddy). Daughter of Jason, Sr., and Caroline. She conceives Miss Quentin by Dalton Ames. About two months later she marries Sydney Herbert Head, who divorces her when he becomes aware of her premarital experience. She then departs Jefferson, leaving her daughter in her mother's care. Thereafter Caddy sends money home regularly for her daughter's support, but Jason, Jr., hoards it for himself.

24, 26–28, 32, 37–40, 42–47, 52, 55–67, 70, 74–77, 80–85, 87–94, 107, 111, 113–115, 119–121, 124–126, 128, 130–132, 134, 135, 140–142, 147, 152, 153, 155, 167, 169, 171–173, 175, 176, 182, 192, 193, 223, 247, 277

* Compson, Caroline Bascomb. Wife of Jason, Sr., and mother of Quentin, Candace, Jason, Jr., and Benjamin. Neurotic, self-pitying, she spends most of her time in bed "saving her strength," attended by Dilsey Gibson. Her chief pride is her conviction that her family is just as good as her husband's, and she is highly resentful of the remarks that Jason, Sr., makes about her brother Maury Bascomb. She believes Jason, Jr., to be the only true Bascomb among her children.

25, 27, 29, 50, 73, 76, 87, 96, 112, 192, 201, 204, 216, 217, 222, 270, 271, 283, 284, 286–288, 291, 293–299, 302, 304, 314–316, 332

† Compson, Jason, Jr. Second son of Jason, Sr., and Caroline. From the first he is the unsympathetic member of the family (to all but his mother), teasing Benjy, "telling on" the others. As a man, head of the house, he seems to believe that because Caddy's conduct robbed him of a banking career with S. H. Head, he is entitled to anything he can get and by whatever means. Brutal

to Miss Quentin, Caddy's daughter, he steals the money that Caddy sends home monthly for her. (The third section of *The Sound and the Fury* embodies his viewpoint.)

29–32, 38–40, 42–46, 52, 55, 56, 58–60, 64, 67, 71, 73, 75, 79, 81–94, 96, 99, 112, 113, 120–123, 127, 128, 190, 192–194, 200–204, 211, 213, 215, 217, 220–222, 225-228, 230–232, 254, 255, 263, 267, 270–273, 278, 279, 284, 287–289, 291, 293–302, 315–321, 324–329, 335, 336

Compson, Jason Richmond, Sr. Husband of Caroline. Genteel except for his sarcasm toward his brother-in-law Maury [Bascomb], he divides a large part of his time between quietly drinking and philosophizing cynically, restrainedly. His drinking, which increases after Caddy Compson's trouble, finally kills him.

28, 44, 45, 47, 56, 58, 60, 62, 80, 96, 123, 192, 200, 216, 225, 288

† **Compson, Quentin.** First son of Jason, Sr., and Caroline, and one of Faulkner's most complex characters. While a student at Harvard, he commits suicide by drowning, partly because of his sister's illicit sex life, and partly because his father's nihilistic philosophy has weakened his grip on life. (The second section of *The Sound and the Fury* is narrated through him.)

31, 37–47, 58, 59, 62, 64, 65, 81, 85–87, 90, 92–95, 107, 112–116, 120, 124, 126–131, 159, 160, 164–167, 170–174, 176, 178, 179, 181, 184, 186, 193, 199, 215, 216, 218, 220, 224, 246, 277–279, 299, 315

† **Compson, Miss Quentin.** Illegitimate daughter of Caddy Compson and Dalton Ames, and object of the younger Jason Compson's hatred because he associates her with his failure to get a job with the banker Head. She stays out of school to meet boys and finally takes $7,000 from Jason (most of which he had actually stolen from her) and runs away with Charlie, the carnival man in the red tie.

30, 49–51, 65, 67–69, 85, 86, 88–92, 201–204, 208, 212, 214, 216, 221, 224, 226, 229, 236–238, 240, 254, 270, 271, 274–276, 280, 287, 292–296, 298–302, 314, 315, 324

Daingerfield, Miss. One of the girls present at Mrs. Bland's picnic the day Quentin Compson commits suicide.
　　164, 165, 167

Damuddy. Compson children's nickname for their grandmother. Her death is kept a secret from the children for a time. (She is probably their maternal grandmother, though there is no clear evidence of this.)
　　39, 42, 45, 46, 55, 57, 82, 92, 93, 109, 170

Deacon. Old Negro character who acts many roles to secure odd jobs from Harvard students. His love for display assures his presence in every local parade.
　　101, 115–120

† **Dilsey.** *See* Gibson, Dilsey.

Earl. Owner of the store in which Jason Compson, Jr., works. He is an example of old-school Southern loyalty to the institution of quality, family, and ladyhood, and he, therefore, respects Mrs. Compson. Because of this sentiment he allows Jason to continue in his employ even though Jason treats him with contempt; moreover, he protects Jason in his lie about having invested $1,000 of Mrs. Compson's in the store.
　　206–208, 211–213, 228, 229, 233–236, 243, 244, 252, 257, 258, 262, 265, 267, 268

† *Frony.* Married daughter of Dilsey and Roskus Gibson.
　　48–53, 55–58, 63, 64, 75, 86, 272, 305–307, 309, 313, 314

† **Gibson, Dilsey.** One of Faulkner's noblest characters, chief among those who "endure." Nominally cook for the Compsons, she, with the aid of her own irresponsible family, keeps the Compsons' lives in some semblance of order. (The fourth section of *The Sound and the Fury* embodies her viewpoint.)
　　27, 29–32, 38, 39, 43–53, 56, 61–68, 71, 74–81, 83, 85–87, 89–93, 105, 107, 109, 132, 171, 188, 201–205, 214, 216–218, 222, 224, 225, 236, 238, 240, 253, 260, 269–274, 281–307, 309–311, 313–317, 329–334

Gibson, Roskus. Husband of Dilsey, probably. He, too, works on the Compson place; but he does not like doing so because, being superstitious and given to "trances," he senses that no good will come of his association with such a family.

    29, 30, 37, 39, 40, 47–51, 53, 62, 65, 89, 90, 105, 113, 118, 119, 268

† *Gibson, T. P.* Son of Dilsey and Roskus, probably. He takes care of Benjy Compson before Luster is big enough to do so.

    29–32, 40–42, 47–59, 61, 64–66, 70, 71, 101, 168, 169, 177, 194, 214, 215, 250, 314, 329, 332, 334

Gibson, Versh. Oldest son of Dilsey and Roskus. He is predecessor of T. P. as nurse-companion to Benjy Compson.

    26–28, 33, 38, 39, 41–50, 52, 55–58, 63–67, 76, 80, 81, 87–89, 92, 120, 131, 133, 134

Hatcher, Louis. Negro who gives Caddy Compson driving lessons, and who goes 'possum hunting with Quentin Compson and Versh Gibson.

    112, 133, 134

Hatcher, Martha. Louis' wife.

    133

Head, Sydney Herbert. Caddy Compson's fiancé, some ten or twelve years her senior, who gives her a car and promises Jason Compson, Jr., a job in his bank. He had been expelled from his club for cheating at cards and from Harvard for cheating on examinations, and he tries to buy Quentin Compson's silence about these matters. After a short marriage to Caddy he divorces her when she gives birth to a child not his, which she had conceived before their marriage.

    112–114, 124, 129, 238, 239, 278

Henry. Smart student in Quentin Compson's class in Jefferson.

    107

Holmes, Miss. Young girl on Mrs. Bland's picnic.

    166

Hopkins. Man in telegraph office interested in the younger Jason Compson's stock-market activities.
211

Job, Uncle. Old Negro who works for Earl, the younger Jason Compson's employer. Though Jason often curses him for his slowness, he remains unperturbed.
207, 208, 229, 263, 265–267

Julio. Brother of the little Italian girl who takes up with Quentin Compson. He attacks Quentin because he thinks Quentin has kidnapped her.
157–162, 164

Junkin, Professor. Official at Miss Quentin Compson's school who reports her absence to Jason Compson, Jr.
198

Kenny. One of the three boys whom Quentin Compson watches fish on the day of his suicide.
141

Laura, Miss. Schoolteacher of Quentin Compson in Jefferson.
107

Lorraine. The younger Jason Compson's Memphis mistress, who often comes to visit him in Jefferson after his mother's death.
211, 250, 263, 323

† *Luster.* Son of Frony. He takes care of the thirty-three-year-old Benjy Compson, whom he often teases. At night he and Benjy watch Miss Quentin slide down the tree to keep appointments with men.
23, 24, 26, 28, 30, 32–37, 39, 40, 49–52, 54, 55, 65, 67–70, 72–80, 84–86, 88, 91–93, 204, 236, 238, 239, 268, 270–273, 284–294, 300–305, 313, 314, 316, 329–336

Mac. Man in the Jefferson drugstore who discusses baseball with Jason Compson.
269

* *MacKenzie, Shreve.* Quentin Compson's Canadian roommate at Harvard, who is present at Bland's picnic even though Mrs. Bland thinks he lacks the necessary family qualifications. Quentin leaves him a farewell note.

>96–98, 100, 101, 112, 118, 120, 125, 126, 160–167, 182–186, 189, 190, 192, 193, 197

Mike. Operator of a gymnasium where Gerald Bland learned to box.

>184

Mink. Employee of the Jefferson livery stable. At Jason Compson, Jr.'s orders he drives the hack in which Jason holds the infant Miss Quentin so that Caddy Compson may see her child. In this way Jason justifies himself in collecting the $100 that Caddy has paid him for allowing her to see Miss Quentin.

>222, 223

Myrtle. Daughter of the Jefferson sheriff who refuses to accompany Jason Compson, Jr., in his pursuit of Miss Quentin because evidence is lacking that Miss Quentin took the money. (The sheriff, moreover, suspects the truth about whose money it is.)

>317, 318

Natalie. Playmate of the Compson children, the girl whom Quentin Compson kissed. When Caddy Compson saw Natalie and Quentin "dancing" sitting down, Quentin pushed Natalie, who then went home angry.

>153, 155

Parker. Operator of the restaurant where Quentin Compson has his last breakfast.

>102

Patterson. Justifiably jealous husband. He sees Benjy and Caddy Compson deliver Maury Bascomb's letter to Mrs. Patterson and takes it from her. Later he blacks Maury's eye and bloodies his mouth.

>33, 62

Patterson boy. Playmate and partner of young Jason Compson, Jr., in a kite-selling venture until he had trouble with Jason, the treasurer, over finances.
193

Patterson, Mrs. Patterson's wife, to whom Maury Bascomb sends love notes.
32, 33

* *Peabody, Doc.* A 300-pound doctor who used to let the Compson children hang onto his buggy and ride.
147

Rogers. Owner of the restaurant in Jefferson where Earl eats.
228, 233

Russell, Ab. Farmer near Jefferson. It is on or near his property that Miss Quentin Compson and the carnival man hide from Jason Compson, Jr., and let the air out of his tires.
257, 259, 260

Sartoris, Colonel. (Colonel John probably, officer in the Civil War, whose exploits were legendary.) Quentin Compson thinks of death and his grandfather as being two old friends waiting in a high place somewhere for Colonel Sartoris to come to them from his still higher place.
194

Shegog, Reverend. Inspired Negro preacher from St. Louis who preaches on Easter Sunday in Dilsey Gibson's church in Jefferson.
306, 307

Simmons. Acquaintance of Jason Compson, Jr. It is from him that Jason obtains the keys to the old opera house, where some blank checks from a defunct bank are kept. On one of these Jason writes a phony check supposedly from Caddy Compson so that he can tear it up in front of his mother, leaving intact the genuine check for him to appropriate for himself.
234

Snopes, I. O. Cotton speculator who is present when Jason Compson, Jr., comes to the Western Union office to dabble a bit.
  235

Spoade. A Harvard senior. He is also present at Mrs. Bland's picnic. In four years he has never been known to arrive at school completely dressed. Friendly but crude, he calls Shreve MacKenzie "Quentin's husband" because these two are roommates and Quentin [Compson] is not interested in girls.
  97, 98, 110, 111, 114, 160–167, 183–186, 190

Thompson. Owner of the café where Spoade comes at ten each morning for two cups of coffee.
  98

Turpin, Buck. Man who receives $10 from the carnival people for their privilege of playing in Jefferson. (He probably owns the lot where the circus locates.)
  248

Vernon. Myrtle's husband. He is present at the home of his father-in-law, the sheriff of Jefferson, when Jason Compson, Jr., comes for assistance in apprehending Miss Quentin Compson.
  317

Walthall, Parson. Methodist preacher in Jefferson, who, to the great chagrin of Jason Compson, Jr., interferes with the plan to kill off the pigeons that have become a nuisance in the town.
  264

Wilkie. Negro servant of the Blands in the time of Gerald's grandfather.
  166

Wright (Doc). Cotton speculator who is often present in the telegraph office when Jason Compson, Jr., goes there to play the stock market.
  211, 234, 235

THE SOUND AND THE FURY:
Appendix[*]

COMPSON: 1699–1945

IKKEMOTUBBE. A dispossessed American king. Called "l'Homme" (and
sometimes "de l'homme") by his fosterbrother, a Chevalier of France,
who had he not been born too late could have been among the brightest
in that glittering galaxy of knightly blackguards who were Napoleon's
marshals, who thus translated the Chickasaw title meaning "The Man";
which translation Ikkemotubbe, himself a man of wit and imagination
as well as a shrewd judge of character, including his own, carried one
step further and anglicised it to "Doom." Who granted out of his vast
lost domain a solid square mile of virgin North Mississippi dirt as truly
angled as the four corners of a cardtable top (forested then because these
were the old days before 1833 when the stars fell and Jefferson Mississippi
was one long rambling onestorey mudchinked log building housing the
Chickasaw Agent and his tradingpost store) to the grandson of a Scottish
refugee who had lost his own birthright by casting his lot with a king
who himself had been dispossessed. This in partial return for the right
to proceed in peace, by whatever means he and his people saw fit, afoot
or ahorse provided they were Chickasaw horses, to the wild western land
presently to be called Oklahoma: not knowing then about the oil.

JACKSON. A Great White Father with a sword. (An old duellist, a
brawling lean fierce mangy durable imperishable old lion who set the
wellbeing of the nation above the White House and the health of his new
political party above either and above them all set not his wife's honor
but the principle that honor must be defended whether it was or not
because defended it was whether or not.) Who patented sealed and
countersigned the grant with his own hand in his gold tepee in Wassi
Town, not knowing about the oil either: so that one day the homeless
descendants of the dispossessed would ride supine with drink and
splendidly comatose above the dusty allotted harborage of their bones in
speciallybuilt scarletpainted hearses and fire-engines.

---

[*] Reproduced here by kind permission of the copyright owner, Random House, Inc.,
(Copyright © 1946).

These were Compsons:

QUENTIN MACLACHAN. Son of a Glasgow printer, orphaned and raised by his mother's people in the Perth highlands. Fled to Carolina from Culloden Moor with a claymore and the tartan he wore by day and slept under by night, and little else. At eighty, having fought once against an English king and lost, he would not make that mistake twice and so fled again one night in 1779, with his infant grandson and the tartan (the claymore had vanished, along with his son, the grandson's father, from one of Tarleton's regiments on a Georgia battlefield about a year ago) into Kentucky, where a neighbor named Boon or Boone had already established a settlement.

CHARLES STUART. Attainted and proscribed by name and grade in his British regiment. Left for dead in a Georgia swamp by his own retreating army and then by the advancing American one, both of which were wrong. He still had the claymore even when on his homemade wooden leg he finally overtook his father and son four years later at Harrodsburg, Kentucky, just in time to bury the father and enter upon a long period of being a split personality while still trying to be the schoolteacher which he believed he wanted to be, until he gave up at last and became the gambler he actually was and which no Compson seemed to realize they all were provided the gambit was desperate and the odds long enough. Succeeded at last in risking not only his neck but the security of his family and the very integrity of the name he would leave behind him, by joining the confederation headed by an acquaintance named Wilkinson (a man of considerable talent and influence and intellect and power) in a plot to secede the whole Mississippi Valley from the United States and join it to Spain. Fled in his turn when the bubble burst (as anyone except a Compson schoolteacher should have known it would), himself unique in being the only one of the plotters who had to flee the country: this not from the vengeance and retribution of the government which he had attempted to dismember, but from the furious revulsion of his late confederates now frantic for their own safety. He was not expelled from the United States, he talked himself countryless, his expulsion due not to the treason but to his having been so vocal and vociferant in the conduct of it, burning each bridge vocally behind him before he had even reached the place to build the next one: so that it was no provost marshal nor even a civic agency but his late coplotters themselves who put afoot the movement to evict him from Kentucky and the United States and, if they had caught him, probably from the world too. Fled by night, running true to family tradition, with his son and the old claymore and the tartan.

JASON LYCURGUS. Who, driven perhaps by the compulsion of the flamboyant name given him by the sardonic embittered woodenlegged indomitable father who perhaps still believed with his heart that what he wanted to be was a classicist schoolteacher, rode up the Natchez Trace one day in 1811 with a pair of fine pistols and one meagre saddlebag on a small lightwaisted but stronghocked mare which could do the first two furlongs in definitely under the halfminute and the next two in not appreciably more, though that was all. But it was enough: who reached the Chickasaw Agency at Okatoba (which in 1860 was still called Old Jefferson) and went no further. Who within six months was the Agent's clerk and within twelve his partner, officially still the clerk though actually halfowner of what was now a considerable store stocked with the mare's winnings in races against the horses of Ikkemotubbe's young men which he, Compson, was always careful to limit to a quarter or at most three furlongs; and in the next year it was Ikkemotubbe who owned the little mare and Compson owned the solid square mile of land which someday would be almost in the center of the town of Jefferson, forested then and still forested twenty years later though rather a park than a forest by that time, with its slavequarters and stables and kitchengardens and the formal lawns and promenades and pavilions laid out by the same architect who built the columned porticoed house furnished by steamboat from France and New Orleans, and still the square intact mile in 1840 (with not only the little white village called Jefferson beginning to enclose it but an entire white county about to surround it because in a few years now Ikkemotubbe's descendants and people would be gone, those remaining living not as warriors and hunters but as white men—as shiftless farmers or, here and there, the masters of what they too called plantations and the owners of shiftless slaves, a little dirtier than the white man, a little lazier, a little crueller—until at last even the wild blood itself would have vanished, to be seen only occasionally in the nose-shape of a Negro on a cottonwagon or a white sawmill hand or trapper or locomotive fireman), known as the Compson Domain then, since now it was fit to breed princes, statesmen and generals and bishops, to avenge the dispossessed Compsons from Culloden and Carolina and Kentucky, then known as the Governor's house because sure enough in time it did produce or at least spawn a governor—Quentin MacLachan again, after the Culloden grandfather —and still known as the Old Governor's even after it had spawned (1861) a general—(called so by predetermined accord and agreement by the whole town and county, as though they knew even then and beforehand that the old governor was the last Compson who would not fail at everything he touched save longevity or suicide)—the Brigadier Jason Lycurgus II who failed at Shiloh in '62 and failed again though not so badly at Resaca in '64, who put the first mortgage on the still intact square mile to a New England carpetbagger in '66, after the old town had been burned by the Federal General Smith and the new little town, in time to be populated mainly by the descendants not of Compsons but of Snopeses, had begun to encroach and then nibble at and into it as the failed brigadier spent the next forty years selling fragments of it off to keep up the mortage on the remainder: until one day in 1900 he died quietly on an army cot in the hunting and fishing camp in the Tallahatchie River bottom where he passed most of the end of his days.

And even the old governor was forgotten now; what was left of the old square mile was now known merely as the Compson place—the weedchoked traces of the old ruined lawns and promenades, the house which had needed painting too long already, the scaling columns of the portico where Jason III (bred for a lawyer and indeed he kept an office upstairs above the Square, where entombed in dusty filingcases some of the oldest names in the county—Holston and Sutpen, Grenier and Beauchamp and Coldfield—faded year by year among the bottomless labyrinths of chancery: and who knows what dream in the perennial heart of his father, now completing the third of his three avatars—the one as a son of a brilliant and gallant statesman, the second as battle-leader of brave and gallant men, the third as a sort of privileged pseudo-Daniel Boone-Robinson Crusoe, who had not returned to juvenility because actually he had never left it—that that lawyer's office might again be the anteroom to the governor's mansion and the old splendor) sat all day long with a decanter of whiskey and a litter of dogeared Horaces and Livys and Catulluses, composing (it was said) caustic and satiric eulogies on both his dead and his living fellowtownsmen, who sold the last of the property, except that fragment containing the house and the kitchengarden and the collapsing stables and one servant's cabin in which Dilsey's family lived, to a golfclub for the ready money with which his daughter Candace could have her fine wedding in April and his son Quentin could finish one year at Harvard and commit suicide in the following June of 1910; already known as the Old Compson place even while Compsons were still living in it on that spring dusk in 1928 when the old governor's doomed lost nameless seventeen-year-old great-greatgranddaughter robbed her last remaining sane male relative (her uncle Jason IV) of his secret hoard of money and climbed down a rainpipe and ran off with a pitchman in a travelling streetshow, and still known as the Old Compson place long after all traces of Compsons were gone from it: after the widowed mother died and Jason IV, no longer need-ing to fear Dilsey now, committed his idiot brother, Benjamin, to the State Asylum in Jackson and sold the house to a countryman who operated it as a boarding house for juries and horse- and muletraders, and still known as the Old Compson place even after the boardinghouse (and presently the golfcourse too) had vanished and the old square mile was even intact again in row after row of small crowded jerrybuilt individuallyowned demiurban bungalows.

And these:

QUENTIN III. Who loved not his sister's body but some concept of Compson honor precariously and (he knew well) only temporarily supported by the minute fragile membrane of her maidenhead as a miniature replica of all the whole vast globy earth may be poised on the nose of a trained seal. Who loved not the idea of the incest which he would not commit, but some presbyterian concept of its eternal punishment: he, not God, could by that means cast himself and his sister both into hell, where he could guard her forever and keep her forevermore intact amid the eternal fires. But who loved death above all, who loved only death, loved and lived in a deliberate and almost perverted anticipation of death as a lover loves and deliberately refrains from the waiting willing friendly tender incredible body of his beloved, until he can no longer bear not the refraining but the restraint and so flings, hurls himself, relinquishing, drowning. Committed suicide in Cambridge Massachusetts, June 1910, two months after his sister's wedding, waiting first to complete the current academic year and so get the full value of his paid-in-advance tuition, not because he had his old Culloden and Carolina and Kentucky grandfathers in him but because the remaining piece of the old Compson mile which had been sold to pay for his sister's wedding and his year at Harvard had been the one thing, excepting that same sister and the sight of an open fire, which his youngest brother, born an idiot, had loved.

CANDACE (CADDY). Doomed and knew it, accepted the doom without either seeking or fleeing it. Loved her brother despite him, loved not only him but loved in him that bitter prophet and inflexible corruptless judge of what he considered the family's honor and its doom, as he thought he loved but really hated in her what he considered the frail doomed vessel of its pride and the foul instrument of its disgrace; not only this, she loved him not only in spite of but because of the fact that he himself was incapable of love, accepting the fact that he must value above all not her but the virginity of which she was custodian and on which she placed no value whatever: the frail physical stricture which to her was no more than a hangnail would have been. Knew the brother loved death best of all and was not jealous, would (and perhaps in the calculation and deliberation of her marriage did) have handed him the hypothetical hemlock. Was two months pregnant with another man's child which regardless of what its sex would be she had already named Quentin after the brother whom they both (she and the brother) knew was already the same as dead when she married (1910) an extremely eligible young Indianian she and her mother had met while vacationing at French Lick the summer before. Divorced by him 1911. Married 1920 to a minor movingpicture magnate, Hollywood California. Divorced by mutual agreement, Mexico 1925. Vanished in Paris with the German occupation, 1940, still beautiful and probably still wealthy too since she did not look within fifteen years of her actual fortyeight, and was not heard of again. Except there was a woman in Jefferson, the county librarian, a mousesized and -colored woman who had never married, who had passed through the city schools in the same class with Candace Compson and then spent the rest of her life trying to keep Forever Amber in its orderly overlapping avatars and Jurgen and Tom Jones out of the hands of the highschool juniors and seniors who could reach them down without even having to tiptoe from the back shelves where she herself would have to stand on a box to hide them. One day in 1943, after a week of a distraction bordering on disintegration almost, during which those entering the library would find her always in the act of hurriedly closing her desk drawer and turning the key in it (so that the matrons, wives of the bankers and doctors and lawyers, some of whom had also been in that old highschool class, who came and went in the afternoons with the copies of the Forever Ambers and the volumes of Thorne Smith carefully wrapped from view in sheets of Memphis and Jackson newspapers, believed she was on the verge of illness or perhaps even loss of mind) she closed and locked the library in the middle of the afternoon and with her handbag clasped tightly under her arm and two feverish spots of determination in her ordinarily colorless cheeks, she entered the farmers' supply store where Jason IV had started as a clerk and where he now owned his own business as a buyer of and dealer in cotton, striding on through that gloomy cavern which only men ever entered—a cavern cluttered and walled and sta-lagmitehung with plows and discs and loops of tracechain and single-trees and mulecollars and sidemeat and cheap shoes and horselinament and flour and molasses, gloomy because the goods it contained were not shown but hidden rather since those who supplied Mississippi farmers or at least Negro Mississippi farmers for a share of the crop did not wish, until that crop was made and its value approximately computable, to show them what they could learn to want but only to supply them on specific demand with what they could not help but need—and strode on back to Jason's particular domain in the rear: a railed enclosure cluttered with shelves and pigeonholes bearing spiked dust-and-lint-gathering gin receipts and ledgers and cottonsamples and rank with the blended smell of cheese and kerosene and harnessoil and the tremendous iron stove against which chewed tobacco had been spat for almost a hundred years, and up to the long high sloping counter behind which Jason stood and, not looking again at the overalled men who had quietly stopped talking and even chewing when she entered, with a kind of fainting desperation she opened the handbag and fumbled something out of it and laid it open on the counter and stood trembling and breathing rapidly while Jason looked down at it—a picture, a photograph in color clipped obviously from a slick magazine—a picture filled with luxury and money and sunlight—a Cannebière backdrop of mountains and palms and cypresses and the sea, an open powerful expensive chromiumtrimmed sports car, the woman's face hatless between a rich scarf and a seal coat, ageless and beautiful, cold serene and damned; beside her a handsome lean man of middleage in the ribbons and tabs of a German staffgeneral—and the mousesized mousecolored spinster trembling and aghast at her own temerity, staring across it at the childless bachelor in whom ended that long line of men who had had something in them of decency and pride even after they had begun to fail at the integrity and the pride had become mostly vanity and selfpity: from the expatriate who had to flee his native land with little else except his life yet who still refused to accept defeat, through the man who gambled his life and his good name twice and lost twice and declined to accept that either, and the one who with only a clever small quarterhorse for tool avenged his dispossessed father and grandfather and gained a principality, and the brilliant and gallant governor and the general who though he failed at leading in battle brave and gallant men at least risked his own life too in the failing, to the cultured dipsomaniac who sold the last of his patrimony not to buy drink but to give one of his descendants at least the best chance in life he could think of.

'It's Caddy!' the librarian whispered. 'We must save her!'

'It's Cad, all right,' Jason said. Then he began to laugh. He stood there laughing above the picture, above the cold beautiful face now creased and dogeared from its week's sojourn in the desk drawer and the handbag. And the librarian knew why he was laughing, who had not called him anything but Mr Compson for thirty-two years now, ever since the day in 1911 when Candace, cast off by her husband, had brought her infant daughter home and left the child and departed by the next train, to return no more, and not only the Negro cook, Dilsey, but the librarian too divined by simple instinct that Jason was somehow using the child's life and its illegitimacy both to blackmail the mother not only into staying away from Jefferson for the rest of her life but into appointing him sole unchallengeable trustee of the money she would send for the child's maintenance, and had refused to speak to him at all since that day in 1928 when the daughter climbed down the rainpipe and ran away with the pitchman.

'Jason!' she cried. 'We must save her! Jason! Jason!'——and still crying it even when he took up the picture between thumb and finger and threw it back across the counter toward her.

'That Candace?' he said. 'Dont make me laugh. This bitch aint thirty yet. The other one's fifty now.'

And the library was still locked all the next day too when at three oclock in the afternoon, footsore and spent yet still unflagging and still clasping the handbag tightly under her arm, she turned into a neat small yard in the Negro residence section of Memphis and mounted the steps of the neat small house and rang the bell and the door opened and a black woman of about her own age looked quietly out at her. 'It's Frony, isn't it?' the librarian said. 'Dont you remember me—— Melissa Meek, from Jefferson——'

'Yes,' the Negress said. 'Come in. You want to see Mama.' And she entered the room, the neat yet cluttered bedroom of an old Negro, rank with the smell of old people, old women, old Negroes, where the old woman herself sat in a rocker beside the hearth where even though it was June a fire smoldered—a big woman once, in faded clean calico and an immaculate turban wound round her head above the bleared and now apparently almost sightless eyes—and put the dogeared clipping into the black hands which, like the women of her race, were still as supple and delicately shaped as they had been when she was thirty or twenty or even seventeen.

'It's Caddy!' the librarian said. 'It is! Dilsey! Dilsey!'

'What did he say?' the old Negress said. And the librarian knew whom she meant by 'he', nor did the librarian marvel, not only that the old Negress would know that she (the librarian) would know whom she meant by the 'he', but that the old Negress would know at once that she had already shown the picture to Jason.

'Dont you know what he said?' she cried. 'When he realised she was in danger, he said it was her, even if I hadn't even had a picture to show him. But as soon as he realised that somebody, anybody, even just me, wanted to save her, would try to save her, he said it wasn't. But it is! Look at it!'

'Look at my eyes,' the old Negress said. 'How can I see that picture?'

'Call Frony!' the librarian cried. 'She will know her!' But already the old Negress was folding the clipping carefully back into its old creases, handing it back.

'My eyes aint any good anymore,' she said. 'I cant see it.'

And that was all. At six oclock she fought her way through the crowded bus terminal, the bag clutched under one arm and the return half of her roundtrip ticket in the other hand, and was swept out onto the roaring platform on the diurnal tide of a few middleaged civilians but mostly soldiers and sailors enroute either to leave or to death and the homeless young women, their companions, who for two years now had lived from day to day in pullmans and hotels when they were lucky and in daycoaches and busses and stations and lobbies and public restrooms when not, pausing only long enough to drop their foals in charity wards or policestations and then move on again, and fought her way into the bus, smaller than any other there so that her feet touched the floor only occasionally until a shape (a man in khaki; she couldn't see him at all because she was already crying) rose and picked her up bodily and set her into a seat next the window, where still crying quietly she could look out upon the fleeing city as it streaked past and then was behind and presently now she would be home again, safe in Jefferson where life lived too with all its incomprehensible passion and turmoil and grief and fury and despair, but here at six oclock you could close the covers on it and even the weightless hand of a child could put it back among its unfeatured kindred on the quiet eternal shelves and turn the key upon it for the whole and dreamless night. *Yes* she thought, crying quietly *that was it she didn't want to see it know whether it was Caddy or not because she knows Caddy doesn't want to be saved hasn't anything anymore worth being saved for nothing worth being lost that she can lose*

JASON IV. The first sane Compson since before Culloden and (a childless bachelor) hence the last. Logical rational contained and even a philosopher in the old stoic tradition: thinking nothing whatever of God one way or the other and simply considering the police and so fearing and respecting only the Negro woman, his sworn enemy since his birth and his mortal one since that day in 1911 when she too divined by simple clairvoyance that he was somehow using his infant niece's illegitimacy to blackmail its mother, who cooked the food he ate. Who not only fended off and held his own with Compsons but competed and held his own with the Snopeses who took over the little town following the turn of the century as the Compsons and Sartorises and their ilk faded from it (no Snopes, but Jason Compson himself who as soon as his mother died—the niece had already climbed down the rainpipe and vanished so Dilsey no longer had either of these clubs to hold over him—committed his idiot younger brother to the state and vacated the old house, first chopping up the vast oncesplendid rooms into what he called apartments and selling the whole thing to a countryman who opened a boardinghouse in it), though this was not difficult since to him all the rest of the town and the world and the human race too except himself were Compsons,

inexplicable yet quite predictable in that they were in no sense whatever to be trusted. Who, all the money from the sale of the pasture
having gone for his sister's wedding and his brother's course at Harvard,
used his own niggard savings out of his meagre wages as a storeclerk to
send himself to a Memphis school where he learned to class and grade
cotton, and so established his own business with which, following his
dipsomaniac father's death, he assumed the entire burden of the rotting
family in the rotting house, supporting his idiot brother because of their
mother, sacrificing what pleasures might have been the right and
just due and even the necessity of a thirty-year-old bachelor, so
that his mother's life might continue as nearly as possible to what
it had been; this not because he loved her but (a sane man always)
simply because he was afraid of the Negro cook whom he could
not even force to leave, even when he tried to stop paying her weekly
wages; and who despite all this, still managed to save almost three
thousand dollars ($2840.50 as he reported it on the night his niece stole
it); in niggard and agonised dimes and quarters and halfdollars, which
hoard he kept in no bank because to him a banker too was just one more
Compson, but hid in a locked bureau drawer in his bedroom whose bed
he made and changed himself since he kept the bedroom door locked
all the time save when he was passing through it. Who, following a
fumbling abortive attempt by his idiot brother on a passing female child,
had himself appointed the idiot's guardian without letting their mother
know and so was able to have the creature castrated before the mother
even knew it was out of the house, and who following the mother's
death in 1933 was able to free himself forever not only from the idiot
brother and the house but from the Negro woman too, moving into a
pair of offices up a flight of stairs above the supplystore containing his
cotton ledgers and samples, which he had converted into a bedroom-
kitchen-bath in and out of which on weekends there would be seen a big
plain friendly brazenhaired pleasantfaced woman no longer very young,
in round picture hats and (in its season) an imitation fur coat, the two
of them, the middleaged cottonbuyer and the woman whom the town
called, simply, his friend from Memphis, seen at the local picture show
on Saturday night and on Sunday morning mounting the apartment stairs
with paper bags from the grocer's containing loaves and eggs and oranges
and cans of soup, domestic, uxorious, connubial, until the late afternoon
bus carried her back to Memphis. He was emancipated now. He was
free. 'In 1865,' he would say, 'Abe Lincoln freed the niggers from the
Compsons. In 1933, Jason Compson freed the Compsons from the niggers.'

BENJAMIN. Born Maury, after his mother's only brother: a handsome
flashing swaggering workless bachelor who borrowed money from almost
anyone, even Dilsey although she was a Negro, explaining to her as he

withdrew his hand from his pocket that she was not only in his eyes the same as a member of his sister's family, she would be considered a born lady anywhere in any eyes. Who, when at last even his mother realised what he was and insisted weeping that his name must be changed, was rechristened Benjamin by his brother Quentin (Benjamin, our lastborn, sold into Egypt). Who loved three things: the pasture which was sold to pay for Candace's wedding and to send Quentin to Harvard, his sister Candace, firelight. Who lost none of them because he could not remember his sister but only the loss of her, and firelight was the same bright shape as going to sleep, and the pasture was even better sold than before because now he and TP could not only follow timeless along the fence the motions which it did not even matter to him were humanbeings swinging golfsticks, TP could lead them to clumps of grass or weeds where there would appear suddenly in TP's hand small white spherules which competed with and even conquered what he did not even know was gravity and all the immutable laws when released from the hand toward plank floor or smokehouse wall or concrete sidewalk. Gelded 1913. Committed to the State Asylum, Jackson 1933. Lost nothing then either because, as with his sister, he remembered not the pasture but only its loss, and firelight was still the same bright shape of sleep.

QUENTIN. The last. Candace's daughter. Fatherless nine months before her birth, nameless at birth and already doomed to be unwed from the instant the dividing egg determined its sex. Who at seventeen, on the one thousand eight hundred ninetyfifth anniversary of the day before the resurrection of Our Lord, swung herself by a rainpipe from the window of the room in which her uncle had locked her at noon, to the locked window of his own locked and empty bedroom and broke a pane and entered the window and with the uncle's firepoker burst open the locked bureau drawer and took the money (it was not $2840.50 either, it was almost seven thousand dollars and this was Jason's rage, the red unbearable fury which on that night and at intervals recurring with little or no diminishment for the next five years, made him seriously believe would at some unwarned instant destroy him, kill him as instantaneously dead as a bullet or a lightningbolt: that although he had been robbed not of a mere petty three thousand dollars but of almost seven thousand he couldn't even tell anybody; because he had been robbed of seven thousand dollars instead of just three he could not only never receive justification—he did not want sympathy—from other men unlucky enough to have one bitch for a sister and another for a niece, he couldn't even go to the police; because he had lost four thousand dollars which did not belong to him he couldn't even recover the three thousand which did since those first four thousand dollars were not only the legal property of his niece as a part of the money supplied for her support and maintenance by her mother over the last sixteen years, they did not exist at all, having been officially recorded as expended and consumed in the annual reports he submitted to the district Chancellor, as required of him as guardian and trustee by his bondsmen: so that he had been robbed not only of his thievings but his savings too, and by his own victim; he had been robbed not only of the four thousand dollars which he had risked jail to acquire but of the three thousand which he had hoarded at the price of sacrifice and denial, almost a nickel and a dime at a time, over a period of almost twenty years: and this not only by his own victim but by a child who did it at one blow, without premeditation or plan, not even knowing or even caring how much she would find when she broke the drawer open; and now he couldn't even go to the police for help: he who had considered the police always, never given them any trouble, had paid the taxes for years which supported them in parasitic and sadistic idleness; not only that, he didn't dare pursue the girl himself because he might catch her and she would talk, so that his only recourse was a vain dream which kept him tossing and sweating on nights two and three and even four years after the event, when he should have forgotten about it: of catching her without warning, springing on her out of the dark, before she had spent all the money, and murder her before she had time to open her mouth) and climbed down the same rainpipe in the dusk and ran away with the pitchman who was already under sentence for bigamy. And so vanished; whatever occupation overtook her would have arrived in no chromium Mercedes; whatever snapshot would have contained no general of staff.

And that was all. These others were not Compsons. They were black:

T.P. Who wore on Memphis's Beale Street the fine bright cheap intransigent clothes manufactured specifically for him by the owners of Chicago and New York sweatshops.

FRONY. Who married a pullman porter and went to St Louis to live and later moved back to Memphis to make a home for her mother since Dilsey refused to go further than that.

LUSTER. A man, aged 14. Who was not only capable of the complete care and security of an idiot twice his age and three times his size, but could keep him entertained.

DILSEY.
       They endured.

AS I LAY DYING (1930)

Albert. Man who works at the soda fountain in Moseley's drugstore.
484, 488, 489

Alford, Dr. Jefferson doctor.
517

* *Armstid.* Farmer who gives the Bundrens shelter overnight after they have lost their mules in the flooded river. (He is the narrator of chapter 43.)
398, 399, 401, 402, 470–473, 482, 505, 511, 515

Armstid, Lula. Armstid's wife. The night the Bundrens spend with the Armstids, Lula takes care of Cash, who has broken his leg.
471, 475, 476

Bundren, Mrs. The duck-shaped woman who lends Anse Bundren the shovels with which to dig Addie's grave and who becomes Addie's successor within hours after the burial. With her graphophone in hand she defiantly accompanies Anse to meet her new family, looking at them "like she dared ere a man."
512, 532

Bundren, Addie. One-time school teacher who marries Anse. She has two children, Cash and Darl, by Anse; then, feeling betrayed by Anse's empty word, "love," she has Jewel by the preacher Whitfield. After Jewel's birth, she bears Dewey Dell and Vardaman by Anse to make up to him for Jewel. Early she exacts from Anse the promise that when she dies he will take her body to Jefferson and bury it in her family cemetery. (Narrator of chapter 40.)
340, 342, 352–354, 363, 364, 366, 369–372, 375, 386, 396, 413, 417, 429, 441, 444–446, 461, 470, 501, 529

Bundren, Anse. A poor farmer trying to function as the head of a family. Anse is capable only of a confused selfishness manifested in the form of a mumbling hesitancy to do anything positive. He persists in fumbling his way to Jefferson with his wife's decomposing body for a variety of half-formed reasons: Dewey Dell's personal desire to get to town; Anse's wish for store-bought teeth; and his stubborn, unconscious desire to do something positive for once. Addie's body is scarcely in the ground before he has bought his teeth with money taken from Dewey Dell and married the duck-shaped owner of the graphophone from whom he has borrowed the shovels with which to dig Addie's grave. (Narrator of chapters 9, 26, and 28.)

351–354, 357–362, 364, 366–370, 389, 390, 398–400, 402, 404, 411, 414–417, 419, 424–427, 435, 438, 448–450, 462–467, 469, 473, 474, 476–481, 515, 516

Bundren, Cash. Bundren's oldest son, a carpenter who thinks primarily in terms of his humble craft. He starts to work on his mother's coffin some time before she actually dies and completes it after her death. For the second time in his life he breaks his leg, this time when the family wagon overturns as the Bundrens attempt to cross the rain-swollen, bridgeless river. Subsequently he nearly loses his leg when it is put into a cement cast. At the last he becomes reconciled to Darl's being taken to the asylum; yet, unlike the other Bundrens, he seems by then to have gained a deeper insight into life and thinks of Darl with compassion. (Narrator of chapters 18, 22, 38, 53, and 59.)

340, 343, 344, 346, 347, 349, 350, 354, 355, 358, 360, 361, 363, 367, 368, 370, 371, 373, 374, 378, 380, 381, 384–386, 388–390, 392–395, 397, 400, 402, 406, 408, 409, 411–414, 416, 419, 422, 425–427, 429–434, 438–446, 448–452, 457, 458, 463–466, 470–472, 474, 478, 479, 481–483, 491–496, 504, 507, 509, 511, 513, 525, 526, 529, 532

Bundren, Darl. Bundren's second son. With the exception of Addie, whose well of affection became poisoned, Darl is the only one of the Bundrens ever capable of love. His poetic imagination labels him as queer; he is "the one folks talk about." He is despised by Dewey Dell because, having seen her together with Lafe, he knows about her pregnancy. He is hated by Jewel Bundren because he, Darl, wounded by Addie's tacit rejection of him and her concentrated love for Jewel, makes remarks to Jewel about his parentage. These remarks infuriate Jewel without his understanding them, because only Darl, thanks solely to his penetrating imagination, is aware of Addie's secret—that Jewel is not the son of Anse. En route to Jefferson, Darl plays into the hands of Dewey Dell and Jewel when, in an effort to cremate Addie's remains and thus put an end to the obscene pageant which now includes buzzards in its ranks, he sets fire to the barn where his mother's decomposed body is housed. Dewey Dell and Jewel learn that the burning is Darl's act, and as soon as Addie's corpse has been interred, they cause their brother to be sent to the insane asylum in Jackson. (Narrator of chapters 1, 3, 5, 10, 12, 17, 21, 23, 25, 27, 32, 34, 37, 42, 46, 48, 50, 52, and 57.)

339, 343, 344, 348, 349, 351, 352, 354–356, 361, 363, 365, 371, 375, 380, 389, 391, 393, 404, 405, 407, 409–412, 422, 423, 425–427, 429, 438, 439, 442, 447–451, 456, 460, 464–466, 470, 474, 476, 478, 481–483, 490, 493–498, 504, 506, 507, 509–513, 524–527, 532

Bundren, Dewey Dell. Anse's only daughter. Pregnant by Lafe, a young farmer, she is too intent on her own problem to fully realize her mother's death. Driven by her desire to get medical aid in town with the $10 Lafe has given her, she furiously pushes Anse on toward Jefferson when he might have turned back. In Mottstown her request for medical aid is turned down by an indignant druggist, and in Jefferson she is tricked by a young drug clerk into submitting to his intimacies in return for some pills which are worthless. Loathing Darl because he knows of her affair with Lafe, she is even more vicious than Jewel in physically aiding the authorities to overpower Darl when they come to take him to the Jackson insane asylum.

347, 355, 358, 359, 365, 366, 369, 371, 372, 374, 375, 378–380, 385, 386, 393, 399, 405, 408, 410, 413, 422, 427–430, 432, 435, 442, 443, 446, 452, 455–458, 467, 470, 471, 482, 483, 490–493, 495–498, 501, 504–507, 509, 511, 513, 514, 524–528, 531, 532

Bundren, Jewel. Addie's son by Whitfield. Of Jewel's illegitimacy only Darl is aware. Jewel's nature is one in which fury permanently resides. There is even a ferocity in his nearest approach to love—love for the horse that he buys from a neighbor whose fields he clears at night when he should have been sleeping. After the Bundren's mules are lost in the flood, Anse virtually steals Jewel's horse to give in partial trade for a new team of mules to take the Bundrens to Jefferson. On two occasions when Addie's body is nearly lost, once in the flood and once in the burning barn, it is Jewel who, in a sort of rage, retrieves the corpse. And finally, his fury reaches new heights when he falls upon his brother Darl as the authorities manacle Darl to transport him to the state insane asylum. (Narrator of chapter 4.)

339, 340, 344–352, 354–356, 359, 361, 365–367, 371, 373, 375, 378, 380, 393, 394, 396, 404–409, 413, 415, 418, 422, 423, 425–430, 432–435, 439–446, 448–450, 452–458, 460, 467, 474–478, 481–483, 493–497, 499–501, 504–514, 524, 525, 527, 529–532

Bundren, Vardaman. Youngest son of Anse and Addie. He thinks Dr. Peabody has killed his mother, so he stampedes the doctor's horses. Confusing his dead mother with a big catfish he catches on the day of her death, he comes to believe that Addie and the fish are one; and after Addie is in her coffin he bores holes in it so she can breathe, unintentionally driving the auger into her head. His chief reason for wanting to go to Jefferson is to somehow get the red toy train that he has seen in one of the store windows there. While at Gillespie's farm he sees Darl set fire to the barn and tells Dewey Dell. (Narrator of chapters 13, 15, 19, 24, 35, 44, 47, 49, and 56.)

358, 359, 364, 367, 371, 372, 374, 376, 378, 380–382, 384, 398, 408, 411, 422, 423, 427, 429, 432, 434, 435, 442, 443, 446, 452, 453, 455, 467, 481, 492–495, 498, 504–507, 509, 511, 514, 523, 527, 530–532

Gillespie. Farmer on the road to Jefferson who lets the Bundrens stay with him. He is the owner of the barn that Darl sets afire in order to cremate Addie's body and thus end the horrible funeral procession.

497–503, 505, 509, 511, 513

Gillespie, Mack. Gillespie's son. He helps put Addie Bundrens' coffin in the barn when the wind changes and he helps get the stock out of the barn when it is on fire.

    498–501

Grimm, Eustace. Man who works for Snopes. Eustace brings to Armstid's place the two mules for which Anse Bundren has traded Jewel Bundren's horse.

    480, 481

Grummet. Mottstown hardware-store owner from whom the Bundrens buy ten cents' worth of cement to put on Cash Bundren's leg.

    488, 489

Houston. One of those present at Addie Bundren's funeral.

    401, 402

Jody. Worker in the drugstore in Mottstown. He serves as lookout while MacGowan makes arrangements with Dewey Dell Bundren and is quite interested in the girl himself.

    517–519, 521, 522

Lafe. A young farmer and Dewey Dell's lover. He gives her $10 with which to buy medicine for "the female trouble" that is the consequence of their lovemaking.

    355, 380–382, 487, 488

Lawington, Miss. Woman who advises Cora Tull about getting a good breed of chickens and who tells Cora about a possible sale for cakes which does not materialize.

    341–343

Littlejohn. A neighbor of the Bundrens who is present at Addie Bundren's funeral.

    401, 402, 416, 421

MacCallum, Stuart. Rafe's twin, a farmer who has been trading with Samson for twelve years but whose first name Samson cannot recall. [Rafe is not identified further in the novel.]

    415, 416, 421

* *MacGowan, Skeet.* Clerk in the Jefferson drugstore who tricks Dewey Dell Bundren into submitting to intimacies in return for some worthless pills. (Narrator of chapter 55.)
    517, 520, 521

Moseley. A Mottstown druggist who refuses to sell Dewey Dell Bundren any medicine for her "trouble." Instead he advises her to marry Lafe. He watches the Mottstown marshal trying to hurry the Bundrens out of town in their wagon with its horrible odor. (Narrator of chapter 45.)
    484

* *Peabody, Dr.* A Jefferson doctor, seventy years old, weighing 225 pounds, who, summoned too late by Anse Bundren, arrives at the Bundrens' house just in time to see Addie die. Later he saves Cash's leg after the Bundrens have put it in a cement cast; and at the very last he comes to the Bundrens' aid once more when he pays their hotel bill in Jefferson. (Narrator of chapters 11 and 54.)
    364, 366, 374, 380, 386, 387, 395, 398, 399, 401–403, 410, 474, 511–513, 515, 529–531

* *Quick, Lon (old).* A farmer located near the Bundrens. He owns a descendant of one of Flem Snopes's spotted horses, which he trades to Jewel Bundren in return for Jewel's tremendous labor in clearing his field for planting.
    415, 433, 434, 451, 456

* *Quick, Lon (young).* Son of Lon, Sr. He is one of those who attend Addie Bundren's wedding. It is young Lon who finds Peabody's lost buckboard.
    398, 399, 401, 402, 415, 456

Samson. A farmer who puts the Bundrens up overnight when Addie Bundren's body has reached its most offensive state of decay. (Narrator of chapter 29.)
    404, 414, 415, 423

Samson, Rachel. Wife of Samson. She is outraged over the treatment of Addie Bundren's body and scores Samson and all men for their treatment of women.
    416–420

Snopes. Flem Snopes's cousin. He is a farmer living near Armstid's place. Snopes trades Anse Bundren a team of mules for Jewel Bundren's horse and other considerations.
473, 475–477, 480, 481, 483

Snopes, Flem. The man who twenty-five years ago brought some spotted horses from Texas to Frenchman's Bend. The horses were all sold at auction but were so wild that Lon Quick, Sr., was the only buyer who ever caught his. The horse Quick gives Jewel Bundren is a descendant of the one he bought from Flem.
433, 480

* *Suratt*. Owner of a talking machine which Cash Bundren believes he could have bought for $5.
478, 512, 530

Tull, Cora. Vernon's psalm-singing wife, vocally aggressive in matters of religion, and in ordering her husband about. (Narrator of chapters 2, 6, and 39.)
340, 351, 359–361, 386–391, 393–395, 399, 404, 405, 410, 430, 437, 448, 449, 459, 465, 467, 468, 528

Tull, Eula. One of Tull's daughters who come with their parents to visit the ailing Addie Bundren. Eula is fond of Darl Bundren.
343, 361

Tull, Kate. Eula's sister. Kate is fond of Jewel Bundren.
341–343, 361

Tull, Vernon. Farmer neighbor of the Bundrens who is very helpful. Among other kindnesses he aids the Bundren family in their effort to ford the swollen river and later dives into the water with Jewel and Darl Bundren to help recover Cash's tools, which are swept away when the Bundrens' wagon overturns. (Narrator of chapters 8, 16, 20, 31, 33, and 36.)
340–342, 344, 345, 348–353, 356, 357, 366, 368, 373, 378, 386–388, 393–395, 398, 399, 409, 411–413, 416, 423, 424, 427, 429, 435, 439, 440, 442, 443, 446–448, 452–458, 468–470

Varner, Uncle Billy. Storeowner and neighbor of the Bundrens. Also a horse doctor, he sets Cash Bundren's leg by very primitive means when Dr. Peabody cannot be reached.
 401, 402, 474, 515

Varner, Jody. Son of Uncle Billy, who says Jody was born in 1888, when the bridge (which later is washed away) was new.
 401

Whitfield. A preacher, one-time lover of Addie Bundren, and father of Jewel Bundren. He has, according to Cora Tull, often wrestled with Addie's soul. When he learns that Addie is dying he, so he says, realizes his sin and resolves to confess it to Anse Bundren. On arrival at the Bundren home, however, he finds Addie already dead and concludes that his confession is no longer necessary, that God will accept the intention for the deed. A short time later, in his mighty voice, he preaches the funeral service. (Narrator of chapter 41.)
 400, 401, 403, 404, 425–427, 429, 441, 459, 460, 468

SANCTUARY (1931)

Benbow, Belle Mitchell. Horace's wife, a divorcée. She goes to her mother's in Kentucky when Horace Benbow leaves her. When he returns, after Goodwin's trial, Belle, notified by Narcissa Sartoris of Horace's defeat, is at home before him, reading a magazine in bed. She is utterly indifferent to his return, her only emotion being vexation over his concern for her daughter's welfare.

    15, 16, 26, 28, 127, 128, 155, 212, 318, 359

Benbow (?), "Little" Belle Mitchell. Belle's daughter by her first marriage. She inspires in her stepfather Horace a mixture of vague sexual feeling and genuine paternal concern for her. She is probably unaware of the former and vexed by the latter; for, to her, he is almost a nonentity. If he comes upon her and a startled male embracing, she explains, "It's only Horace."

    14, 16, 28, 127, 199, 267, 358–360

* **Benbow, Horace.** Sensitive, verbose lawyer, who suddenly leaves his wife, unable to endure her coarse ways. As he travels afoot, he comes on the bootleggers' place, where he meets Popeye and Goodwin. Later, though scarcely the heroic type, he makes a valiant effort to defend Goodwin against a false murder charge. Opposed on every hand, especially by Narcissa Sartoris, he loses the case and returns, crushed, to his wife in Kinston.

    4–6, 11, 12, 14–16, 19–29, 126–132, 136–141, 143, 144, 146–148, 150, 153–157, 159–161, 192, 193, 197, 199, 201–219, 221–224, 240–250, 252, 254–259, 261, 265, 313, 314, 317–319, 321–332, 334–343, 348–355, 357–360

Binford. Miss Reba Rivers' landlord and lover for eleven years. When he died (two years before *Sanctuary* begins), Miss Reba, heartbroken, acquired two dogs and named them "Miss Reba" and "Mr. Binford."

    185, 307

Bud, Uncle. Small boy who accompanies Miss Myrtle, with whom he is visiting, to Miss Reba's. As the women drink away their woes, Uncle Bud also gets drunk, on beer he steals from them, and becomes sick.

301, 302, 304, 305, 308–310, 312

Doc. One of three young men whom Gowan Stevens takes in his car when he is in search of liquor after the dance in Oxford.

34–38

Drake, Judge. Temple's old father, who comes to court to get her after she has given false testimony at Goodwin's trial. Later he takes her to Paris.

62, 212

Drake, Hubert (Buddy). Temple's youngest brother. He, with his three brothers and their father, escorts Temple from the courtroom during Goodwin's trial.

63

Drake, Temple. Only daughter of Judge Drake. She has a bad reputation in Oxford, where she is attending the university. En route via train to a baseball game, she leaps from the moving coach to keep an engagement with the drunken Gowan Stevens, who takes her to Lee Goodwin's house. There she becomes involved with the bootleggers and is indirectly responsible for the death of Tommy, a half-wit. After being perversely violated by Popeye she accompanies him to a Memphis bordello, where, under his supervision, she takes a lover named Red. Lusting for Red, she attempts to run away with him and thus gets him killed by Popeye. Though she leads Horace Benbow to think that she will testify against Popeye, she gives false evidence against Lee Goodwin instead, thereby causing Lee to be convicted of murdering Tommy. At the last, with her father, she is sojourning in Europe, utterly bored with her life there.

31, 33, 34, 41, 46–49, 53, 55–58, 62–73, 75–78, 80–92, 94–98, 101–104, 107–110, 118, 120, 121, 123, 162–164, 166, 167, 170–181, 184–186, 188–190, 205, 207, 212, 256, 257, 269–275, 277–280, 285, 290, 339, 341, 342, 344, 361, 378, 379

* *Du Pre, Genevieve (Miss Jenny).* Ninety-year-old great aunt of Narcissa's deceased husband, she lives with Narcissa Sartoris. Though she is opposed to Horace Benbow's rather childish flight from home, she disapproves of Narcissa's ruthlessness and gives Horace some much-needed moral support in his fight for justice.
25–29, 127–129, 138–141, 150, 151, 153–155, 197–198, 219, 223, 350

Fonzo. See Snopes, Virgil.
226–238

Frank. Sweetheart of Ruby La Marr before she met Goodwin. He was killed by Ruby's father in her presence.
67

Gene. Bootlegger who supplies free drinks consumed at Red's funeral.
293–297

Goodwin, Lee. Ruby La Marr's common-law husband, a bootlegger who uses the old Frenchman's place as a hideout. Tried for a murder committed by Popeye, he refuses to give evidence against the murderer because, though proven a man of courage, he is afraid of Popeye's pistol, which never misses. Goodwin is convicted, and is later burned to death by a mob.
8, 9, 11, 12, 16, 20, 22, 23, 38, 43, 48, 52, 54, 57, 60, 65, 71, 76, 78–80, 84–88, 90–94, 110, 113, 116–120, 124, 129, 130, 135–137, 143, 144, 147, 150, 151, 155–158, 193–196, 224, 265, 323, 324, 326–336, 338, 344, 345, 350

Goodwin (?), Pap. An old man, blind, deaf, and dumb, who lives with the bootleggers and frightens Temple Drake as he taps his way from place to place. He is probably Lee Goodwin's father.
52, 53, 124, 156, 157

Graham, Eustace. District attorney who prosecutes Lee Goodwin. He is an ambitious man with an average mind who has always taken advantage of the allowances people make because of his clubfoot. During the trial he frequently introduces irrelevant material to impress the jury.
223, 314–316

Harris. Livery-stable owner who was in a poker game with Graham and passed when he recalled that Graham had dealt the cards.
316

Isom. Negro worker for the Sartorises. He drives Narcissa's car and chauffeurs Horace Benbow when the latter is in Jefferson.
145, 146, 148, 150, 158, 220

Joe. Proprietor of the Grotto Café, where he sponsors Red's funeral, complete with dance band, liquor, and mourners.
297, 298

Jones, Herschell. Man who has been calling on Narcissa Sartoris until Gowan Stevens comes along.
26

La Marr, Ruby. Goodwin's common-law wife and mother of his child, she cooks and keeps house for Lee and his men. Years before, she had given herself to an attorney to get Lee out of Leavenworth. Now she expects to do the same with Horace Benbow. (She is often called "Mrs. Goodwin.")
9, 10, 78, 88, 125, 137, 157, 160, 217, 323, 324, 327

Lorraine, Miss. Thin woman, member of the drinking party at Miss Reba Rivers' on the day of Red's funeral.
305–312

Luke. Bootlegger outside Oxford from whom Gowan buys liquor on the night of the dance.
35, 36

Minnie. Negro maid at Miss Reba's.
173–176, 184, 185, 234, 236, 237, 249–252, 254, 269, 271–275, 300–303, 309–312, 321, 322

Mitchell, Harry. Belle's first husband and Little Belle's father.
126

Myrtle, Miss. Member of the drinking party at Miss Reba's on the day
of Red's funeral. Miss Myrtle brings Uncle Bud with her.
303–311, 322

Popeye. Bootlegger born of a syphilitic father. He is impotent and so
weak of stomach that alcohol will kill him. His principal occupation is smoking numberless cigarettes. He inspires constant fear
among those who know him because he is eager and able to use
his ever-present automatic pistol. In Goodwin's barn he kills
Tommy, violates Temple Drake with a corncob, and later sets her
up at Miss Reba's [Rivers] in a private room, where he brings Red
to make love to Temple while he looks on. At last he kills Red
and leaves for Pensacola on his yearly visit to his mother. In
Birmingham he is arrested for killing a man in a small Alabama
town, where he, Popeye, has never been. He is subsequently tried,
convicted, and hanged for a murder that occurred on the same
night at the same hour that he killed Red in Memphis.
*1–11, 17, 22, 23, 50–52, 55–58, 80, 84, 85, 87, 88, 91–93, 95,
115–117, 120, 121, 123, 129, 137, 143, 147, 156, 158, 162–167,
169–171, 175, 190, 194, 196, 251–253, 256, 261, 265, 270, 273,
277, 280, 282–286, 290, 307, 310, 311, 313, 361, 363–365, 368–
378*

Quinn, Doctor. Doctor whom Miss Reba Rivers coerces into attending
Temple Drake.
173, 176

Red. Temple's lover, who is killed by Popeye because, at Temple's instigation, she and Red attempt to steal away from Popeye so that,
in the words of Temple, "It'll just be us." Later, during the excitement at the Grotto Café while Red's funeral is in progress, his
corpse falls out of the coffin and, when his cap falls off, Popeye's
calling card is exposed: a small blue hole in the center of Red's
forehead.
279, 283–287, 290, 293–295, 297, 310

Rivers, Reba. Proprietor of the bordello where Popeye brings Temple
Drake. Miss Reba is a successful "madam"; she caters to important
people and keeps the police in line, all the while lamenting her

sorrows—all physical ones—and fussing over her two dogs, "Mr. Binford" and "Miss Reba."
170–173, 175, 176, 178–180, 184, 185, 187–191, 231, 232, 234, 236, 248–257, 259, 261, 264, 269, 272–274, 276, 300–309, 311, 312, 321, 322

Sartoris, Benbow (*Bory*). Ten-year-old son of Narcissa.
27, 28, 140, 153, 155

Sartoris, Narcissa Benbow. Widowed sister of Horace Benbow, seven years his junior. She ruthlessly opposes at every turn Horace's efforts to help justice prevail in the Goodwin affair because she fears for her own social standing in the community, and finally hurries Horace home to his wife Belle, the woman she has always detested.
27–29, 127, 128, 131, 141, 145, 148, 151–155, 158, 159, 197, 198, 218, 219, 222, 223, 242, 244, 316, 349

Shack. One of two insipid university students on the Oxford-bound train with Horace Benbow who cheat the conductor out of their fare.
203

Snopes, Clarence. Coarse, unethical state senator, who seeks to fraternize with Horace Benbow, believing the latter's interest in Ruby La Marr and Temple Drake is carnal and that he and Horace, therefore, have much in common where women are concerned. As a result of his preoccupation with houses of prostitution, Clarence discovers Temple's refuge and informs Horace for a price.
208–214, 223, 238, 239, 242–249, 313, 317, 319, 320

Snopes, Virgil. Kinsman of Clarence, Virgil comes to Memphis with Fonzo to attend barber college. Seeking a cheap hotel, they, in their country-bred innocence, stumble onto Miss Reba's place, where they rent a room, thinking her large house is a hotel. Though they never discover the true nature of Miss Reba's establishment, they, with the help of Clarence Snopes, soon learn their way about other Memphis brothels, ever fearful, however, that Miss Reba

will find out about their adventures and regard them as unfit to
live in her "home."
226–239

* **Stevens, Gowan.** Young man proud of his attendance at the University of Virginia, where he learned to drink "like a gentleman."
When Narcissa [Sartoris] rejects his proposal of marriage he turns
to Temple Drake, whom he takes for a drunken ride to Goodwin's
for more liquor. Near Goodwin's place he wrecks his car, and he
and Temple spend the night as captives of the bootleggers. For
the fourth time in twenty-four hours Gowan gets drunk and is
badly beaten by Van, one of Lee Goodwin's men. Next morning,
in a stupor, Gowan leaves the bootleggers' place in search of a car
for hire. By the time he finds one his head has cleared to the
extent that he cannot bear to face Temple and so leaves her at
Goodwin's.
*26–29, 33–38, 40–42, 44, 46–48, 50–59, 61–63, 65, 66, 71, 75,
77, 79, 84–86, 88, 90, 92, 94–96, 99, 100, 153, 163, 197, 198*

Tommy. Feeble-minded but kindhearted man who works for Goodwin.
He is shot to death by Popeye when he attempts to protect
Temple Drake from him.
*20–24, 48, 55, 56, 75–88, 90–93, 95, 115, 117–121, 129, 134,
156, 196, 323, 344, 345*

Tull. Farmer who lives two miles from Goodwin's. At Tull's house
Ruby La Marr phones the sheriff that Tommy has been murdered.
100, 124, 125

Van. One of the bootleggers who beats up Gowan Stevens and is later
checked by Goodwin from furthering his designs on Temple Drake.
76–79, 85–88, 91, 93, 101, 194, 196

Walker, Mrs. Ed's wife, who gives Ruby La Marr and her child a night's
lodging on the jail premises when the hotel ejects Ruby.
215

Walker, Ed. Jefferson jailer.
218

LIGHT IN AUGUST (1932)

(See the genealogical chart of the Burden family on page 318.)

Alice. Twelve-year-old girl who helped look after Joe Christmas when they were both inmates of an orphanage.
127–129

Allen, Bobbie. Waitress in a cheap restaurant near McEachern's farm who has been brought from Memphis by Max Confrey as a combination waitress and prostitute. The seventeen-year-old Christmas has his first affair with her. After Christmas strikes Simon McEachern, she rejects him and flees with Max and Mame Confrey.
168, 171, 180, 201, 203, 205, 207, 208

* *Armstid.* Farmer who takes Lena Grove to his home overnight and the following morning transports her to Varner's store, where she can get a ride to Jefferson.
6–12, 14, 18–20, 22, 23

Armstid, Martha. Wife of Armstid. Though indignant about Lena Grove's illegitimate pregnancy, for which she apparently blames the whole masculine world, she gives her some hard-earned egg money to help the girl on her way.
10, 12–15, 17–20, 22

Atkins, Miss. Dietitian at the orphanage where Christmas lived. She thinks the five-year-old Christmas has heard her and Charley making love and understood what they were doing and that he will inform on her. After vainly trying to bribe the child, who does not understand what she is doing, the desperate woman tells the matron that he is a Negro, and the two women soon see to it that he is adopted by the McEacherns.
133, 134

Beard, Mrs. Owner of the boardinghouse where Byron Bunch lives and where Lena Grove stays when she first comes to Jefferson.
43, 76, 78–80, 283, 395

Bedenberry, Brother. Negro preacher who, while he is preaching, is assaulted by Christmas after Joanna Burden's murder.
305, 306

Brown, Joe. See Burch, Lucas.
32–42, 48–51, 73, 74, 80, 81, 83, 84, 86–98, 101, 102, 106, 255–260, 277, 279, 286, 287, 290, 303, 304, 331, 344, 369, 399, 400, 403–405, 410–414, 416, 417

Buford (Bufe). Deputy who helps the sheriff on the Burden murder case. Buford is in charge of Christmas when he escapes just before being killed.
276, 310, 433

Bunch, Byron. Worker at the Jefferson planing mill six days a week and leader of a country church choir on Sundays. He is Hightower's only link with the outside world and eventually draws him into aiding Lena Grove and attempting to save Christmas. Byron meets Lena because of the similarity between his name and that of Burch, her seducer. Without knowing it, he falls in love with Lena almost instantly and begins to serve her selflessly: finds a home for her, persuades Hightower to deliver her baby, and makes the supreme sacrifice in bringing Brown [Burch] to her. Believing that Lena is now lost to him and that he is in disgrace in Jefferson, he is about to leave town forever when he sees Brown fleeing from Lena's cabin. In an effort to make Brown return, Byron fights him and is badly beaten. Shortly, he sees Brown hop on a freight train and knows that he himself is free to go back to Lena. At the last, though Lena is still apparently oblivious to him, he accompanies her and protects her as before, because, in his own words, "I done come too far now . . . I be dog if I'm going to quit now." (His journey with Lena is described in chapter 21.)
22, 27, 29–34, 36, 38, 39, 41–47, 50, 55–57, 59, 62–76, 78–80, 82, 83, 85, 93, 282–287, 289–291, 294–299, 302–304, 342–

345, 348–351, 353–355, 361, 366–376, 380–384, 388–391, 393–395, 397–402, 413, 415–418, 422, 465, 477

Burch, Lucas (Brown, Joe). "Fun-loving" man who seduces Lena Grove in Alabama and, when she becomes pregnant, leaves for Mississippi, telling her that he must go for business reasons but will send for her. In Jefferson he changes his name to Brown and, for a time, works alongside Joe Christmas at the planing mill. He leaves this job to help Christmas with his bootlegging and goes to live with Joe in one of Miss Joanna Burden's cabins. Sometime later Brown, drunk, is found in the blazing Burden house by a countryman, Hamp Waller, and tries vainly to prevent the man from going upstairs, where Hamp finds Joanna's body, almost decapitated. Brown then disappears; but when he hears of the $1,000 reward offered for Joanna's murderer he hurries to town to inform on Joe and is himself taken into custody. Realizing that his own activities and his feeble efforts to explain them render him suspect, he plays his trump card: Christmas is a Negro, and he berates the lawmen who "Accuse the white and let the nigger run." With the sheriff now convinced that Christmas is the guilty one, Brown redoubles his desperate efforts to collect the reward. Before Christmas is apprehended, however, Brown flees the community because Bunch brings him, still in custody, face to face with Lena and her baby, which he fathered. He would sacrifice all chances of the reward to avoid domestic entanglements.

4, 6, 9, 10, 13, 15–17, 22, 25, 45, 46, 77, 79, 80, 288, 299, 303, 304, 380, 390, 399, 408, 415

Burden, Beck. Daughter of the elder Calvin and Evangeline. She, along with her brother Nathaniel and her sisters Sarah and Vangie, is forced to listen to their father read the Bible every Sunday. He can read only in Spanish, because all his formal education took place when he was a Catholic in Spanish California. Unfortunately, the children do not understand this language.

232

Burden, Calvin. Youngest of Nathaniel Burrington's ten children, he ran away to California at the age of twelve. Unable to even spell

his right name, he pronounced it "Burden." A hater of slavery, he taught his children to despise slaveholders and hell, and he himself killed a man in an argument over the racial question. He lost an arm in '61 while fighting with Kansas guerrillas. Afterward he moved with his family to Jefferson, where he was killed by Colonel John Sartoris over a question of Negro suffrage.
228–230, 232

Burden, Calvin. Son of Nathaniel and Juana Burden, and grandson of the elder Calvin. At the age of twelve he served as ring-bearer at the wedding of his father and mother, who had been unable to marry sooner because of the scarcity of ministers where they had been living. At the age of twenty, fourteen years before the birth of his half-sister Joanna, he was killed along with his grandfather by Colonel John Sartoris over a question of Negro voting.
233–238, 251

Burden, Evangeline. Wife of the elder Calvin and mother of Nathaniel Burden.
233

Burden, Joanna. Daughter of Nathaniel and his second wife. Because of her extensive activities on behalf of Negroes she is regarded by the white people as a foreigner, an outsider, in Jefferson, her birthplace, where she lives on the old family property long after all the other Burdens have gone. She permits Joe Christmas to live in one of her cabins, and after a time they become lovers, she becoming savage and perverted in their relationship. Meanwhile Brown has come to live with Christmas on the Burden property, a perfect place to cache their bootleg whisky. At about this time, Joanna suddenly abandons her way of life with Christmas and turns to religion. She attempts to convert him and make him a sort of missionary to the Negroes. When he refuses to pray with her she tries to shoot him. The ancient pistol she aims at him fails to go off and he slashes her throat and sets the house afire. Shortly a passer-by takes her body from the blazing structure.
32, 39, 42, 44, 45, 72, 73, 77, 81, 85, 86, 88, 214, 238, 278, 279, 420

Burden, Juana. Nathaniel's first wife, a Spanish woman whom he met in Mexico. She looks so much like the deceased wife of her father-in-law that he calls out the name "Evangeline" the first time he sees her.
    233

Burden, Nathaniel. Son of the elder Calvin. He ran away at the age of fourteen and returned sixteen years later to the home of his father, where he could get a minister to marry him to the mother of his twelve-year-old son. Eight years later he buried his son and his father in Jefferson, both slain by Colonel Sartoris, against whom Nathaniel claimed no vengeance because he understood that Sartoris was obliged to act as his homeland had trained him to act. Nathaniel told his daughter Joanna that the Negro race was "doomed and cursed to be forever and ever a part of the white race's doom and curse for its sins."
    230, 232, 233, 278

Burden, Sarah. The elder daughter of the elder Calvin.
    232

Burden, Vangie. Daughter of the elder Calvin. (Her name was probably Evangeline, after her mother.)
    232

Burrington, Nathaniel. New England minister, father of the elder Calvin Burden.
    228

Burrington, Nathaniel, II. Joanna Burden's nephew, who lives in St. Exeter, New Hampshire. He offers a $1,000 reward for the capture of Joanna's murderer.
    257, 258

Bush, Lem. Neighbor of the Hines family. He took Milly Hines to the circus in his wagon but did not bring her back because she ran away with one of the circus men.
    352

Carruthers, Miss. Organist for the church in Jefferson when Hightower II preached there. Though she has been dead for twenty years, Hightower still thinks of her as being alive and on duty.
346

Charley. Young intern whom the child Christmas is supposed to have heard making love to Miss Atkins. Christmas, hiding in Miss Atkins' clothes closet when she and Charley are together, is oblivious to everything but the sickness caused him by the pink toothpaste he has stolen and eaten.
113, 118, 119

Christmas, Joe. (*See* McEachern, Joe.) Illegitimate son of Milly Hines and a dark man said to be a Negro. After spending the first five years of his life in a white orphanage, where he got his name because he was left there on Christmas night, Joe is adopted by Simon McEachern, with whom he lives until the age of seventeen, accepting Simon's harsh discipline with a certain respect as being part of a relationship between males and therefore straightforward, predictable. However, when Simon pursues him to a country dance-hall and insults his mistress, Bobbie Allen, Joe knocks him unconscious with a chair, perhaps killing him. Later that night Joe is rejected by Bobbie and beaten and robbed by her associates. Haunted by these events and ever certain that he is part Negro, Joe begins a fifteen-year period of furious wandering, perversely proclaiming his mixed ancestry and thus provoking fights with men, whites and Negroes alike, and venting his bitterness on the women of both races to whom he makes love. He is proud that no white woman has ever thrown him out. At thirty-three he comes to work in a planing mill in Jefferson, Mississippi, and becomes the lover of Joanna Burden, white, on whose property he lives. Sometime later he quits his job to expand his bootlegging activities. When Joanna fails to convert him to her newly revived religion and attempts to shoot him, he slashes her throat and sets fire to her house. He is at last caught but escapes and flees to Hightower's home, where he is killed and castrated by Percy Grimm, a fanatical racist.
29, 31–42, 48–50, 73, 74, 80, 81, 83, 86–98, 102, 106, 109, 110, 124, 132, 135, 136, 173, 214, 215, 227, 234–236, 240, 244, 258–

*260, 265, 267–270, 277, 279, 284, 286, 287, 303, 307, 312, 319,
320, 322, 325–329, 331, 332, 343, 345, 359, 360, 362–364, 376,
388, 391, 399, 412, 418, 419, 421, 423, 427, 436–438, 465, 466*

Cinthy. Negro, wife of Pomp and cook for the first Gail Hightower, at whose home she remained until convinced of his and her husband's death. Still a slave, by choice, she moved into the home of the first Gail's son, where she remained, finally becoming the "third phantom" in the second Gail's life by giving the boy numberless extravagant accounts of his grandfather's exploits.
457–459

Confrey (?), Mame. Probably wife of Max, whom she aids, often directs, in all of his ventures.
175, 180, 185, 187, 198

Confrey, Max. Proprietor of a small restaurant near McEachern's place. Max imports Bobbie Allen to work for him as a combination waitress and prostitute.
175, 179–182, 185–187, 198, 199, 201–203, 205

Conner, Buck. Town marshal of Jefferson, active in handling the Burden murder case.
92, 93, 286

Dollar. Owner of the Mottstown store in front of which Doc Hines sits while his wife visits the jail in an effort to see Christmas. Dollar observes that Doc acts as if hypnotized.
338

Gillman. Owner of the sawmill of which Hines was foreman for a time.
359

Grimm, Percy. Young captain in the State National Guard. He is a chauvinist, frustrated because he was too young to serve in World War I. He atones by maintaining a "sublime and implicit faith in physical courage and blind obedience, and a belief that the white race is superior to any and all other races . . . and that the American uniform is superior to all men. . . ." When Christmas is brought captive from Mottstown to Jefferson, Percy, splendid in his captain's uniform, coerces the sheriff into making him a deputy. When Christmas escapes, Grimm pursues him skillfully and joyfully to Hightower's house, where he shoots Joe and castrates him so that he will "let white women alone, even in hell."

400, 425, 426, 428–439

Grove, Lena. A country girl six months pregnant by Lucas Burch. She leaves her brother's Alabama home and serenely sets out on foot to find Burch, who has promised to send for her when he is settled. At length she arrives in Jefferson, Mississippi, where Lucas is living. Because of a similarity in names she meets Byron Bunch, who falls in love with her and "protects" her so well that she does not meet her lover until after their baby is born. She knows from Byron's description of the man called Joe Brown, however, that Lucas is in town. When Lucas Burch, alias Joe Brown, flees from her, she resumes her travels, unperturbed, in the company of Byron Bunch. She does not mind having Byron attend her, but she does not seem to mind his absence. What she is most concerned about, apparently, is traveling, seeing the country, before the time comes when she must settle down. (Her journey with Byron is described in chapter 21.)

1–3, 14, 15, 17–20, 22, 45, 76, 78–80, 299, 371, 372, 403, 406, 416

Grove, McKinley. Brother of Lena, twenty years her senior, who, when their father dies, takes Lena into his home in Doanes Mill, Alabama. A hard-working, "bloodproud" man, he shows Lena no mercy when he sees that she is pregnant.

2

Halliday. Man in Mottstown who recognizes and captures Joe Christmas.

331, 332, 336

Hightower, Gail, I. Grandfather of Gail II, he was a bold, hearty man, who taught himself law. On the day his son married he surrendered the key of the family home to his son and daughter-in-law, and drove away, never to visit them because of a very delicate

sense of behavior inherent in him. During the Civil War he was shot to death robbing a chicken roost while a member of Van Dorn's Cavalry, sent to destroy Grant's stores in Jefferson.
451, 452

Hightower, Gail, II. The only child of an invalid mother and an austere father, almost a stranger, whom the boy feared. To Gail these two were as phantoms, their actions less real than the martial exploits of his grandfather, a mighty hero as described by still another "phantom," Cinthy, a Negro slave. In his heated imagination, young Gail II "skipped a generation," dying spiritually twenty years before he was born, the instant his grandfather, Gail I, was shot to death robbing a chicken roost in Jefferson while a member of Van Dorn's Cavalry. Because he felt that he must live in the town where his grandfather met death, Gail II came as a minister directly from the seminary, bringing with him his young wife, who had helped the innocent Hightower manipulate himself into the appointment he desired. Here he spent the first years in the supposed glory of his grandfather's past, preaching hysterical sermons in which religion and galloping cavalry became fused inextricably. His wife, apparently frustrated in marriage, made several mysterious trips out of town alone and finally lost her life when she fell from the window of a Memphis hotel in which she and a man were registered as husband and wife. Jefferson gossip had it that Hightower was not a "natural" husband, but evidence late in the story suggests that the Hightowers' marital problems may have resulted from Gail's extreme innocence and his obsession with the glorious past of Gail I. Finally his congregation rejected him, and he endured much persecution for a time; but he remained in his lonely Jefferson house, living "outside life," until his only regular visitor, Byron Bunch, "restores" him by bringing people's problems to him. In this way the man who thinks he "has bought immunity" from life finds that he still has compassion for suffering humanity: he tries to "save" Byron from Lena Grove but fails; later he delivers Lena's baby; then he makes a heroic but abortive effort to save Christmas from slaughter by saying that he and Joe were together on the night of Joanna Burden's murder.
43, 44, 53–55, 57–59, 62, 67–69, 71–74, 76, 77, 80, 82, 83, 85,

93, 282, 283–285, 289–300, 342–345, 349–351, 353, 354, 358, 361, 365–375, 377, 379, 380, 381, 385–388, 391, 392, 395, 401, 407, 416, 419, 421–423, 438

Hines, Mrs. Eupheus' wife, who for thirty-three years has not known whether her grandson is dead or alive. When she realizes who the murderer is, she pleads with Hightower to furnish an alibi for Joe. She is present at the birth of Lena Grove's baby, and confuses it in her mind with her own grandson, Joe Christmas.

327, 337, 349, 373, 376–378, 380

Hines, Eupheus (Uncle Doc). Slightly mad old man who preaches white supremacy in the churches of the Negroes who help to support him. Many years before, he killed the man who had run away with his daughter Milly because the man, it was said, was part Negro. Later he refused to call a doctor to attend Milly in labor, and she died. Shortly afterward, Hines placed Milly's infant on the doorstep of a white orphanage, where he himself worked for five years as a janitor and as "God's instrument . . . to watch the working out of His will" on Joe Christmas. After McEachern adopts Joe, Hines does not see his grandson until Joe comes captive to Mottstown, where Hines is living. Once again old Doc functions as God's instrument and harangues the populace to lynch Joe.

322–324, 326–330, 332, 333, 338, 341, 351–354, 356–365

Hines, Milly. Daughter of Eupheus, she ran away with the employee of a circus, who looked Mexican but was said to be part Negro. She died in giving birth to their child.

330, 352, 356–358, 360, 376

Jupe. Negro man who was in the path of Christmas when he walked aimlessly through the Negro section of Jefferson.

109

Kennedy, Watt. Sheriff who pursues Christmas.

45, 275, 390, 404, 405, 412, 429

McEachern, Mrs. Simon's wife. A small timid "gray" woman, she loves Joe Christmas and, though she fears Simon, she tries to protect

Joe from him and sneaks food to Joe when Simon is punishing him. From the beginning Joe has hated her well-meant conspiracies, her soft kindnesses. He steals money and later takes it openly from her little secret hoard rather than allow her to give it to him.

134, 138, 139, 141, 144, 152, 155, 171, 178, 179, 185, 188, 189, 196, 247

McEachern, Joe. See Christmas, Joe.

139, 144, 146, 147, 148, 151–155, 162–164, 166–174, 181–183, 185, 188, 189, 191–197, 199–202, 204, 205

McEachern, Simon. Stern, Calvinistic farmer who, ignorant of Joe Christmas' parentage, adopts him. He beats Joe without rancor whenever the boy fails to learn his Bible lessons and whenever Joe otherwise offends against Simon's rigid standard of conduct. On the night of the dance, after seeing Joe steal away from the house to be picked up in an auto, he follows on horseback in nightshirt and trousers. By sheer instinct he comes to the scene of the dance, a country schoolhouse, which he enters in puritanical outrage. He confronts Joe and Bobbie Allen, whom he calls "harlot," and is felled by his foster son, who departs, leaving Simon unconscious, perhaps dead.

136–144, 146, 149, 151–155, 157, 162–164, 166, 170, 171, 173, 179, 185, 187–189, 191–194

McLendon, Captain. Man in a barbershop who discusses with Maxey the highjacking activities of Christmas and Brown.

81

Mame. See Confrey, Mame.

Maxey. Man in barbershop who hears the drunken Joe Brown talk about his and Christmas' highjacking of a truck of liquor.

81

Metcalf. Mottstown jailer.

334, 335

Mooney. Planing-mill foreman where Christmas, Brown, and Bunch work.

    32–35, 37–41, 391

Peebles, E. E. Miss Joanna Burden's Negro attorney.

    261, 278

Pomp. Husband of Cinthy. Negro servant of Gail Hightower I, he followed his master to the war and, believing that the Yankees were holding Gail prisoner, lost his life when he attacked a Union officer.

    452

Russell. Sheriff's deputy in Mottstown.

    334, 335

Salmon. Renter of cars in Mottstown. Mrs. Hines wants him to take her and Eupheus to Jefferson but thinks his rates are too high.

    338, 339

Sartoris, Colonel John. Confederate soldier who killed Joanna Burden's half brother and her grandfather in Jefferson when they tried to implement Negro suffrage there.

    235, 240, 241, 420

Simms. Owner or superintendent of planing mill who hires Christmas and Brown.

    31, 32, 38

✱ *Stevens, Gavin.* Young district attorney, Harvard graduate, Phi Beta Kappa, whose grandfather publicly congratulated Colonel Sartoris for killing the Burdens. He makes arrangements for Christmas' body to be shipped to his grandparents and theorizes on how Mrs. Hines came to think of Lena Grove's baby as being "Joey" Christmas.

    419–421, 433

Thompson, Pappy. Old Negro man assaulted by Christmas when the latter disrupts a meeting in a Negro church after the Burden murder.
306

Thompson, Roz. Pappy's grandson, who wants to kill Christmas for hitting Pappy. As Roz enters the darkened church where Christmas waits, Christmas fractures his skull with a bench leg.
306, 307

Varner, Jody. Son of Will Varner. He tells Lena Grove that the man working at the Jefferson planing mill is named Bunch, not Burch.
21–23

Varner, Will. Jody's father.
11, 19, 24

Vines, Deacon. Negro deacon who sends a man for the sheriff when Christmas breaks into the church.
307

Waller, Mrs. Hamp's wife, who telephones the sheriff about the Burden house being on fire.
90

Waller, Hamp. Countryman who enters the burning house and brings Miss Joanna Burden's body out.
90

Winterbottom. A shrewd farmer, who is selling Armstid a cultivator when Lena Grove walks by, en route to Jefferson.
6–8

Atkinson. Partner of Ord in the manufacture of airplanes.
168, 207, 214, 232

Bullitt, Mrs. Bob's wife.
31

Bullitt, R. Q. (Bob). Flyer competing in New Valois airmeet.
31–33, 52, 60, 160

Burnham, Lieutenant Frank. One of the competing pilots, who is burned to death when his plane crashes.
27, 52, 55, 57, 60, 64, 73, 142, 144, 150, 152, 153

Chance, Vic. Airplane builder who would like to gratify Shumann and build him an airplane, but is prevented since neither man has the necessary money.
47

Cooper. Writer on the Reporter's paper who fills in for the latter at the airfield.
178

Despleins, Jules. French stunt flyer in the New Valois airmeet.
27, 142, 229

Feinmann, Colonel H. I. Jewish lawyer, chairman of the Sewage Board of New Valois, and operator of the local airfield. Feinmann is more concerned with pleasing his public than with protecting his flyers.
12, 14, 29, 32, 58, 64, 73, 74, 141, 150–152, 170, 214–216, 220, 222–226, 228, 232

Grady. One of the reporters on duty at the scene of Shumann's crash, who urges his fellows to stop talking about Shumann's sex life, to "let the guy rest." Grady does, however, continue to speculate as to why the flyers live as they do.
291

Grant, Joe. One of the flyers competing in the airmeet.
31

Hagood. City editor of the Reporter's paper. He storms at the Reporter for getting involved with the flyers and neglecting his job but reveals his sympathy by not discharging him, and even lends him large sums of money.
62, 85–87, 89–91, 93–99, 143, 162, 178, 179, 181, 187, 203–205, 230, 231, 238, 239, 241, 242, 266, 269–271, 314, 315

Hank. Announcer at the Feinmann Airport.
151

Holmes, Jack. Professional parachute jumper and Laverne's alternate lover. He may or may not be the father of the little boy called Jack Shumann. When Shumann is killed, Jack takes Laverne on his own and continues his old life at the various airmeets.
71, 82, 97, 98, 112, 113, 117, 123, 125, 128, 129, 147, 160, 165–167, 175, 182, 187, 246, 264, 296, 301, 303, 311

Hurtz. The Reporter's newest stepfather, who takes his bride to Santa Monica, California, for their honeymoon.
270

Jackson, Art. A stunt flyer whom Jiggs joins in the role of parachute jumper after Shumann's death.
39, 264, 282, 295, 296

Jiggs. Shumann's mechanic, who shares the common lot of Shumann's strange family. He takes money needed for living expenses and buys a pair of fancy boots which he pawns after Shumann's death to buy presents for Laverne and her son. Finally Jiggs decides to be a parachute jumper and teams up with Art Jackson, stunt flyer.

7–24, 29, 30, 32–38, 40, 56–59, 62, 66–73, 78–82, 84, 96–104, 112–133, 145–149, 155–159, 163, 164, 167, 175–177, 180–193, 217–220, 245–254, 257, 263–266, 268–274, 276, 278–283, 295–297

Joe. Proprietor of a café where the Reporter and his associates often go for refreshments.
205, 206, 299

Jug. Photographer on the Reporter's paper.
142, 143, 162, 230, 236

Laverne (Mrs. Shumann). A woman who was actively exposed when very young to the more seamy aspects of adult life. Her code of sexual ethics, therefore, is distorted; and she lives openly with two men, Roger Shumann and Jack Holmes, not knowing which is the father of her son. When Roger is killed, she surrenders her son into the keeping of Roger's parents and goes away with Jack Holmes, carrying in her womb a second child, which she knows belongs to Jack.
19, 20, 32–34, 57, 82, 98, 102, 103, 117, 125, 131, 148, 187, 198–200, 276, 277, 303, 311, 315

Leblanc. Policeman on duty at the airport when Holmes floors Jiggs and the Reporter. Knowing Leblanc, the Reporter prevails on him not to take the drunken Jiggs into custody and later borrows $5 from the officer.
156, 157, 182

Legendre, Dr. Doctor that Hagood recommends to the Reporter for a prescription for sleeping pills.
270

Leonora. Negro woman who cleans the Reporter's apartment.
138, 264, 300

Mac. The desk sergeant to whom the Reporter pays Jiggs's fine for vagrancy.
181

Marchand. One of Matt Ord's helpers, a Cajun whom the Reporter and Roger Shumann trick into surrendering Ord's defective airplane.
212, 215, 216, 218, 219, 227, 243

Monk. One of the airplane crew members at Feinmann's.
39

Myers, Al. One of the competing pilots.
31, 33, 53, 60, 64, 160

Ord, Mrs. Wife of Matt.
171

Ord, Matt. Former racing pilot, now a builder of airplanes. He does everything in his power to prevent Shumann from flying a plane that both men know to be defective.
97, 165, 167–175, 188, 189, 192, 207, 213–215, 218–229, 232–234, 243, 244, 292

Ott, Jimmy. Racing pilot.
31, 32, 60, 160

Pete. Restaurant man who sells the Reporter some gin with paregoric in it so it will pass for absinthe.
83

Reporter. The reporter assigned by Hagood to cover the New Valois airmeet. He meets the Shumann company and falls so deeply in love with Laverne that to serve her and hers is all he asks. He surrenders his home to the flyers and borrows money for their needs. He even signs Shumann's note for a second airplane when Roger's first one is wrecked. When Laverne, blaming him in part for Shumann's death, tells him to go away, he is crushed. Even so, thinking that Laverne and her son will continue together, he conceals a sum of money in the boy's toy airplane. When he learns that Laverne is to leave her son with Shumann's parents and go away with Holmes, the Reporter is grieved. (His real name is spoken of as being an incredible one and is never mentioned in the novel.)

27, 41–43, 50–53, 58, 59, 61, 64–66, 74, 76–79, 83, 84, 89, 90, 92–96, 99–104, 109, 111, 115, 119–122, 124, 132, 143–148, 156–159, 162–172, 175–183, 189, 201–208, 210–220, 228, 230, 231, 233–235, 238–251, 253–255, 257–262, 264–272, 274, 276, 278–280, 282, 283, 286, 288–290, 293–300

Sales, Mac. Airplane inspector who is coerced through a technicality into permitting Roger Shumann to fly Ord's defective airplane.

173, 220, 223–226, 230

Shumann, Dr. Carl S. Roger's father, who was greatly disappointed when he learned that young Roger was interested in racing machines instead of in medicine. He mortgaged his farm, however, to provide Roger with aircraft, and he finally accepts the care of Laverne's child (hoping it is Roger's too), provided she will never come near the child as long as he, Carl Shumann, is alive. When he breaks Jack's toy plane and discovers the Reporter's money, the doctor burns it, thinking Laverne has earned it as a prostitute.

212, 214, 304, 306, 309–313

Shumann, Jack. Laverne's son. His father is either Roger Shumann or Jack Holmes. To the oft-repeated question "Who's your old man today, kid?" little Jack will come at his questioner, fists flying.

22, 23, 64, 77, 78, 82, 193, 293

Shumann, Roger. Dr. Carl's son, who scorned a medical career to become a racing pilot. He shares his common-law wife with Jack Holmes and assumes the paternity of Laverne's boy, who may or may not be his. After wrecking his own airplane he, aided by the Reporter, tricks Matt Ord into letting him use a plane known to be defective. In a valiant effort to win a large purse for "his family" he loses his life when Ord's plane comes apart over a lake and plunges into the water. At the end Roger's body is still unrecovered.

12, 14, 20, 23, 31–33, 35, 44, 46–48, 52, 57, 59, 62, 64, 65, 69–71, 78, 79, 81, 82, 84, 98, 102, 103, 112–117, 119–131, 147–151, 154–156, 160, 163–172, 174–177, 179–191, 193, 196–200,

211–216, 220, 222–229, 232–234, 237, 240, 253, 255–257, 259, 272, 274–276, 290, 292–294, 296, 302, 303, 306–309, 311, 314, 315

Shumann, Mrs. Roger. See Laverne.

Smitty. One of the Reporter's fellow workers on the newspaper.
204, 205

ABSALOM, ABSALOM! (1936)

(Chapter vii of this novel incorporates an extensively revised version of the short story "Wash" [from *Doctor Martino*; reprinted in *Collected Stories of William Faulkner*]. In indexing this novel the present tense is used only for detailing events that occur during the lifetime of Quentin Compson, who, with Shrevlin McCannon, pieces together the parts of the Thomas Sutpen narrative.)

Akers. A coon hunter who nearly stepped on one of Sutpen's Negroes who had covered himself with mud for warmth. One evening five years later, after having seen Sutpen's four wagons loaded with house furnishings, Akers stepped into the bar at Holston House and reported as follows: "Boys, this time he stole the whole durn steamboat!"
36, 44

Benbow, Judge. Self-appointed executor of Goodhue Coldfield's estate, he sold the family store for Miss Rosa Coldfield. Since the indigent spinster would not accept cash from the sale, the judge overpaid her through the years by leaving baskets of food on her porch and by paying for services and articles that she demanded in the stores but would not admit she had bought, including a $200 headstone for the grave of Judith Sutpen.
46, 170, 211, 212

Benbow, Percy. Judge Benbow's son, who, after his father's death, opened the Judge's Coldfield portfolio marked "Private" and found that the judge had for forty years kept strict book on all money that he had won and lost on horse races and had put his winnings to Miss Rosa Coldfield's nonexistent account.
212

Bon, Charles. Son of Eulalia and Thomas Sutpen. Unaware of his father's identity and of his mother's elaborate plan for revenge, he went to the university at Oxford, Mississippi, when he was about twenty-eight years old. There, as his mother had planned, he met Henry Sutpen and went home with him, where he inspired Judith Sutpen's love. Afterward, learning that Thomas Sutpen was his father as well as Judith's, he was willing to leave Judith forever if his father would but acknowledge him. This Sutpen would never do; but when he learned that Bon planned to marry Judith, he informed Henry that Bon was Henry's brother. Since Henry finally decided to accept the idea of incest, Sutpen then told him that Bon was part Negro. Miscegenation Henry could not permit, and so after the war the two veteran soldiers rode together to the gates of Henry's home, where Bon, refusing to give up Judith, met his death at Henry's hand.

67, 70, 71, 74, 75, 78, 79, 82, 87, 89–99, 101–115, 117–123, 126, 133, 141, 148, 158, 162, 182, 190, 192, 201, 203, 216, 265–270, 276, 295, 296, 300–307, 309, 311, 314, 318–320, 322, 326–329, 332, 334–346, 348–351, 353–358, 364, 374, 377, 378

Bon, Charles Etienne Saint Valery. Son of Charles Bon and his octoroon mistress. Motherless at the age of twelve and speaking no language save French, he came to Sutpen's to live with Judith Sutpen and Clytie [Clytemnestra]. Unaware of the implication of "nigger," and shielded by Judith and Clytie from knowledge of his Negro blood, he eventually worked out his role for himself. Because he was bitter over his heritage, this role was a perverse one. Though he could have passed for white, he married a coal-black, apelike, mentally retarded woman whom he flaunted in the faces of "all who would retaliate," thus earning himself countless beatings by strangers, white and black. After a year's absence he returned to Sutpen's, his wife already far advanced in pregnancy. Thereafter, except for an infrequent drinking bout in the Negro district, he lived like a hermit in one of the Negro cabins at Sutpen's, consorting with neither white nor black. About four years after the birth of his son, Etienne fell ill of yellow fever and died in Sutpen's big house. (Valery is spelled Velery in the appendix to the novel.)

191, 205, 208, 215

Bon, Eulalia. See Sutpen, Eulalia Bon.

Bond, Jim. Slack-mouthed, feeble-minded son of Charles Etienne Bon and his mentally-retarded wife. As the old Sutpen house, behind which he is living in a shack, burns down, we finally find him, twenty-six years old, "the last of his race, seeing it too now and howling with human reason now since now even he could have known what he was howling about."
214–216, 371, 376, 378

Clytemnestra (Clytie). Thomas Sutpen's daughter by one of his Negro slaves. With Judith she scratched a living from Sutpen's land and kept their home intact while Thomas was away at war. When Etienne Bon lost his mother she fetched him from New Orleans, watched over him constantly, and taught him to farm. Later, when Judith and Etienne were ill of yellow fever, Clytie risked her life to minister to them until they both died. Then for the next twelve years she scrimped to make the last payment on Etienne's headstone, meanwhile raising Etienne's feeble-minded son, Jim Bond. At the end, Clytie, a little dried-up woman not much bigger than a monkey, guards the secret of Henry Sutpen's presence in his old home until Rosa Coldfield discovers him there; and when Clytie sees the ambulance coming for him, she thinks officials are about to arrest him for the ancient murder of Charles Bon, whereupon she sets fire to the big house and perishes in it along with the invalid, Henry.
61, 62, 70, 87, 94, 101, 125, 126, 128, 132, 142, 150, 152, 154–159, 162–164, 168, 172, 180, 183, 186, 187, 190, 191, 194, 195, 199–201, 203, 204, 208–210, 216, 266, 271, 274, 276, 277, 281, 285, 350, 351, 353, 358, 369–371, 374, 375, 378

Coldfield, Goodhue. Keeper of a small store before the Civil War and, for a time, partner of Thomas Sutpen. During their association Coldfield, in a moment of uncertainty, permitted Sutpen to use a bill of lading unethically, thinking that such an act would fail anyway. It did succeed, however, and Coldfield, a man of great moral strength, broke up the partnership. Later he preached against secession calmly and logically; but when war was declared, his logic departed. He closed his store and withdrew from life, solaced only by his Bible. When his store was looted by Confederate troops, he nailed himself in his attic, where he lived on food hoisted up to him by Rosa Coldfield, all the while lamenting the waste that accompanies war. After three years of this self-imprisonment, he starved himself to death.

43, 44, 46–53, 55, 57, 59, 63, 64, 66, 71, 73, 77, 78, 80, 82, 211, 212, 259, 262

Coldfield, Miss Rosa. Goodhue's younger daughter, who hated him because her mother died in giving birth to her. Even so she became the dutiful mistress of her father's household after the paternal aunt, who raised her and whom Rosa despised, eloped from Goodhue's home with a horse-and-mule trader; and during the years her father hid in his attic from the war he hated, she faithfully provided him with food. After the deaths of her father and Ellen Sutpen, Rosa went to Sutpen's to live with Judith Sutpen and Clytie [Clytemnestra]. Some months after the war, when Thomas Sutpen, whom Rosa had from childhood regarded as an ogre, returned home a widower, she was prepared to accept from him what at first seemed an offer of marriage, since, in her opinion, his valorous conduct in the war had slain the ogre in him. He was at least human, she thought, until he proposed that they be married only if she first provided him with a son to replace the vanished Henry. Outraged, she returned to her father's old home to live on charity which she would not acknowledge. In 1909 she sends for Quentin Compson; and, her original hatred of Sutpen long since restored, she gives the youth her account of Thomas which presents him as a fiend. She then asks Quentin to accompany her to Sutpen's home, where she has not been in forty-three years, because she somehow knows that there is "something living in that house"; and she does not mean Clytie. Once at Sutpen's, she discovers the invalid Henry and summons an ambulance for him. Though she is said to have "died of outrage" in 1866, her actual death occurs in January, 1910.

7, 9, 11–14, 27, 33, 36, 37, 40–43, 48, 51, 59–71, 73–77, 79–85, 87, 88, 94, 102, 104, 126, 133, 138, 139, 141, 142, 149, 150, 159, 164, 166, 168, 170, 171, 173, 174, 176, 180, 190, 196, 209–211, 216, 269, 277–280, 284, 296, 302, 304, 322, 325, 350, 358, 362, 364, 367–371, 374–376

Compson, General. Quentin's grandfather, a one-armed veteran of the Civil War. He came to know Sutpen and lent the penniless man seed cotton. General Compson, through his son, supplied Quentin with a kindlier version of Thomas Sutpen than does Miss Rosa Coldfield.
  33–35, 37–41, 208

Compson, Jason. Son of General Compson and father of Quentin, he transmits the General's story of Sutpen to his son Quentin. (Jason narrates pages 43–58.)
  12, 31, 43, 59, 89, 128, 132, 174, 187, 188, 190, 191, 207, 277, 278, 335, 336

Compson, Quentin. Jason's son, a student at Harvard, who, with the aid of his roommate Shrevlin McCannon, pieces together the Sutpen story, parts of which have been supplied by various people. Quentin himself has previously come upon an important part of the story at first hand when he helps Miss Rosa Coldfield discover the dying Henry Sutpen.
  7–14, 20–22, 31, 33, 35–38, 40, 41, 43, 59, 61, 88, 89, 128, 129, 132, 172–174, 176, 178, 179, 181, 185, 187–193, 207, 210, 211, 215, 217, 218, 220, 221, 238, 255, 258–261, 265, 266, 274, 275, 277, 280, 292–295, 299, 311, 314, 321, 322, 324, 325, 328, 334–336, 344–346, 359–366, 369–371, 373–378

de Spain, Major. Sheriff who came with a posse to the scene of Thomas Sutpen's murder. He was forced to kill Wash Jones when Wash rushed toward him with the scythe he had used to kill Sutpen.
  291, 292

Hamblett, Jim. Justice who tried Charles Etienne Bon for fighting with Negroes. He was well into his oration of indictment when General Compson, understanding the implications surrounding Charles Etienne's brawls, quashed the indictment and paid the fine.
  203

Holston, Alexander. One of the founders of Jefferson, who opened the establishment that still bears his name, Holston House.
  31–33, 36, 43–45, 63, 275

* *Ikkemotubbe.* Chickasaw Indian who sold Thomas Sutpen the 100 miles of Yoknapatawpha bottom land that came to be known as "Sutpen's Hundred."
  54

Jones, Melicent. Daughter of Wash and mother of Milly. She is rumored to have died in a Memphis brothel. (Named only in the novel's genealogy appendix.)

Jones, Milly. Sixteen-year-old granddaughter of Wash. She bore the sixty-year-old Thomas Sutpen a daughter and was insulted by him because the child was not a boy. Shortly after, she died by the hand of Wash, who wished to protect her by this act.
  185, 286

Jones, **Wash.** Squatter, living in an abandoned fishing shack on Thomas Sutpen's property. He admired and looked up to Sutpen and wanted to be identified with him even to the extent of letting Sutpen have his granddaughter Milly, providing Sutpen would "do right by her," as Wash felt sure he would do. When Milly bore Sutpen a daughter, not a son, Sutpen repudiated her; and Wash, the eyes of his small, lowly world upon him, killed Sutpen with a scythe. A short time later he killed Milly to save her from the suffering he imagined was in store for her, and then he died at the hands of the sheriff, de Spain, as he rushed at de Spain with the murder weapon.
  26, 81, 87, 125, 133, 134, 150–152, 154, 156, 161, 166, 168, 171, 172, 177, 181–187, 271, 276–278, 280–292, 358

Luster. Negro lad who, with Quentin Compson and some other boys, is frightened away from the Sutpen property by Clytie [Clytemnestra] and who later refuses to go within 50 yards of the old house.
  187, 213–215

* *McCannon, Shrevlin (Shreve).* Quentin's Canadian roommate at Harvard, who helps Quentin put together the Sutpen story. He cannot understand the Southern mind, but his objective outsider's viewpoint (at times expressed almost brutally) constitutes a solid contribution to the task that faces the two young men. (Only his nickname, "Shreve," appears in the novel; his full name is given in the novel's genealogy appendix.)

173, 174, 176, 181, 187, 207, 215–218, 220, 223, 232, 246, 247, 255, 256, 258–262, 265–267, 270, 274, 275, 277, 280, 286, 289, 292–295, 299, 303, 311, 314, 316, 321, 324, 329, 333–336, 339, 344–346, 351, 358–361, 373, 374, 376–378

McCaslin, Theophilus. Old man who assisted at Charles Bon's funeral by helping to carry the coffin and by giving a Confederate yell in lieu of the proper Catholic words, which no one present knew.

152, 275

Pettibone. Owner of the big plantation for whom Thomas Sutpen's father worked. His materially rich life helped to inspire Thomas' dream of wealth and power.

231

Sartoris, Colonel John. Man of valor and decision. With Thomas Sutpen he raised a Jefferson regiment in '61 and rode away with Sutpen as his second-in-command beneath the regimental colors which the two of them had designed. After the Second Battle of Manassas, Colonel Sartoris was replaced by Sutpen at the annual election of regimental officers.

80, 121, 124, 126, 152, 189

Sutpen, Ellen Coldfield. Goodhue Coldfield's older daughter, twenty-seven years Rosa's senior. She married the mysterious Thomas Sutpen and moved into his big house, where she bore him a son and a daughter. Passive, confused, she feared her husband from the beginning. After some years of marriage, corrupted by Sutpen's role of arrogant ease, she flowered (like his, it was a forced blooming) into the part of regal lady of the manor, and in this role she spoke convincingly of Charles Bon as son-in-law, complement for her household, and social mentor for Henry Sutpen. Her airy dream exploded on the Christmas Eve that Thomas and his son quarreled and Henry and Charles Bon rode away. She then seemed to have retired into that darkened room where she remained for two years. At the end of this time she asked Rosa Coldfield to take care of Judith and died.

9, 11, 13, 15–18, 20–30, 46, 48, 49, 51–58, 60, 62–66, 68, 70–76, 78–82, 84–87, 93, 97, 99, 101–106, 121, 125, 126, 134–136, 138, 140–142, 145–147, 149, 164, 165, 171, 188, 211, 269, 271, 279, 281, 320–322, 326, 329, 330, 363, 367

Sutpen, Eulalia Bon. Thomas Sutpen's first wife, a wealthy Haitian-born woman who bore him a son and whom he put aside when he discovered she had Negro blood. Thereafter, dominated by a scheme for revenge, she arranged to have her polished son go to the university at Oxford, Mississippi, preceded by a letter of introduction to Henry Sutpen, who was also a student there. The final outcome of the association between the two young men was much as she could have wished it, though she probably never survived the final working-out of her plot, because by that time she had very likely been murdered by her attorney. (Her name is mentioned only in the novel's genealogy appendix, but important references to her appear on pages 296–313, 339.)

Sutpen, Henry. Son of Thomas and Ellen. He was much more sensitive than was his sister Judith. At Oxford he was captivated by the polished Charles Bon and tried to imitate him in dress and manner. Through him Charles and Judith met and became engaged. When Henry was told by his father that Charles was his half brother, he gave Thomas the lie and left home in anger, knowing even then that his father had told the truth. As the two young men served together in the army, Henry, still devoted to Charles, gradually began to accept the idea of incest. When at length their path crossed that of Thomas, Thomas summoned Henry to his tent, where he told him that Charles was part Negro. Hoping now that Charles would not go through with the marriage, Henry bided his time until the war's end, when, assured that Charles would not back out, Henry killed him at the Sutpen gate and disappeared. Years later, a sick old man, he returns home secretly to die. His end comes when Clytie [Clytemnestra] sets fire to the old house in which he is lying helpless.

18, 21, 25–27, 29, 30, 62, 65, 67, 70, 71, 73–76, 78, 79, 86, 87, 89–115, 117–123, 126, 132, 133, 135, 136, 138–141, 145–147,

152, 155, 157, 159, 162, 201, 208, 216, 265–271, 276, 277, 292–
295, 309, 313, 314, 317–322, 325–329, 332–337, 340–347, 349–
359, 364, 373, 374, 378

Sutpen, Judith. Daughter of Thomas Sutpen, whose strong nature she
inherited. Falling desperately in love with Charles Bon, she
awaited him through the war years and lost him at the hands of
her brother, perhaps without knowing why. Without apparent
emotion she buried him and later her father. Finally she raised
the son of her fiancé by his octoroon mistress, nursed him on his
deathbed, caught his sickness, yellow fever, and died shortly before
he did.

15, 18, 21, 22, 25, 26, 30, 59, 61, 62, 65–67, 69–71, 73, 75–77,
79, 80, 84, 86, 87, 90–92, 94, 96–99, 101–105, 107–109, 119–
127, 135–142, 145–147, 151, 152, 154–159, 162–164, 167, 168,
170, 183–185, 188, 190–195, 197, 199–201, 203–211, 216, 266–
271, 276, 277, 281, 283, 285, 320, 322, 328–330, 332–334, 337,
341–343, 347, 350, 353, 354, 358, 370, 377

Sutpen, Thomas. Son of a poor West Virginia mountain farmer. He
came to believe early that material possessions were all-important;
and when, delivering a message for his father to the wealthy
Pettibone, he was directed by a haughty servant to go to the rear
door, the purpose of his life was confirmed: to establish a dynasty
of material wealth. From then on, with great singleness of purpose, he directed his every act to that end. Beginning his mission
in the West Indies, he put away his wife and son when he discovered that she had Negro blood, taking only some wild Negro
slaves with him to America. By devious means (including the
exchange of Spanish coins), he acquired 100 miles of virgin
bottom land 12 miles from Jefferson, and with his slaves and a
captive French architect he built a massive house on this land.
This done, he married a woman of good family and had a son
and a daughter by her. His design was then threatened by the
appearance of Charles Bon, his first son, who won Judith Sutpen's
love—all a part of Sutpen's first wife's plan for revenge. Rather
than openly acknowledge Charles Bon as his son and thus prevent
Judith's marriage to Charles, he attempted to achieve this end
by secretly telling his son Henry of the relationship. When, in the

midst of war, he realized that Henry would permit the incestuous union, he told him of Bon's Negro blood. This act made it necessary for Sutpen to start again insofar as family was concerned, for Henry disappeared, after killing Charles, and stern Judith remained a spinster for life. Sutpen, his wife Ellen dead, proposed to Rosa Coldfield, his sister-in-law, that they be married on condition she first provide him with a son. Outraged, she rejected his proposal and he, at sixty, tried for a son with Milly, sixteen-year-old granddaughter of Wash Jones. When Milly had a daughter Sutpen insulted her, perhaps as a means of provoking Wash to kill him, which Wash did. According to Quentin's grandfather, General Compson, who knew Sutpen better than anyone else, Sutpen's basic fault was one of innocence. "Where did I fail?" was the question that he honestly asked General Compson.

9, 11–14, 16, 30, 32–41, 43–45, 47–56, 59, 63, 68, 70, 72, 74, 79, 80, 82, 84, 85, 87, 90, 92–94, 96, 97, 99, 101–107, 120, 121, 124–126, 134, 145, 154–158, 162, 165, 182, 183, 188, 190, 209, 218–220, 238, 239, 243, 245, 247, 249, 252, 256, 257, 259–262, 266–270, 272, 273, 276, 280–290, 301, 302, 304, 305, 309, 313, 329, 331–333, 335, 344, 348, 353, 377

Willow, Colonel. Officer who made the report about Henry Sutpen's wound to Thomas Sutpen.

353

THE UNVANQUISHED (1938)

(The first six chapters of *The Unvanquished*, previously published separately as short stories, were revised for the book ["Ambuscade," *Saturday Evening Post*, September 29, 1934; "Retreat," *Saturday Evening Post*, October 13, 1934; "Raid," *Saturday Evening Post*, November 3, 1934; "Skirmish at Sartoris," *Scribner's*, April, 1935; "The Unvanquished" (entitled "Riposte in Tertio" in the book), *Saturday Evening Post*, November 14, 1936; and "Vendée," *Saturday Evening Post*, December 5, 1936]. The last chapter, "An Odor of Verbena," had not been published previously. *See the genealogical chart of the Sartoris family on page 316.*)

Benbow, Judge. Judge who arranges for Redmond to sell his half of the railroad to Colonel John Sartoris.
259

Benbow, Cassius Q. (Uncle Cash). Former Benbow Negro. He runs off with the Yankees during the war. Later he is candidate for marshal, but his election is prevented by Colonel John Sartoris and his followers.
228, 229, 232, 234, 241, 253

Bowden, Matt. One of Grumby's renegade group. Disgusted with his leader's action, especially the killing of Granny, he delivers Grumby into the hands of Bayard Sartoris and Ringo.
208

Bowen, Captain. Officer in the Union Army.
132

Breckbridge, Gavin. Drusilla Hawk's [Sartoris] betrothed, who is killed at Shiloh.
101, 219, 227, 263

Bridger. One of Grumby's men who deserts Grumby to follow Bowden.
205, 207

Burdens. Two Missouri men who come to Jefferson with a patent from Washington to organize the Negroes as voters. They try to get Cash Benbow elected as marshal and are killed by Colonel John Sartoris, who allows them to fire the first shot.
229, 232, 234, 236

Compson, General. Confederate officer in the Civil War.
282

Compson, Mrs. Old lady in Jefferson who lends Rosa Millard clothing and an umbrella. Mrs. Compson inspires sympathy because her husband is generally regarded as queer, one of his idiosyncrasies being that he often shoots potatoes off the heads of Negro children.
52, 80, 87, 88, 92, 117, 120–122, 127, 147, 148, 153, 155, 156, 178, 180, 211, 218, 220–224, 226, 227

* *Cook, Celia.* Young girl who, as she watched General Forrest ride down an Oxford street, scratched her name on the windowpane with a diamond ring.
17

Dick, Colonel Nathaniel G. Union officer who pretends not to know that the two boys, Bayard Sartoris and Ringo, who have shot one of his horses, are hiding under Granny Millard's skirts. Later, partly through generosity, partly by accident, he repays Granny with interest for her stolen silver, mules, and servants.
88, 89, 120, 124, 125, 145, 146

* *Du Pre, Virginia Sartoris (Aunt Jenny).* Colonel John Sartoris' sister, whose husband is killed early in the Civil War. After Rosa Millard's death she comes to her brother's home. She supports Bayard Sartoris in his refusal to shoot Redmond.
247, 251, 253, 254, 259, 263, 265, 267, 270–273, 275, 276, 278, 279, 281, 291, 292

Fortinbride, Brother. Former private in Colonel John Sartoris' regiment. He is sent home from the war to die but lives on and preaches at Colonel John's church. He helps Rosa Millard distribute money and mules to the poor and later conducts her funeral.
152–154, 156–158, 177–180

Granny. *See* Millard, Rosa. To Bayard and Ringo Rosa is always "Granny."

Grumby. Craven leader of a group of Southern renegades who terrorize their own people, especially the women and children. He is responsible for Granny's death and so is killed by Bayard Sartoris and Ringo, who nail his body to the door of the compress where Granny was shot and nail his hand to her wooden headstone.
    170–172, 183, 184, 187, 191–193, 195, 198, 201, 204–208, 210, 218, 248, 251, 254, 261, 283, 287

Habersham. Worker in Jefferson bank who signs Colonel John Sartoris' peace bond.
    253

Habersham, Martha. His wife, who helps Aunt Louisa Hawk keep an eye on Colonel John Sartoris and Drusilla Hawk and who is finally very active in getting them married.
    215, 216, 223–225, 227, 232, 234, 235, 241, 253

Harris, Plurella. An alias that Ringo invents for Granny to use in her plan to trick the Yankees out of livestock.
    146, 149

Harrison. Union sergeant who searches the Sartoris house after Bayard Sartoris and Ringo have shot one of his group's finest horses.
    34, 36

Hawk, Dennison, Jr. (*Cousin Denny*). Drusilla's young brother. He is ten years old when we first meet him during the last weeks of the war. When he grows to manhood he marries and reads law in Montgomery, where Drusilla joins him after she leaves the Sartoris home.
    98–103, 106, 113, 116, 147, 156, 220, 230, 232, 233, 236, 292

Hawk, Dennison, Sr. (*Uncle Dennison*). Father of Drusilla and Dennison, Jr. He named their home Hawkhurst. Hawk died before the war began.
    15, 97, 230, 231

Hawk, Louisa. Wife of Dennison, Sr., and sister of Rosa Millard. She is convinced that her daughter Drusilla and Colonel John Sartoris are living in sin and goes to John's home to put things right.
105, 106, 170, 215–223, 227, 230–236, 239–241

Hilliard. Livery-stable man in Oxford from whom Ringo obtains a fine horse when he comes to tell Bayard Sartoris about Colonel John Sartoris' death.
250

Holston, Mrs. Old Jefferson lady whose porter witnesses the killing of the two Burdens.
237

Jingus. Negro servant of the Hawk family in whose cabin the Hawks live after their house is burned by the Yankees.
98–101

* *Joby.* Ringo's grandfather. He grumbles over much of the labor Granny Millard assigns him but is loyal to the Sartoris family.
4, 8, 12–14, 16, 18, 19, 22, 24–27, 29, 42–51, 61, 63, 65–67, 80, 81, 84, 88–90, 135, 141, 162, 163, 165, 166, 174, 183, 212, 213, 221, 224–227, 231, 251, 265, 279

Lena, Missy. Negro servant of the Hawk family. It is in her cabin that Ringo sleeps when he is at Hawkhurst.
112

Loosh. Negro, Joby's son and Ringo's uncle. Loosh is the only one of his family to get caught up in the idea of freedom for the Negro. He reveals the hiding place of the Sartoris silver to the Yankees and goes off with them but returns to Sartoris after the war.
4–6, 8–10, 12–14, 16, 19, 22–27, 41, 42, 44–46, 48–51, 84, 85, 89, 90, 104, 125, 142, 155, 246, 279

Louvinia. Joby's wife, who is cook for the Sartorises and ever faithful to them. Loosh's behavior is her shame.
8, 12, 13, 15, 16, 19, 20, 23–27, 29, 30, 31, 34–38, 42–48, 51,

58, 82–84, 86, 88–90, 99, 106, 133, 134, 141, 142, 155, 174, 211, 212, 221, 226, 227, 236, 241, 270, 273, 275, 276, 278, 279, 281, 293

McCaslin, Amodeus (Uncle Buddy). Twin brother of Theophilus. He wins a card game played with Theophilus to determine which shall go to war. He becomes a sergeant in Tennant's brigade in Virginia. Amodeus and his brother have a distinctive concept of land: they believe that land does not belong to people but people belong to the land. They also have a plan for freeing their slaves.
52–57

McCaslin, Theophilus (Uncle Buck). Seventy-year-old twin of Amodeus who loses the card game played to determine which of them shall go to war. Later Uncle Buck helps Bayard Sartoris and Ringo trail Ab Snopes and Grumby.
52–61, 89, 159, 172, 179–202, 207, 211–213, 254, 259

Marengo (Ringo). Constant companion of young Bayard Sartoris. Both boys are the same age and both nursed at the same Negro breast. For these reasons Ringo occupies a special position in the Sartoris family and, being very intelligent, he often does Granny Millard's thinking for her, especially in the business of selling the Yankees their own mules. Later he helps Bayard get his revenge on Grumby; and still later, thanks to Ringo's indifference to the color line, he seeks to help Bayard avenge Colonel Sartoris' death and is at first disturbed when Bayard lets Redmond go unharmed.
3–10, 12, 13, 15–24, 27–33, 38–41, 43–48, 51, 52, 61–63, 65–83, 85–95, 97–103, 105–108, 110, 112, 117, 118, 122–126, 128–136, 138–149, 151–153, 156–163, 165, 166, 168–170, 172–175, 178–180, 182, 183, 185–190, 192–197, 199–205, 207–213, 216, 218, 219, 221, 224–230, 232, 235, 236, 241, 244–246, 248–252, 254, 267, 271, 279, 282, 283, 289, 290

Millard, Miss Rosa (Granny). Louisa Hawk's sister and Colonel John Sartoris' mother-in-law. She keeps John's house going during the most trying days of the Civil War. Though the times force her to alter her ethical standards somewhat, she never does so for selfish reasons. For a time she is able to trick the Union forces out of a great many mules, and by disguising the U.S. brand she sells the mules back to the Yankee army. She distributes the mules and money she gains from this deceit among her poor neighbors. Finally she is killed by Grumby over some horses he has stolen.

7–12, 16–18, 20–22, 26–38, 41–52, 61–67, 70, 71, 74, 77, 80–82, 84–99, 101, 103–106, 114, 117, 118, 120–158, 162–171, 173, 175, 177–181, 183, 184, 186, 187, 194, 198, 199, 203, 209, 211–213, 217–219, 221–223, 230, 231, 233, 246–248, 250, 251

Mitchell, Unc Few. A Negro "loony" to whom Louvinia alludes when she is describing the pretense of deafness that Colonel John Sartoris puts on when the Yankee troops are looking for him.
83

Newberry, Colonel. Union commander of an Illinois regiment from whom Granny Millard gets her last order of mules before her deceit is found out.
141, 145, 147, 149

Philadelphy. Negro, Loosh's wife, who unwillingly goes with him to join the Yankees.
4–6, 16, 24, 25, 27, 85, 86, 125

* *Redmond, Ben.* A lawyer, Colonel John Sartoris' former partner in building a railroad. He sells out to John because the two cannot agree. Sartoris defeats him for the State Legislature just to spite him. This act and John's constant goading drive Redmond to kill John. Later, when, with pistol in hand, Ben faces the unarmed Bayard Sartoris, he fires two shots at nothing, walks away, boards a train, and leaves Jefferson forever.
251, 254, 258–261, 266, 268, 283

Ringo. *See* Marengo.

Sartoris, Bayard. Colonel John's son, who, as a boy, lives by his reckless father's exploits. As a college man, however, he begins to outgrow Colonel John's concepts of violence; and when the Colonel is shot to death, Bayard refuses to seek the revenge that is expected of him. Rather, he faces, unarmed, the killer Redmond, who fires two shots aimlessly and then leaves Jefferson forever.

8, 23, 26, 29, 30, 38, 39, 46, 61, 72, 73, 77, 78, 82, 84, 102, 105, 116, 199, 200, 224, 227, 233, 243, 244, 257, 261, 262, 264, 271, 273, 276, 280–282, 286

Sartoris, Uncle Bayard. Brother of Colonel John Sartoris and Virginia Du Pre (Miss Jenny).

271

Sartoris, Drusilla Hawk. Daughter of Dennison Hawk, Sr. When Breckbridge, her betrothed, is killed at Shiloh, she sheds femininity and rides, manlike, with the regiment of her cousin by marriage, Colonel John Sartoris. After the war she lives innocently with Colonel John and his family; but, appearances being against her, she is coerced into marrying John, a man she admires but probably does not love. When Bayard returns home after his father's death, he meets Drusilla, who is dedicated to the glory of revenge with Bayard as the instrument. Realizing that Bayard intends no vengeance, she is ashamed of him, but before she leaves Sartoris she has become reconciled to his conduct.

100–106, 109–113, 116, 118, 120–122, 170, 212, 213, 215–222, 224–242, 247, 252–254, 261, 263, 265, 269–273, 275, 276, 278, 284, 288, 291, 292

Sartoris, Colonel John. Organizer and commander of the first Jefferson regiment. His dashing exploits in the Civil War make him a sort of superman to the Southerners and a very dangerous person to the Yankees, who put a price on his head. After the war he continues living by force for a time, as when, on his wedding day, he kills the Burdens to prevent their getting Cassius Benbow elected marshal. At last, however, he tires of killing and faces Redmond, an old rival whom he has long tormented, and allows himself to be killed.

6, 7, 10, 12, 23, 27, 40, 42, 44, 49, 57, 59–61, 64, 70, 71, 74, 76, 77, 83–85, 101, 105, 115, 120, 139, 140, 174, 212, 213, 220, 226, 227, 229, 231, 233, 236, 237, 240, 242, 245, 256, 260, 264, 268, 271, 285

Riverside City College Library.
Riverside, California

* *Simon.* Ringo's father and son of Joby. He has been trained to succeed his father as house servant, but he accompanies Colonel John Sartoris to the war as his faithful body servant.
  18, 19, 277, 279

Snopes, Ab. Unscrupulous forager. Though he tells people that he is in Colonel John Sartoris' regiment, he never gets dangerously close to hostilities. Instead he sells to one Yankee troop mules that Rosa Millard has procured from another after, of course, the U.S. brand has been changed. Later he prevails on Rosa to deal with Grumby, knowing there is danger involved. When Grumby kills Rosa, Ab joins Grumby's men in flight but is soon left behind, tied to a sapling, for Bayard Sartoris to punish. Bayard whips him, and Buck McCaslin, now ill and wounded, takes Ab back home.
  135–141, 143, 146–149, 151, 152, 157–159, 163, 164, 166, 168–171, 173, 177, 180, 182–186, 192, 193, 195, 197–201, 211, 212

Sutpen, Colonel. Civil War officer. In '61 he rides away with the first Mississippi regiment as second-in-command to Colonel John Sartoris, and after the Second Battle of Manassas he is elected to lead the regiment. The war ended, he, unlike Sartoris and many others, chooses to forsake violence and restore his war-ravaged lands.
  255, 256

White, Jed. One of Sartoris' old regiment. He rides to the Sartoris home to tell the family that Bayard is safe after facing Redmond.
  288, 292

Wilkins, Mrs. Wife of Professor Wilkins. She is acquainted with Rosa Millard.
  243, 245, 246, 281

Wilkins, Professor. One of Bayard's instructors in law with whom young Sartoris lives while he is in Oxford. It is Wilkins who informs Bayard of Colonel John Sartoris' death. (Colonel Sartoris refers to him as "Judge Wilkins.")
  243, 244, 246–249, 266

Worsham, Doctor. Preacher at John Sartoris' church before the war.
153, 154, 156

Wyatt, George. One of Colonel John Sartoris' old troop. He is active
in support of John Sartoris when John upsets the Burdens' election
plans; and he is in charge of several former soldiers ready to see
justice done when Bayard Sartoris goes to face Redmond after
Colonel John's death.
237–239, 241, 254, 258, 260, 261, 267–270, 276, 283, 284,
287, 288

THE WILD PALMS (1939)

(*The Wild Palms* includes two complementary stories, "The Wild Palms" and "The Old Man," which are printed in alternating chapters, but which are treated separately here.)

Bradley. A neighbor at the lake who, sensing that Charlotte Rittenmeyer and Harry Wilbourne are not married, is somewhat insolent when he calls on them to leave some supplies at their cabin.
99, 106, 107, 109

Bradley, Mrs. His wife who, with Bradley, leaves the lake shortly after the arrival of Charlotte Rittenmeyer and Harry Wilbourne.
108

Buckner (Buck). Manager of the Utah mine where Wilbourne goes to work. He finally leaves his job, knowing there will be no more pay for him.
179, 180, 182–187, 190–192, 194–198, 200, 203, 204, 209, 219

Buckner, Mrs. Billie (Bill). Buck's wife, upon whom Harry Wilbourne successfully performs an abortion.
179, 182, 183, 190, 193, 209

Callaghan. Owner of a Utah mine. To meet legal requirements he hires Harry Wilbourne as mine doctor so that he, Callaghan, can continue selling stock in the mine he knows to be worthless.
182, 195, 201

Cofer. The real estate agent of a small Mississippi seacoast town who rents Dr. Richardson's beach house to Harry Wilbourne and the dying Charlotte Rittenmeyer.
11, 17

Crowe. Host at the New Orleans party where Charlotte Rittenmeyer and Harry Wilbourne meet.
36, 44

De Montigny. Owner of the tuxedo that Flint borrows so he can lend
his own to Wilbourne.
35, 36

Doc. Part owner of McCord's lakeside cabin.
97

Flint. An intern, who, because it is Harry Wilbourne's birthday, persuades him to celebrate by going to Crowe's party.
34–37, 40, 44, 45

Gillespie. Partner with McCord and Doc in ownership of the lakeside
cabin.
97

Gower. District attorney who prosecutes Harry Wilbourne after Charlotte Rittenmeyer's death.
318, 319

Hogben. Man who runs the ore train at the Utah mine. He must make
a trip every thirty days to keep his franchise.
188, 202

Louisa. Maid in a San Antonio brothel where Harry Wilbourne goes in
search of some medicine that will serve to abort Charlotte Rittenmeyer.
211

McCord (Mac). Chicago newspaperman who befriends Charlotte Rittenmeyer and Harry Wilbourne, helping them to keep alive their
ideas of love although he does not entirely agree with them. He
lends them his cabin at the lake resort and helps get Charlotte a
job in Chicago; but he is strongly opposed to Harry's taking the
job in Utah, and his misgivings are justified.
*88, 90, 96–104, 113, 116–118, 120, 121, 123, 124, 129–134,
136, 138, 139, 141, 226*

Martha. Wife of the doctor whose beach house Charlotte Rittenmeyer
and Harry Wilbourne rent. In the face of her tenants' tragedy,
Martha's hard common sense, though selfishly motivated, is a wel-

come contrast to her husband's Baptist morality, which overshadows his medical training. While the doctor storms at Wilbourne for his sin, Martha prepares Wilbourne a cup of coffee.
  6, 8, 293

Pete. Mexican employee in the San Antonio brothel where Wilbourne goes in search of medicine for Charlotte Rittenmeyer.
  214

Ralph. Charlotte Rittenmeyer's brother, who once worked on a newspaper with McCord.
  223

Richardson, Doctor. The doctor who is in attendance on Charlotte Rittenmeyer when she dies.
  294, 301, 307

Rittenmeyer, Ann. Younger daughter of Francis and Charlotte.
  222

Rittenmeyer, Charlotte. Older daughter of Francis and Charlotte.
  222

Rittenmeyer, Charlotte (Mrs. Wilbourne). Believing that any state resembling marriage can be the death of love, Charlotte forsakes her solid home and two daughters to go away with Harry Wilbourne, a poor intern. She and Harry hold various jobs, always moving on when a concern for security begins to show itself. Since children are also a threat to her idea of love, Charlotte's pregnancy is a tragedy; and she prevails on Harry to perform the abortion that results in her death.
  20, 31, 38, 49, 53, 58, 81, 88, 89, 97–102, 104, 106–108, 114, 117, 119–124, 130–132, 141, 179–182, 191–193, 196–204, 210, 220-222, 224, 285, 287, 288, 294, 296, 305

Rittenmeyer, Francis (Rat). Charlotte's husband, who, though too prudent to be a proper mate for her, is nevertheless capable of intense devotion. Being a Catholic, he will not grant his wife a divorce, but he does permit her to try her experiment with Harry Wilbourne provided he hears from her monthly; and he gives

Harry a check to be used only for Charlotte's return fare home in case of emergency. After Charlotte's death, Rat, true to his promise to Charlotte, tries to save Wilbourne: first, he pays Harry's bond and implores him to flee to Mexico; next he makes a plea in court on Harry's behalf. Failing in these attempts, he finally comes to Harry's cell bringing cyanide, which Harry refuses to take.

38, 40, 42, 43, 47, 53, 55–58, 221–223, 225, 226, 228, 288, 297, 311–313, 319, 320, 322, 323

Wilbourne, Dr. Harry's father, who left his son $2,000 for his medical studies.

31

Wilbourne, Henry (Harry). Young intern. At twenty-seven, innocent of love, he is captivated by Charlotte Rittenmeyer, and after finding $1,278 in the street, leaves his internship only a few months before completing the requirements for a medical degree. During the next two years he is the loving, though sometimes fearful, disciple of Charlotte and her principles of unmarried love. Finally he allows Charlotte to persuade him to perform an abortion on her, but he blunders and so causes Charlotte's death. In prison for his deed, he refuses to run away or commit suicide because memory is all he has left of his life with Charlotte. One needs the corporeal body in order to remember, and so "between grief and nothing" he will take grief.

12, 13, 15, 18, 20–22, 31, 32, 34–38, 42, 44–47, 52–58, 81, 88, 89, 96, 97, 99–104, 106–108, 118, 120, 123, 124, 128–131, 139, 141, 179–197, 199–202, 204–206, 211–214, 216, 218, 219, 221, 223, 227, 279, 281, 286, 288–294, 296–304, 308, 311–313, 318, 320, 322, 323

THE OLD MAN (1939)

Bledsoe. Man who works with the livestock in the prison at Parchman.
326

Buckworth. Deputy warden at Parchman who reports the Convict dead.

The latter's safe return poses a problem which can be solved only by Buckworth's removal. Since Buckworth has too many voting relatives for him to be fired outright, he is transferred to the Highway Patrol, where he can do no harm.

331

Cajan, the. Alligator hunter who befriends the Convict and the girl. The Convict enters into partnership with the Cajan, and kills alligators with a knife for the hides. During the ten days of the partnership, the Convict is deterred from his primary goal—returning to prison because he had "done forgot how good making money was. Being let to make it." The business is suddenly eliminated when a levee is dynamited, and the Convict, with the girl and her baby, continues his efforts to return to prison.

253, 254, 256, 257, 259–263, 265–269

Convict, the (also referred to as "the tall convict"). Young man sentenced to fifteen years for attempted train robbery. He had not wanted the money but merely the satisfaction of having executed successfully a plan sifted from two years of reading paperbacked novels that purported to tell how various crimes are performed. His outrage, therefore, is not at the authorities who imprison him but at the writers who misinformed him. When the great flood of 1927 strikes, he is taken from the security of prison to help fight the flood waters and is subsequently selected to go in a rowboat to the rescue of a man on a cotton house and a woman in a tree. After rescuing the woman he becomes lost in the flood and is given up for dead. During the next few weeks he fights and labors for his very existence and that of the woman, who, far advanced in pregnancy when found in her tree, soon gives birth. The Convict's one goal is to get back to prison as soon as possible with his burdensome passenger and his rowboat, the property of the state. When he finally does surrender himself he reports: "Yonder's your boat and here's the woman. But I never did find that bastard on the cottonhouse." In order to save face the state officials, having duly reported the Convict dead, now add ten years to his sentence. At the end, the Convict's disillusionment with the female sex and his relief at being safely in prison once more are succinctly expressed in the one word, "Women!"

27, 28, 71–77, 143, 151–153, 156–158, 161, 162, 165, 167,

168, 229, 231–234, 237–239, 242, 243, 245–250, 256, 259–263, 265–275, 277, 331–339

Hamp. Man in the Warden's office when Buckworth suggests that the returned convict be tried by a fake judge and jury; he says that Hamp can be judge and the Convict will be none the wiser. (Hamp may be the name of the Warden or the Governor's emissary, both of whom are present.)
  328

Waldrip, Mrs. Vernon. Brand new name of the Convict's ex-sweetheart, who once entertained ideas of being a successful criminal's moll. After the convict is imprisoned she visits him once; and, though he writes faithfully, she answers but once, when she sends a picture postcard showing the hotel where she is honeymooning with her husband, Vernon Waldrip.
  339

THE HAMLET (1940)

(*The Hamlet* incorporates extensively revised versions of "Fool about a Horse" [pp. 33–53; from *Scribner's,* August, 1936], "The Hound" [pp. 250–296; from *Doctor Martino*], "Spotted Horses" [pp. 309–379; from *Scribner's,* June, 1931], and "Lizards in Jamshyd's Courtyard" [pp. 383–421; from *Saturday Evening Post,* February 27, 1932]. Part of the story of "Barn Burning" [*Harper's,* June, 1939] is told in *The Hamlet* [pp. 15–21], but it is not taken over as a whole; it appears in *Collected Stories of William Faulkner* [but the four others do not].)

Armstid, Mrs. Henry's work-worn wife, who sometimes helps her husband pull a plow in lieu of a horse. Henry takes 5 dollars she has earned weaving, to buy a pony; Hipps, however, knowing the circumstances, refuses to sell to him, giving Flem Snopes the money to hold for Mrs. Armstid, but Flem pockets it instead. Later, she brings suit to recover the money, but Lump Snopes, appearing in court instead of Flem, swears he saw Flem give the 5 dollars back to Hipps, who has left town by then.
    358–362, 370–372, 374

* **Armstid, Henry.** A poor farmer near Frenchman's Bend who breaks his leg trying to catch a wild pony he thinks he has bought from Hipps (secretly a partner of Flem Snopes); later he mortgages all he owns to buy from Flem a third interest in the old Frenchman's place and loses his mind digging for treasure that is not there.
    166, 167, 331–333, 335, 336, 343–346, 348–352, 355, 357–362, 367, 370, 372–374, 376, 383–401, 407–414, 417–420

Benbow, Judge. Judge in Jefferson who once said of Will Varner that a milder-mannered man never bled a mule or stuffed a ballot box.
    5

Bolivar, Uncle Dick. Old man whom Ratliff engages to locate, by means of his divining rod (a forked peachtree branch), the

treasure supposedly buried on the old Frenchman's place. He succeeds only in locating three bags of silver coins which Flem Snopes has buried on the land to fool Ratliff, Armstid, and Bookwright.
391–394, 397, 398, 407

Bookwright, Odum. A bachelor who spends much of his time lounging about Varner's store; he is one of three men whom Flem Snopes tricks into buying some worthless property, the old Frenchman's place.
65, 68, 70, 78–82, 88, 90, 92–94, 97, 166, 167, 170, 184–187, 224, 301, 302, 304, 305, 315, 341, 352, 355, 366, 367, 372, 376, 383–393, 395–400, 403, 407–414, 417

Cain. Jefferson storekeeper who sells Ab Snopes a milk separator.
44, 45, 53

de Spain, Major. One-time landlord of Ab Snopes. He charged Ab 20 bushels of corn for ruining Mrs. de Spain's 100-dollar French rug. Ab sued in return, and a local judge reduced the charge by one half. Ab was nevertheless still furious with his landlord. That night, de Spain's barn burned to the ground and, though their guilt was never proved, evidence pointed to Ab and his son Flem as the agents. The next day a willing de Spain allowed Ab to cancel their contract.
15–21

de Spain, Mrs. Major de Spain's wife, whose expensive rug is purposely ruined by Ab Snopes when he tracks manure on it.
17, 18

Doshey. Family name of Eustace Grimm's first wife.
413

Freeman. A very talkative lounger at Varner's store. Having bought one of the Texas ponies auctioned off by Hipps, he is active in the group effort to catch them "one at a time."
309, 313, 315–317, 325, 341–344, 352, 365, 400, 402, 403, 415–417

Freeman, Mrs. Wife of Freeman, probably. She saw Eck Snopes's pony kill himself by running into the rope that Eck had stretched across a narrow lane on the Freeman property.
365

George. One of the deputies who escort Mink Snopes to jail for the murder of Jack Houston.
293

Grimm, Eustace. Young tenant farmer living 10 or 12 miles from Frenchman's Bend. His presence in the hamlet just after Ratliff, Bookwright, and Armstid have found the coins at the old Frenchman's place is a source of great worry to Ratliff: perhaps he and Lump Snopes saw the men dig up the coins, and perhaps Eustace is Lump's agent to contact Flem Snopes, who is in Jefferson, and arrange to buy the old Frenchman's place before Ratliff can make the deal. After Ratliff has bought the property, he recalls that Eustace is Ab Snopes's nephew and concludes that Eustace was part of Flem's scheme to unload the worthless estate on him and his two partners.
400–403, 405–409, 413

Grumby, "Major." Outlaw who killed Mrs. Rosa Millard.
33

* *Hampton.* Sheriff who captures Mink Snopes and takes him to the Jefferson jail.
266, 267, 277, 284, 285, 288, 289

Harris. Grenier County farmer who once took Ab Snopes to court on the charge that Ab had burnt his barn.
11, 15

Hipps, Buck. A Texan (secretly in partnership with Flem Snopes) who auctions off the wild ponies in Frenchman's Bend. Aware that Armstid has taken money from his wife against her will to buy a pony, he refuses to sell to him and turns the money over to Flem Snopes for safekeeping.
310, 312, 314

Hoake (*Old*). Father of Allison [McCarron]. He waited with a loaded shotgun across his knees to receive his daughter and her husband, McCarron, when they returned from a ten-day elopement.
153

Holland, Anse. Man who once rented farms to Ab Snopes and Ratliff's father. He was the owner of the old sorghum mill and straight plow stock that Ab Snopes, without Anse's knowledge, traded to Kemp for a horse.
30, 34–36, 51, 53

* Houston, Jack. Farmer, murdered by Mink Snopes. He left home at the age of sixteen to escape the attentions of Lucy Pate [Houston]. After a series of adventures he settled down with a woman he took out of a brothel, and lived with her for twelve years while working on the railroad in Texas. Three years after his father died, he divided his savings with the woman, and left her to return to the farm he had inherited. Soon after his return he married Lucy, but six months after the wedding she was killed by his stallion. From then on he lives alone, morose and fierce. Because he has penned up Mink's stray yearling and charged him for its keep, Mink kills Houston and stuffs his body down inside a hollow tree trunk. The odor of the corpse reveals the hiding place to the sheriff.
71–74, 79, 103, 104, 180, 181, 184, 191, 192, 200–202, 204, 213, 214, 216, 220, 221, 223–225, 229, 231, 235, 238, 277, 285, 293, 304

* *Houston, Mrs. Lucy Pate.* Houston's childhood friend, who became his wife and was killed by his stallion six months after their marriage.
238

Jim. One of Hampton's deputies, driver of the surrey with the captive murderer Mink Snopes in it.
293

Jim. Negro man who is very skillful at disguising horses and mules. Assistant of Pat Stamper.
47

Kemp, Beasley. Man who traded Ab Snopes a horse that he had bought from Herman Short for 8 dollars.
35–43, 50, 51

Labove. Man with whom Will Varner, on a business trip, spends the night. Labove tells him about his son who works in sawmills and plays "the football" in order to pay his way through college. He also says that his son wants to be Governor.
116–118

Labove. His son. He works in sawmills in the summer and plays football, a game he does not like, in the fall at the University of Mississippi, to pay for his education. Labove begins to teach in the single-roomed school at Frenchman's Bend before he has completed his education, and because he is captivated by Eula Varner [Snopes], a student in the school, he stays on as teacher in the hamlet after he has received his degree and been admitted to the bar. At length he attempts to take her by force, but fails, and without bothering to collect his salary he leaves suddenly, knowing that his action has not even impressed Eula sufficiently for her to tell her father about it.
115, 119–121, 124, 128, 130, 132, 138, 143, 156, 406

Littlejohn. One-time owner of a boardinghouse in Frenchman's Bend which still bears his name. He probably died before the novel begins.
11, 32

Littlejohn, Mrs. His widow, perhaps. She now operates the boardinghouse where Ratliff stays when in the hamlet. A humorless, hardworking woman, she is nonetheless tenderhearted: she helps the Armstids when Henry's leg is broken, and she looks after Isaac Snopes, who sleeps in her barn. Much public activity (including the auction of Hipps's Texas ponies) takes place in the lot next to Mrs. Littlejohn's; and she, even while doing her endless chores, sees most of it.
60, 87, 93–96, 100, 101, 113, 186–188, 193, 194, 208, 216, 223, 225–227, 229, 231, 278, 304, 305, 312, 313, 319–322, 324, 327–330, 332, 334, 335, 340, 342, 345, 346, 348–350, 352, 353, 355, 356, 358–361, 367

McCallum, Anse. Man who brought home two wild Texas ponies which he made into a good team.

    56, 315–318

McCallum, Old Man Hundred-and-One. A name Ratliff mentions in connection with Flem Snopes and his wife Eula. Ratliff says that a sign painter can make Flem's bedroom look like the grocery store, "so he can know to do what every man and woman that ever seen her [Eula] between 13 and Old Man Hundred-and-One McCallum has been thinking about for 29 days now." (At the time Flem has been married for 29 days.)

    185

McCarron. A gambler who apparently reformed after his marriage to Allison and settled down to being a good overseer on old Hoake's farm. Several years later he is shot to death, probably in a gambling house.

    153, 154

McCarron, Allison Hoake. Daughter of Old Hoake. She braves her father's fury to elope with the man of her choice.

    153

McCarron, Hoake. Their son and bold suitor of Eula Varner [Snopes], who, with her aid, fights off other suitors and gets a broken arm during the battle. After Will Varner has set the arm and retired, Hoake takes Eula's virginity, and in so doing he causes the arm to break free of the splints and the two bone ends to telescope. Later, learning of Eula's pregnancy, he leaves for Texas.

    152, 154, 156–160, 416

McCaslin, Uncle Buck. Man who once said that Ab Snopes's crippled leg resulted from his being shot by Colonel John Sartoris when Ab tried to steal the Colonel's horse. Uncle Buck went on a long chase with Bayard Sartoris to catch Ab and punish him in connection with Miss Rosa Millard's death.

    19, 33

McCaslin, Ike. Farmer for whom Ab Snopes once worked and in whose cotton storehouse Ab and his family lived for a time. He owes Ratliff money for a sewing machine.
11, 403

Millard, Miss Rosa. Colonel John Sartoris' mother-in-law. During the Civil War she and Ab Snopes dealt in horses and mules together. Later she was killed by the renegade, "Major" Grumby.
33, 37

Mitchell, Hugh. One of the town loafers, to whom Ab Snopes bragged about the "Kentucky" horse he had just won in a shrewd trade. Mitchell identified the horse as the one that Herman Short had sold to Kemp five years before. Prior to that, Ab's horse had belonged to Pat Stamper.
38, 40, 42

Odum, Cliff. Man who helped Ab Snopes's first wife transport her cow to Pat Stamper so that she might get her milk separator back from him in return for the animal.
51, 52, 79

* *Peabody, Doc.* Doctor from whom Ratliff got a bottle of whisky for Ab Snopes to deaden the shock of being thoroughly out-traded by Pat Stamper.
45

* *Quick.* Owner of a sawmill. (Evidence in this novel suggests that this is Lon Quick, although old Ben Quick, who also appears in *The Hamlet,* is referred to in *Knight's Gambit* as being the owner of a sawmill.)
65, 80

* *Quick, Uncle Ben.* An old man, owner of the goats with which Ratliff attempts to outwit Flem Snopes.
88, 89, 92, 94, 97

* *Quick, Lon.* Farmer who buys one of the Texas ponies, which he never succeeds in catching. It is he who leaves the gate open, thus allowing the ponies to escape.

184, 303, 304, 309–317, 341, 342, 352, 355, 377, 400

Ratliff, V. K. Itinerant sewing-machine salesman and trader in livestock, secondhand farm tools, and musical instruments. In his buckboard he travels about in four counties, where he knows everybody. Ever on the alert, he seems to be present whenever there is action and carries news of it from place to place, seldom forgetting a name or an incident. He is no mere talebearer, however. Ethical, intelligent, he is soon aware of the threat posed by the unscrupulous Flem Snopes and his relatives, and he seldom rests from his efforts to check them. Tenderhearted, too, is this bland, affable countryman. He gives to Isaac Snopes money that he got from Flem, Isaac's guardian, in an involved goat deal; and he helps make a home for the family of the murderer Mink Snopes. Unfortunately, Ratliff is outwitted to his great cost on one occasion when Flem Snopes takes his half of a Jefferson restaurant in exchange for a one-third interest in the old Frenchman's place.

7, 14–19, 21, 28–34, 48, 54–65, 68, 70, 76–90, 92–99, 101–104, 168, 170, 179–187, 224–226, 229–234, 246, 297–306, 315–318, 342, 346, 348–362, 364, 366–368, 370, 383–414, 416, 417, 420

Rideout. Aaron's brother.

417

Rideout, Aaron. Ratliff's cousin, equal partner with Ratliff in a Jefferson restaurant.

417

Sam. Negro boy who works for the Varners.

30, 159, 163–165, 415

Sartoris, Bayard. Colonel John's son, who tracked Ab Snopes down and beat him in connection with the death of Miss Rosa Millard.

33

Sartoris, Colonel John. Confederate officer who, according to Uncle Buck McCaslin, shot Ab Snopes for trying to steal his horse during the Civil War.

    19, 33, 37

Short, Herman. Man who swapped Pat Stamper a horse and buggy for the horse that he later sold to Kemp for 8 dollars.

    38–40

Snopes, Mrs. Ab's second wife, who comes with him to sharecrop on one of Varner's farms.

    15–17

Snopes, Ab. Flem's hard-bitten father. According to Ratliff, who knew him some years before *The Hamlet,* he is not naturally mean (though he certainly appears so). A series of bitter experiences gradually soured him on life. During the Civil War he was badly beaten by Bayard Sartoris and some others because of his connection with Rosa Millard's death. Later, Colonel Sartoris crippled Ab permanently when he shot him in the heel for stealing his horse. Even then, Ab's spirit was not entirely curdled, for he had his horse-trading to fall back on. Then Pat Stamper thoroughly bested him in a horse trade that cost Ab his wife's milk separator and, a little later, his wife Vynie also. He has established a reputation for burning the barns of his successive landlords with whom he cannot get along. His current landlord is Will Varner.

    8, 10, 15–20, 23, 30–56, 299, 413

Snopes, Eckrum (Eck). One of Flem's cousins, who, though ignorant of blacksmithing, comes to work for I. O. Snopes in the blacksmith shop formerly operated by Will Varner. A little stupid, probably, but innocent and honest, Eck is a credit to the other Snopeses. When he and I. O., under pressure from Ratliff, decide "in family conference" to take Whitfield's advice about Isaac Snopes's cow, Eck agrees to pay the lion's share for the animal because he, having a large family, stands to lose more Snopes honor than does I. O. And later, feeling sorry for Isaac, he buys him a toy cow so that Isaac will not be too lonely. Still later, when the pony Hipps gives Eck causes Tull to be injured, Eck is at once willing to pay damages, but the court clears him, since he has no bill of sale for the pony.

73, 79, 227, 232–234, 275, 303, 305, 312–314, 317–325, 328, 330, 331, 333, 343–346, 348, 352–358, 365–367, 370, 373, 375–379, 415, 416

Snopes, Eula Varner. Daughter of Will Varner, and the youngest of his 16 children. Taller at 10 than her mother, Eula develops early into a girl of overwhelming beauty, a beauty to which she seems oblivious or, being incorrigibly lazy like her father, too indolent to concern herself about. She has never been willing to walk even the shortest distance; and when, at the age of 8, she starts to school, her brother Jody is obliged to take her on his horse, astride which she exposes her voluptuous legs, unaware of or indifferent to the effect she has on all the males about Frenchman's Bend. Even when she is 14 it is possible that she does not know what Labove is about when he attempts to rape her. Two years later, however, she has apparently become aware of sex; for, after helping Hoake McCarron beat off several rivals, she gives him her virginity. When, some three months later, it becomes known that she is pregnant, Hoake flees town; and Eula passively consents to marry Flem Snopes, her face now "a calm, beautiful mask."

107, 112, 113, 155, 157, 160, 161, 166, 304, 350, 351, 404

Snopes, Flem. Chief among the Snopeses. Shortly after Flem's father Ab moves onto one of Will Varner's farms, Flem becomes a clerk in the Varner store, aware, surely, that Jody Varner has hired him as insurance against the barn-burning Snopeses. From this lowly job Flem rises rapidly. He quickly brings efficiency to the store, soon supersedes Jody in the cotton gin, and even begins to help Will Varner settle his accounts with tenants and debtors. Meanwhile Flem has been lending money at a high rate of interest and has acquired a fine herd of cattle. Next he opens a new black-smith shop, putting the old one, now run by I. O. Snopes, out of business. Then Flem invades the Varner empire further when he marries Eula Varner, pregnant by another man, and receives the old Frenchman's place as part of Eula's dowry. As always, Flem is closemouthed, operating behind the scenes. Just as he has never admitted that the cattle were his, so he will never own that he is Buck Hipps's partner nor that he has kept Mrs. Armstid's 5 dollars. After he has buried some silver coins about the old Frenchman's place and thus tricked Ratliff, Bookwright, and Armstid into thinking that a fortune is buried on the property, he sells it to them for a substantial sum and moves on to Jefferson, in search of bigger worlds to conquer.

15, 16, 18–20, 25, 30, 31, 56, 58, 61, 67, 69, 70, 75, 76, 79, 80, 82–88, 92, 96–99, 101, 102, 104, 107, 151, 162, 165–167, 171, 182, 228, 232, 298, 302, 304, 305, 309, 311, 315, 317–319, 322, 324, 325, 334, 337–341, 349, 352, 354–362, 366, 367, 370, 372–375, 379, 382, 384, 388–392, 402, 403, 405–407, 415–417, 420, 421

Snopes, I. O. Nominal lessee of the blacksmith shop, whose ordinary speech is larded with proverbs. He succeeds Labove as school-teacher and serves as counsel for his kinsman Mink Snopes, the murderer. I. O., who everyone thinks is unmarried, disappears one day when his wife shows up with a six-month-old baby whom, according to Eck Snopes's son, I. O. has fathered.

72, 79, 183, 227, 229–234, 275, 303, 304, 306, 364, 368

Snopes, Isaac. Flem's cousin, an idiot in love with a cow, which he steals and runs away with. After Houston, the owner, gives the cow to him in disgust, Isaac lives with it for a time in his home, Mrs. Littlejohn's barn. Here he unknowingly stages performances that the loungers at Varner's flock to see. Finally the animal is taken from him and destroyed. (Pages 188–213 are narrated from his viewpoint.)

86, 87, 98–100, 191, 193, 229

Snopes, Launcelot (Lump). A "real" Snopes, who succeeds his cousin Flem Snopes as clerk at Varner's store, and announces daily when Isaac Snopes and the cow are ready to perform. He aids Flem religiously in the latter's chicanery, even to the point of perjuring himself. After Mink has killed Houston, "Lump" tries desperately to get at the money that the slain man has in his wallet.

Snopes, Mink. Another of Flem Snopes's cousins, who lets his heifer range on Houston's land and kills Houston when he pens up the heifer and wins a judgment of $3 against Mink for pasturage fee. For a few days after shooting Houston and cramming his body into a hollow tree trunk, Mink stays in his cabin, haunted by the wail of Houston's dog and plagued by Lump Snopes, who has solved the murder mystery and wants to get the money he knows Houston had on him. Mink, however, poor as he is, does not want any of the money and refuses to tell Lump where he has put the body. Killing Houston was, for him, apparently a matter of principle. Realizing finally that he may be suspected of the crime, Mink decides to dispose of the body and its telltale odor by throwing it into the nearby river. As he drags the huge decaying corpse from its hiding place, Mink battles Houston's fierce hound; and as he tosses the body into the water, he notices that one of the arms is missing. Back at the hollow tree trunk, still fighting the dog, Mink recovers the arm, but in that instant he is captured by the sheriff, who takes him to the jail in Jefferson. Here he is visited by his two children and his wife, whose pathetic help he scorns. He even refuses bail and counsel. His entire hope lies in the return from Texas of Flem Snopes, who, Mink believes, will somehow save him. Eight months after his arrest, he is sentenced to the state penitentiary for life. Scarcely hearing the judge's words, Mink curses Flem, who has surely protracted his stay in Texas because of his kinsman's trouble.

Snopes, Saint Elmo. I. O.'s oafish son, who steals candy from Varner's store.

Snopes, Mrs. Vynie. Ab's first wife. Having lost his team to Pat Stamper, Ab traded her milk separator to get his animals back; and Vynie was obliged to give Pat their cow to redeem her sepa-

rator. Finally Vynie's father took her to his home and warned Ab that he would get shot if he ever came near her.
34–37, 39, 44, 47, 50–52

Snopes, Wallstreet Panic (Wall). Oldest son of Eckrum, the blacksmith. The boy had no first name until he was about ten, at which time he was given the name Wallstreet Panic in hopes it might make him rich like the people that ran the Wall Street Panic. "Wall" is active in helping his father try to catch the two Texas ponies that Eck has acquired.
303, 306, 318, 322, 323, 346

Stamper, Pat. Peerless horsetrader. He traded Ab Snopes a pair of worthless mules for Ab's doctored-up horse; and when Ab, realizing he had been fooled, wanted to trade back, Stamper gave him his original horse, disguised, in exchange for the mules and Mrs. Snopes's milk separator.
33–36, 38–49

Trumbull. Varner's blacksmith for years. He loses his place to the Snopeses.
67, 71–73, 75, 76

Tull, Mrs. "A strong, full-bosomed . . . woman with an expression of grim and seething outrage," who dominates her husband and their four daughters. She sues Eck Snopes for the damages his pony causes Tull, but she loses the suit because Eck does not have a bill of sale for the pony.
347, 357, 369, 370, 373, 375, 376, 378, 379

Tull, Vernon. Gentle farmer, "Archetype . . . of all men who marry young and father only daughters and are themselves but the eldest daughter of their own wives." When Eck Snopes's pony runs Tull down he is injured so badly that he is unable to work for several days.
10–12, 70, 78–81, 166, 167, 170, 303, 304, 347, 348, 357, 367, 369, 370, 375–379, 415–417

Varner, Mrs. Will's wife, a cheery, bustling woman who loves household routine (cooking, preserving, and so forth) as an end in itself. Her interests are not at all mental, but physical, and her reaction to Jody's uproar about their daughter Eula's pregnancy is one of outrage because her nap has been interrupted.

    11, 89, 108, 109, 111, 112, 116, 148, 150, 161–165, 351, 404, 415, 416

Varner, Jody. The ninth of Will's sixteen children, the only son to remain at home, where he helps look after the family interests. He puts Ab Snopes on as a tenant, thus providing the opening through which the Snopeses first begin to penetrate the Varner empire, and he spends much time regretting his shortsightedness. It is also he who is chiefly concerned about having his sister Eula [Snopes] get an education, and it is he who suffers most keenly for her obliviousness to propriety.

    7–14, 16, 18–21, 23–28, 30–32, 48, 53, 59–61, 64–70, 76, 88, 89, 92, 94, 95, 102, 109–114, 136, 143, 144, 152, 162–164, 183, 269, 276, 310–312, 362–365

Varner, Will. Chief man of the country, fountainhead of advice, farmer, usurer, veterinarian. He is the owner of most of the good land in the country, and he holds mortgages on most of the rest. He also owns the store, cotton gin, and combined grist mill and blacksmith shop. A shrewd man of strength and courage, Varner rewards Flem Snopes's intelligent and successful efforts on his behalf by allowing Flem to penetrate more and more deeply into his kingdom. It is obviously Will who arranges for Flem to marry his daughter Eula. This one act is easily explained: he wants to get his unmarried, pregnant daughter off his hands.

    3–5, 11–13, 28–32, 54, 55, 58, 61, 62, 65, 66, 68–70, 73, 75, 76, 80, 82, 89, 95, 100–102, 104, 108–110, 115, 116, 118–121, 123–126, 130, 132, 134, 139, 143, 144, 146, 149, 151, 152, 155–167, 179–185, 204, 230–232, 245–248, 257, 261, 269, 276, 292, 293, 302, 304, 315, 324, 340, 349–352, 368, 375, 384, 386, 391, 401–407, 415–417, 419

Whitfield. "Harsh, stupid, honest, superstitious and upright minister, holder of no degrees." To cure Isaac Snopes of his passion for the cow he suggests that the animal be slaughtered and a piece of its cooked flesh be fed to the idiot, who thereafter "wont want to chase nothing but human women."

231–233

Winterbottom. Resident of Frenchman's Bend with whom Launcelot Snopes boards and with whom Eustace Grimm takes his meals while he is in the hamlet.

402

INTRUDER IN THE DUST (1948)

Armstead. Family name of early valley settlers who became farmers.
  149

Beauchamp, Lucas. Proud Negro farmer whose grandfather was white.
  He knows and threatens to reveal that Crawford Gowrie is stealing lumber from his brother Vinson Gowrie and their "uncle,"
  Sudley Workitt. After Crawford, fearing exposure, has killed
  Vinson in such a way as to make it appear that Lucas is the
  murderer, the Negro, though expecting a lynching party at any
  moment, operates coolly from behind jail bars and prevails on
  young Chick Mallison to open Vinson's grave as a first step toward his eventual exoneration from the false charge.
    *3, 6–8, 10, 13–15, 17–20, 22–29, 31–34, 36, 37, 39–45, 48,
    49, 58–66, 68–70, 72, 73, 78–87, 90, 101, 109, 117–119, 126,
    128, 130, 137, 138, 142, 144, 147, 152, 153, 155, 162, 178, 179,
    181, 188, 192, 193, 195–204, 208, 210–228, 232, 234, 236, 240–
    247*

Beauchamp, Molly. Wife of Lucas. She is dead when the novel begins.
  15, 22, 23, 25, 87, 119, 242

Bookwright. Family name of early valley settlers who became farmers.
  149

Compson, General. One of the hunters with Major de Spain.
  93

Dandridge, Miss Maggie. Chick Mallison's grandmother.
  15

de Spain, Major. Cousin of Chick's grandfather. The Major once had a
  hunting camp 12 miles out of Jefferson.
  93

Downs. Mrs. An old white woman who tells fortunes, cures hexes, and finds things that are lost.
    71

* *Edmonds, Carothers.* Owner of the property on which Lucas Beauchamp has long been a tenant. He is an old friend of Gavin Stevens.
    3–10, 12, 13, 16–19, 22, 25, 28, 30, 36, 44, 93, 151, 152

Ephraim. Old Negro man, father of Paralee. He intuitively locates a long-lost ring belonging to Chick Mallison's mother. At the same time he tells Chick that if he ever needs to have anything done "out of the common run," not to waste his time on the menfolks but to have the women and children do it.
    63, 70, 71, 112, 130

* *Fathers, Sam.* Son of a Chickasaw chieftain by a Negro woman. Sam had been the best woodsman of all at de Spain's old hunting camp.
    93

Fraser. Family name of early hill settlers and still operators.
    148, 149

Fraser, Squire Adam. Owner of the store near which Vinson Gowrie is killed.
    27, 30, 34, 39, 41, 219, 228, 229

Fraser, Doyle. Son of Squire Fraser.
    37

Gowrie. Family name of early hill settlers and still operators.
    148, 149

Gowrie, Amanda Workitt. Deceased wife of N. B. Forrest Gowrie. Her body lies in the Gowrie burial plot.
    101

Gowrie, Bilbo. Twin of Vardaman. Bilbo and Vardaman are the next to the youngest of Nub Gowrie's sons. *See* Gowrie, Vardaman.
    165

Gowrie, Bryan. Third son of Nub Gowrie. He is the unifying force of the Gowrie family which makes it possible for their farm to support them.

165

Gowrie, Crawford. Second son of Nub Gowrie. He is in the lumber business with his brother Vinson Gowrie and his "Uncle" Sudley Workitt. When Lucas Beauchamp sees him stealing lumber from his partners and threatens to expose him, he kills Vinson in a way calculated to make Lucas appear to be the murderer. Soon after, Crawford sees Vinson's body removed from its grave by Jake Montgomery, who also knows of Crawford's guilt and who, either because he is not getting enough blackmail pay from him, or possibly because he simply hates him, apparently plans to take the body to the sheriff to prove that only Crawford's German Luger pistol could have killed Vinson. Crawford then kills Jake also, and, desperate for time, puts the body into Vinson's grave and throws Vinson's into a bed of quicksand. Later that night Crawford sees Chick Mallison's party looking for Vinson's body but discovering Jake's instead. After they have returned Jake's body to the grave and left, Crawford digs it up again and places it in a shallow grave nearby. Only a little later, his crimes discovered, Crawford commits suicide before Sheriff Hampton can apprehend him.

164, 192, 197, 199, 201, 202, 204, 208, 210, 218–220, 222–230, 237, 243

Gowrie, N. B. Forrest. Husband of Amanda. He is old Nub Gowrie's oldest son.

101, 164

Gowrie, Nub. Fierce old one-armed widower, father of six sons. He will not permit the sheriff to open Vinson Gowrie's grave until he realizes that Vinson's body is not there.

79–81, 139, 160–163, 167, 168, 171, 173, 175, 177–179, 192, 197, 219, 230

Gowrie, Vardaman. Twin of Bilbo. He and Bilbo spend their nights hunting and their days sleeping on the bare planks of the front

gallery of their home. The twins dig up Vinson's grave and find Jake Montgomery's body there.
165

Gowrie, Vinson. Youngest son of Nub Gowrie. He is engaged in many business ventures, one of which is his partnership with his brother Crawford. This association costs him his life, because Crawford, who has been stealing from Vinson, kills him when Lucas Beauchamp threatens to tell him of the theft.
27, 28, 34, 38, 40, 62, 63, 86, 104, 109, 115, 117, 153, 164, 165, 173, 175, 178, 179, 188, 192, 201, 214, 220–225, 227–229, 231, 237

Greenleaf. Family name of early valley settlers who became farmers.
149

Grenier, Louis. One of the founders of Yoknapatawpha County.
75, 76

Grinnup, Lonnie. Simple-minded descendant of Louis Grenier, one of the three founders of Yoknapatawpha County.
76

Habersham, Doctor. One of the three founders of Yoknapatawpha County.
75

Habersham, Miss Eunice. A kinless spinster of seventy. Feeling a special interest in Lucas Beauchamp, perhaps because her grandparents once owned the parents of Molly, Lucas' wife, Miss Habersham is instrumental in proving Lucas innocent of murder. Quick to act upon Chick Mallison's report of Lucas' contention that his innocence can be proved if Vinson Gowrie's body is examined, she accompanies Chick and Aleck Sander to the Gowries' burial place, where they find Jake Montgomery's body in Vinson Gowrie's grave. Miss Habersham's presence at this time makes the boys' subsequent report to Hampton convincing enough for the Sheriff to go to work on the case.
75–78, 80, 82, 87, 89, 90, 92–95, 98–114, 116–119, 121, 127–130, 132, 133, 138, 142, 144, 150, 158, 159, 169, 185, 186, 193, 198, 208, 209, 212, 221, 223, 228, 234, 237, 241–244

Halladay, Jim. District attorney, probably. If so, he resides in Harrisburg.
110

Hampton, Mrs. Wife of Sheriff Hampton.
107

* **Hampton, Hope.** Sheriff of Yoknapatawpha County. A less able man in the sheriff's position might have failed to save Lucas Beauchamp. Hampton, however, armed with information supplied by Miss Habersham and the boys, succeeds in seeing justice done.
31, 34, 40, 44, 52–54, 56, 62, 64, 73, 79–81, 83, 89, 107, 111, 113, 117, 118, 131, 136, 139, 140, 142, 143, 192, 197, 203, 204, 210, 211, 223–225, 229, 231–234, 240, 242, 245

Hogganbeck, Boon. Part Chickasaw Indian. He had been a member of de Spain's hunting camp.
93

Holston. One of the three founders of Yoknapatawpha County.
75, 76

Ingraham. Family name of early hill settlers and still operators, now pronounced Ingrum.
148, 149

Ingrum. See Ingraham.

Ingrum, Willy. The Jefferson Marshal. As Gavin Stevens and Hope Hampton both know, the surest way to spread information is to give it to Willy and tell him to say nothing about it.
136, 140–142, 184, 212, 221, 232, 237

Joe. Negro boy who works for Carothers Edmonds.
7

Legate, Will. Man whom the sheriff stations outside the Jefferson jail to help protect Lucas Beauchamp. Legate is an excellent marksman with a rifle. It is he who secretly transports Lucas from the jail to Hampton's house to prevent a possible lynching.
52–54, 62, 66–68, 79, 80, 83, 114, 115, 117, 121, 138, 142, 224

Lilley. Owner of a small store patronized chiefly by Negroes. He voices his willingness to help lynch Lucas Beauchamp, that is, if the boys need him.
48, 49

Littlejohn. Family name of early valley settlers who became farmers.
149

McCallum. Family name of early hill settlers and still operators.
148

McCallum, Buddy. Farmer near Jefferson and a veteran of World War I. He traded a German Luger automatic pistol to Crawford Gowrie for a pair of foxhounds.
179, 192, 229

McCaslin, Carothers. White grandfather of the Negro Lucas Beauchamp.
7, 9, 17, 69, 226

McCaslin, Uncle Ike. Great-uncle of Carothers Edmonds. Still alive at ninety, he had been a boy hunter at Major de Spain's hunting camp.
93

* *McGowan, Skeets.* Drugstore man in Jefferson from whom Chick Mallison buys tobacco for Lucas Beauchamp when Lucas is in jail.
66

Mallison, Charles, Jr. (Chick). Young nephew of Gavin Stevens. When he falls into an icy creek on the Edmonds' place one November day and is fished out by Lucas Beauchamp and virtually coerced into being a guest at Lucas' Negro cabin, Chick attempts to pay Lucas for his hospitality. Lucas, aggressively unwilling to concede the relationship implied by such an act, spurns the money. In the months that follow, Chick, confused by Beauchamp's behavior, tries in various ways to pay off the Negro for his services; but every favor, every gift Chick bestows on Lucas, the latter repays in kind. It is partly this tension that influences Chick to undertake the frightening assignment of digging up the body of Vinson Gowrie in order to prove Lucas innocent of murder. But another influence, surely, is Chick's growing awareness of the guilt inherent in a society that can set the law aside when its victim is a Negro.

32, 68, 87, 104, 113, 117, 209, 224, 228, 234, 242

Mallison, Charles, Sr. (Charlie; Charley). Chick's father.
32, 105, 124, 127

Mallison, Maggie. His wife. Chick Mallison's mother, sister of Gavin Stevens.
105, 127

Maycox, Judge. Judge whom Gavin Stevens says might issue an order for the opening of Vinson Gowrie's grave.
110, 111

Millingham. Family name of early valley settlers who became farmers.
149

Montgomery, Jake. A kind of "jack-leg" timber dealer. He has been involved in various questionable deals, among them buying from Crawford Gowrie lumber that he knows the latter has stolen. Jake knows also that Crawford has killed Vinson Gowrie; and after Vinson has been buried, Jake, for some reason wanting to see Crawford punished, digs up Vinson's body and starts to bear it away on a mule, apparently with the intention of showing it to Sheriff Hampton to prove that Crawford is the murderer. Crawford witnesses Jake's act, kills him, and puts his body into Vinson's grave. After it has been discovered there and reburied by Chick Mallison's party, Crawford digs it up and disposes of it once again, this time in a shallow grave nearby. It is in this second grave that Jake's remains are found by Sheriff Hampton.
104, 115, 162, 168, 175, 178, 183, 185, 188, 193, 208, 220, 221, 223, 224, 229–232, 237

Mosby, Uncle Hogeye. Negro epileptic from the poorhouse.
184

Paralee. Mother of Aleck Sander and cook for the Stevens–Mallison household.

    12, 38, 39, 63, 70, 71, 75, 85, 96, 116, 123, 124, 126–128, 130, 147

Sander, Aleck. Negro boy and companion of Chick Mallison. Aleck is the third member of Chick's party which goes to the Gowrie cemetery to exhume the body of Vinson Gowrie and prove thereby that Lucas Beauchamp was not Vinson's murderer. Being a Negro, Aleck is taking a very special risk which does not extend to his two companions.

    4–13, 16, 35, 45, 71, 75, 78, 81, 83–86, 89–103, 105, 106, 108, 110–114, 116, 118, 121, 128–132, 141, 143, 144, 147, 149, 150, 158, 159, 169, 170, 174, 175, 185, 193, 209, 230, 237, 242, 243

Skipworth. The constable of Beat Four, where the Gowries live. After Vinson Gowrie has been killed, it is he who takes Lucas Beauchamp into custody and chains him to a bedpost in the Skipworth home.

    34, 37, 40, 228, 240

* **Stevens, Gavin (Uncle Gavin).** County attorney. At the beginning of the Beauchamp affair, Gavin, being white, and a man, lacks the flexibility to accept Lucas' contention of innocence. However, when Chick Mallison, Miss Habersham, and Aleck Sander have opened Gavin's eyes, he is quick to devote all his time and ability to saving Lucas.

    15, 75, 77, 86, 114, 127, 162, 178, 191, 209

Tubbs. Jefferson jailer.

    53, 66, 80, 117

Tubbs, Mrs. His wife.

    118

Urquhart. Family name of early hill settlers and still operators, now pronounced Workitt.

    148

Varner. Owner of a store and principal figure at Frenchman's Bend.
234

Workitt. See Urquhart.
148, 149

Workitt, Uncle Sudley. Kinsman and partner of Vinson and Crawford
Gowrie in a lumber deal. (He is spoken of as their uncle, but he
is really only a distant cousin of their mother.)
28, 220, 222, 223, 225–227

KNIGHT'S GAMBIT (1949)

(The first five sections of *Knight's Gambit*, previously published separately as short stories ["Smoke," *Harper's*, April, 1932 (also in *Dr. Martino*); "Monk," *Scribner's*, May, 1937; "Hand Upon the Waters," *Saturday Evening Post*, November 4, 1939; "Tomorrow," *Saturday Evening Post*, November 23, 1940; and "An Error in Chemistry," *Ellery Queen's Mystery Magazine*, June, 1946], are reprinted in the novel without revision. The last section, "Knight's Gambit," appears in the novel for the first time.)

Ballenbaugh, Boyd. Younger brother of Tyler. He murders Lonnie Grinnup [Louis Grenier] because he knows that Tyler is Lonnie's beneficiary. Boyd is, in turn, killed by Joe, the deaf and dumb orphan whom Lonnie had adopted, in "Hand Upon the Waters." *71, 76–80*

Ballenbaugh, Tyler. Boyd's older brother. He insures Grinnup's life and later pays for Boyd's villainy, in "Hand Upon the Waters." *70, 72–80*

Berry, Ben. Sheriff's deputy, in "An Error in Chemistry." *117–119*

Blake, Jim. Countryman who helps bear Lonnie Grinnup's body away from the coroner's office, in "Hand Upon the Waters." *68*

Bookwright. Farmer from Frenchman's Bend, who kills Buck Thorpe for running off with his daughter, in "Tomorrow." *85, 86, 89, 90, 104, 105*

Canova, Signor. Master of illusion. Professional name of man who calls himself Joel Flint, in "An Error in Chemistry." (*See* Flint, Joel.) *129–131*

Cayley, Miss. Daughter of Hence, she is the girl to whom Max Harriss gives a ring, in "Knight's Gambit."
184–191, 194, 226

Cayley, Hence. Father of the Cayley girl in whom Max Harriss is interested, in "Knight's Gambit."
184

Dodge, Granby. Cousin of the Holland twins and beneficiary of Virginius Holland. Granby, after killing old Anse Holland, hires a man from Memphis to dispose of Judge Dukinfield. Gavin Stevens spoils Granby's plans to inherit the Holland property, in "Smoke."
6, 25, 28, 29, 33–36

Dukinfield, Judge. Executor of old Anse Holland's will. The judge is murdered because he has special information that worries Granby Dodge, in "Smoke."
10–14, 16–20, 23, 24, 26, 28, 31

Dukinfield, Miss Eunice. Daughter of Judge Dukinfield, in "Smoke."
32

Ewell, Bryan. Sheriff's deputy, sent by Hub to watch old man Pritchel, in "An Error in Chemistry."
117, 118

Fentry, G. A. Father of Stonewall Jackson Fentry, in "Tomorrow."
90, 91, 103

Fentry, Jackson and Longstreet. The name Stonewall Jackson Fentry gives the boy whom he raises, until the Thorpe boys, his uncles, claim him, in "Tomorrow."
95, 105

Fentry, Stonewall Jackson. Juryman who will not vote to acquit Bookwright of the murder of Buck Thorpe, whom Fentry had raised as a child, in "Tomorrow."
89, 91–93, 95–97, 102–105

Flint, Ellie Pritchel. Wesley Pritchel's daughter, a weak-minded spinster of forty who marries Joel Flint partly to get away from her eccentric father, in "An Error in Chemistry."
    113, 117, 119, 126

Flint, Joel. A Yankee who kills his wife Ellie and her father, and then impersonates the latter in an effort to profit from the illegal sale of Pritchel's farm, in "An Error in Chemistry." (*See* Canova, Signor.)
    109, 111, 113, 114, 116–124, 128–130

Fraser. Whisky maker of wide repute with whom Monk Odlethrop lives after Mrs. Odlethrop's death, in "Monk."
    42, 43, 45, 47

Frazier, Judge. Judge who tries Bookwright for killing Thorpe, in "Tomorrow."
    88, 89

Gambrell, C. L. Prison warden killed by Monk at Terrel's instigation, in "Monk."
    50, 52, 53, 55, 57, 58

Gauldres, Captain. Argentine army captain, house guest of the Harrisses, who marries the Harriss girl and finally joins the U.S. Cavalry in World War II, in "Knight's Gambit."
    136, 137, 163–165, 168–175, 178–182, 185, 191, 194, 195, 212–221, 223, 224, 226–229, 238, 242

Grenier, Louis (Grinnup, Lonnie). Simple-minded descendant of one of the three founders of Yoknapatawpha, he calls himself Lonnie Grinnup. He is murdered for his insurance, in "Hand Upon the Waters."
    63–66, 71–74, 77, 79–81

Grinnup, Lonnie. See Grenier, Louis.

Harriss. Wealthy New Orleans man, bootlegger on a grand scale, who makes his wife's old home into a massive showplace. He is finally killed, gangland fashion, in "Knight's Gambit."
146, 148, 150–153, 155, 156, 160, 162, 163, 165, 167, 210

Harriss, Miss. Sister of Max. She finally marries Gauldres, in "Knight's Gambit."
135, 184–190, 208, 218

Harriss, Mrs. Wife of Harriss, whom she marries because she believes that Gavin Stevens, her betrothed, does not want her. Twenty years after, however, her husband being dead, she does indeed marry Stevens, in "Knight's Gambit."
153, 161, 162, 167–169, 172, 218, 238, 245

Harriss, Max. Harriss' son, who attempts to have a wild horse kill Gauldres because the latter can outride and outfence him, in "Knight's Gambit."
135, 178, 180–184, 189, 198, 199, 203, 207, 209, 210, 212, 221–226, 228, 229

Hogganbeck, Melissa. Charles Mallison's history teacher, in "Knight's Gambit."
199, 200, 205, 206

Holland. Foreman of the jury on the Bookwright case, in "Tomorrow."
89

Holland, Anselm (old Anse). Father of the twins. He is murdered by Granby Dodge, in "Smoke."
3–11, 13, 17–20

Holland, Anselm, Jr. (young Anse). Son of Anselm, twin of Virginius, in "Smoke."
4–11, 14–23, 25, 28, 30, 34

Holland, Cornelia. Wife of old Anse, mother of the twins, in "Smoke."
17

Holland, Virginius. Young Anselm Holland's twin, in "Smoke."
4–11, 15, 17, 19, 21, 25, 28–30, 32–35

Holston. Name of one of the three founders of Yoknapatawpha County,
in "Hand Upon the Waters."
66

* *Hub.* The sheriff, probably Hub Hampton, in "An Error in Chemistry."
124, 128

Ike. Leader of the men who bear Lonnie Grinnup's body away from
the coroner's office, in "Hand Upon the Waters."
68

Job, Uncle. Negro servant of Judge Dukinfield, in "Smoke."
26, 30–33

Joe. Deaf and dumb orphan raised by Lonnie Grinnup. He avenges the
death of Lonnie by killing Lonnie's murderer, Boyd Ballenbaugh,
in "Hand Upon the Waters."
63–65, 72, 80

Killegrew, Hampton. The night marshal in Jefferson, in "Knight's
Gambit."
203, 204, 222, 226

McCallum, Rafe. Farmer and horse breeder who sells Max Harriss the
wild horse with which Max plans to kill Gauldres, in "Knight's
Gambit." Only Rafe's timely arrival saves Gauldres.
168, 200, 201, 202, 206, 208–217, 219–221, 223

McWilliams. Conductor of train out of Jefferson, in "Knight's Gambit."
243, 245

Mallison, Charles (Chick). Nephew and aide of Gavin Stevens, in
"Knight's Gambit"; narrator of "Monk," "Tomorrow," and "An
Error in Chemistry."

88, 137–142, 145, 149, 151–155, 159, 162–166, 172, 176–178, 187, 203, 205, 207, 209, 210, 212–215, 217, 218, 222, 224, 226, 228, 229, 231, 237, 242, 243

Mallison, Maggie Stevens. Mother of Charles, sister of Gavin Stevens, and one of Mrs. Harriss' girlhood friends, in "Knight's Gambit."
163

Markey, Robert. Memphis lawyer, who had been at Heidelberg with Gavin Stevens. Acting on Gavin's instructions, he has Max Harriss watched while Max is in Memphis, in "Knight's Gambit."
192, 194, 198, 199, 204, 221, 222

Matthew. Countryman who helps bear Lonnie Grinnup's body away from the coroner's office, in "Hand Upon the Waters."
68

Mitchell. Storeowner with whom Lonnie Grinnup's burial money had been deposited, in "Hand Upon the Waters."
68

Monk. See Odlethrop, Stonewall Jackson.

Mossop. Maiden name of Hence Cayley's wife, in "Knight's Gambit."
184

Nate. Negro man, in "Hand Upon the Waters."
74

Odlethrop, Mrs. Supposedly Monk's grandmother, in "Monk."
41, 42

Odlethrop, Stonewall Jackson (Monk). Moron who is sentenced to life imprisonment on a false murder charge. When pardoned, he refuses to leave prison. Later he is executed for the murder of Warden Gambrell, in "Monk."
39–51, 55–57

Paoli. Italian fencing master. Max Harriss was his star pupil, in "Knight's Gambit."
182

Pose. Countryman who helps bear Lonnie Grinnup's body away from the coroner's office, in "Hand Upon the Waters."
68

Pritchel, Wesley. Father-in-law of Joel Flint. He is the violent-tempered owner of a small but good farm which contains valuable clay, in "An Error in Chemistry."
109, 110, 112–115, 117–119, 122–128

Pruitt, Mrs. Mother of Rufus, she aids her son in telling Gavin Stevens about the Fentrys, in "Tomorrow."
92–95

Pruitt, Rufus. Countryman who, aided by his mother, tells Gavin Stevens about Fentry and his infant son, in "Tomorrow."
91–95, 103

* *Quick, Ben*. Owner of the sawmill where S. J. Fentry works, in "Tomorrow."
93

Quick, Isham. Ben's son. He finds a half-drawn pistol in Buck Thorpe's hand after Thorpe has been killed by Bookwright. Later Isham recalls information that explains the Fentry–Thorpe tie-up, in "Tomorrow."
86, 97

Rouncewell, Mrs. Owner of the boardinghouse where the Bookwright jury meets, in "Tomorrow."
89

Sartoris, Benbow. Commissioned officer on duty in England in World War II, in "Knight's Gambit."
239, 240

Smith, Miss. The name Fentry gives as the maiden name of his deceased wife, in "Tomorrow."
95

Stevens, Captain. Father of Gavin Stevens, in "Tomorrow."
91, 103

* **Stevens, Gavin.** County attorney of Yoknapatawpha, Phi Beta Kappa, Harvard and Heidelberg. He solves all the mysteries in *Knight's Gambit* and finally marries the widow Harriss, sweetheart of his youth.
13–16, 18, 19, 21–26, 28–36, 46–48, 50–59, 65–81, 85–94, 96–100, 104, 111–121, 123–125, 127, 128, 130, 131, 136, 184, 202, 210, 213, 214, 217, 234, 238

Terrel, Bill. Convict who incites Monk to murder Warden Gambrell, whom Terrel hates because the warden has twice denied him a parole, in "Monk."
52, 53, 55–59

Thorpe, Buck (Ripsnorter). Brawler, moonshiner, thief, who is found dead with a half-drawn pistol in his hand. He was killed by Bookwright for running off with his daughter, in "Tomorrow."
85, 86, 97, 103–105

Varner, Will. Justice of the peace and storeowner, in "Tomorrow."
86, 97

Warren, Captain. Royal Flying Corps flight commander in World War I. During World War II Chick Mallison asks him how a sixteen-year-old can enlist. Warren tells Chick to wait, in "Knight's Gambit."
197

West, Doctor. Owner of the drugstore where the murderer of Judge Dukinfield buys the rare cigarettes that help Gavin Stevens solve the murder mystery, in "Smoke."
26–28, 31, 33, 34

Whitfield. Preacher who marries S. J. Fentry to the pregnant Thorpe woman and who preaches her funeral shortly afterward, in "Tomorrow."
  100

Workman, Mr. Insurance adjustor, in "An Error in Chemistry."
  121

REQUIEM FOR A NUN (1951)

Coldfield. Old family name in the Yoknapatawpha area.
9

Compson. Old family name in the Yoknapatawpha area.
9

Compson, General. Son of the first Jason and partner in the railroad with Colonel John Sartoris and Redmond, whom he disliked.
237, 238

Compson, Jason. The first Jason, who, according to legend, saved the Natchez Trace bandits from a lynching in Jefferson before the early town had a jail that was safe for prisoners. Later he traded Ikkemotubbe a racehorse for a large piece of Yoknapatawpha land.
13–17, 19, 20, 22–27, 32–34, 36–38, 41, 42, 45, 215, 216, 219, 220

* *Depre, Mrs. Virginia.* Sister of Colonel John Sartoris.
239

Farmer. Jailer during Civil War.
229
* *Farmer, Cecilia.* His daughter. She sat endless hours at the window of her home in the jail building and once with a diamond scratched on the pane her name and the date April 16, 1861. Four years later she married an ex-Confederate officer and went with him to his small hill farm in Alabama.
229

Gombault, Uncle Pete. Old man who during the New Deal years held a political sinecure under the designation U.S. Marshal.
242

Mannigoe, Nancy. Temple Stevens' Negro maid. She murders Temple's baby to prevent it from suffering the consequences of either being left behind or taken on Temple's flight with Pete. For this act she is to be executed. When Temple, after her visit to the governor, comes to Nancy's cell, Nancy knows, without being told, that there will be no reprieve. She has long since abandoned hope and substituted salvation, trust in Jesus. "Just believe," she says.
    50, 51, 78, 82, 93, 118, 121, 122, 124, 125, 132–134, 157, 168, 171, 172, 178–192, 195, 201, 208, 209, 211, 267–283

Mason. Leader of a gang of ruffians who were active in the early days of the settlement.
    5, 104, 223, 226

Mohataha. Chickasaw matriarch, mother of Ikkemotubbe, and sister of Issetibbeha. She took her people from Mississippi to Oklahoma.
    21, 27, 30, 34, 35, 215–217

Mulberry. Negro janitor for several professional men. During reconstruction days he held the title of U.S. marshal. He also peddled illicit whisky, which he cached beneath a mulberry tree.
    242

Murrel, John. Leader of a gang of ruffians after the time of Mason.
    5, 226

* *Peabody, Doctor.* Successor of Dr. Habersham. He was active in the naming of Jefferson.
    15, 19, 20, 22, 23, 25–29, 32, 34, 38, 42, 45

Pete. Brother of Alabama Red. He is blackmailing Temple Stevens. The fact that he strongly resembles Red makes him attractive to her.
    173–181

Pettigrew, Thomas Jefferson. Mail rider for whom the town was named.
    19–24, 26–29, 32, 36, 38, 219, 224

Ratcliffe. Post trader in the settlement that was to become Jefferson.
    15, 20–28, 30, 31, 34–38, 42, 43, 213, 216, 219, 220

Red (Alabama). Temple's lover in *Sanctuary*, killed by Popeye Vitelli.
144, 160, 167, 170, 178

* *Redmond*. Carpetbagger who came from Missouri to settle in Jefferson. Inspired by physical fear, he killed from ambush his partner in the Jefferson-Tennessee railroad, Colonel Sartoris.
233, 238

Sartoris. Old family name in the Yoknapatawpha area.
9

Sartoris, Bayard. Banker son of Colonel John. He was responsible for a law being passed which banned mechanically propelled vehicles from the streets of Jefferson. Later he died in such a vehicle.
242

Sartoris, Colonel John. Father of Bayard. He came to the settlement in its sixth year, a man of substance. In 1861 he raised a regiment of Mississippi infantry and became their colonel until after the second Battle of Manassas, when he was deposed. By 1876 he had built a railroad with General Compson and Redmond. Ten years later he was ambushed and killed by Redmond, who feared him. By then Sartoris had no friends: "only enemies and frantic admirers."
44, 45, 214, 230, 231, 237, 238

Stevens. Old family name in the Yoknapatawpha area.
9

Stevens, Bucky. Older child of Gowan and Temple.
66, 67, 78, 79, 184, 185, 203, 204, 207, 209

* **Stevens, Gavin.** Gowan's uncle and county attorney, who defends Nancy Mannigoe; he takes Temple to the governor so that she may confess her sins.
40, 49, 53–56, 58–64, 66–74, 76–96, 113, 115, 117, 119, 121–123, 125–127, 129–140, 142, 144–147, 149, 151, 152, 155, 156, 160–164, 167, 171–173, 194–196, 198, 199, 201–212, 214, 263–265, 268–273, 276, 278–282, 284–286

* **Stevens, Gowan.** Gavin's nephew. He marries Temple Drake and gives up drinking to atone for abandoning her to the bootleggers in *Sanctuary*.

51, 53–62, 64–66, 68–75, 77, 95, 97, 121, 136, 154, 157, 158, 172, 186, 188, 194–196, 201–205, 207, 209, 286

Stevens, Temple Drake. A judge's daughter who marries Gowan in an effort to nullify her past: the days when she became involved with bootleggers, lived in a brothel, and was responsible for the deaths of two men. The old Temple triumphs, however, when she tries to run away with Pete, the brother of her former lover, Alabama Red, and take her baby with them. She is thwarted when Nancy Mannigoe kills the baby. At Gavin Stevens' instigation she visits the governor and reveals her sordid past, believing that she may save Nancy.

51, 53–69, 71, 72, 76–97, 113–120, 122–140, 142–144, 146–152, 156–161, 168, 170, 172–192, 194, 196, 201–212, 263, 264, 266–268, 270–274, 276, 277, 280, 281, 283–286

Sutpen. Old family name in the Yoknapatawpha area.
9

Sutpen, Thomas. Man who used a captive French architect and wild slaves to build his plantation home and later the courthouse.
37, 40, 41, 44, 45, 214, 225, 227, 228, 238, 244

Tubbs. The Jefferson jailer during Nancy Mannigoe's imprisonment.
267, 269

Tubbs, Mrs. His wife.
266, 267

Vitelli, Popeye. Memphis gangster. [*See* Popeye in *Sanctuary*.]
144–146, 149

Whitfield. Some sort of preacher, probably. His cabin was the first church in Jefferson.
28

A FABLE (1954)

(*A Fable* incorporates [on pages 151–189] a revised version of a separately published episode, *Notes on a Horsethief* [Greenville, Mississippi: Levee Press, 1951; a limited, signed edition of 975 copies]. The story takes place at a time when the Royal Flying Corps was being replaced by the Royal Air Force; hence the mixture of RFC and RAF personnel.)

Angelique. Old blind French woman who rails at Marthe Demont, Marya, and the Corporal's wife because of their relationship to the Corporal, whom Angelique calls "anarchist."
216

Ball. Royal Flying Corps flyer, now deceased.
88, 89, 112, 120

Barker. Hero of the RFC.
88, 120

Beale, Colonel. A British army officer who calls the Corporal "Boggan" because the Corporal looks like a British soldier of that name whom the Colonel saw killed at Mons in 1914.
275, 276, 278–280

Beauchamp, Philip Manigault. Negro, American private, one of three soldiers who volunteer for an assignment in Paris. Only one of these three, Buchwald, knows that they are supposed to kill General Gragnon and make it look as if the Germans did it. To thwart them, Gragnon turns so that he is shot from behind. Since Beauchamp plans to be an undertaker, he is delegated to plug the bullet hole with wax so it will not show.
374

Bidet. French group commander, secretly called "Mama Bidet" by the enlisted men. He hopes to get a marshal's baton as a result of the

military coup that calls for Gragnon's regiment to execute an
attack that is intended to fail.

23, 27, 28, 32, 35, 50

Bishop. Famed RFC flyer.

88, 112, 120

Bledsoe, Sergeant. A British sergeant whom the military Runner is
obliged to knock out in order to further his plan of having the
British and German enlisted men make their own peace by giving
up fighting.

317–319

Blum, Major. French army officer who graduated from the Academy in
1913.

279, 280

Boggan. Name by which Colonel Beale addresses the Corporal. (*See*
Beale, Colonel; also see Brzewski and Stefan.)

276

Bouc, Pierre. See Zsettlani, Piotr.

Bridesman, Captain. Flight commander of young Levine's group. He
is one of those who make the fake attack on the German general
who is supposed to arrive at French headquarters for a conference
with officers of the Allied Countries.

89–91, 95, 97–100, 102–116, 324, 325

Brzewski. Name by which Captain Middleton calls the Corporal. (*See*
Middleton, Captain.)

277

Buchwald. Brooklyn-born American soldier, the only one of the three
volunteers who knows that they are supposed to kill General
Gragnon. It is Buchwald who actually fires the German pistol that
kills Gragnon and who delegates Beauchamp to fill the first bullet
hole with wax. Later, in America, Buchwald becomes a bootlegging

czar; and when he is murdered, has an elaborate gangster-style funeral.
372–380

Burk. Officer in the Royal Air Force.
116, 117, 323

Casse-tête (Horse). One of the two murderers executed with the Corporal. He is a simian-like idiot whose vocabulary consists of the one word *Paris.*
357–361, 384

Collyer. British officer who puts the Villeneuve Blanche, a French dive, out of bounds for his flyers.
93, 94, 99, 100, 109, 112, 114–117, 235

Conventicle. Flight sergeant with young Levine's group.
92, 96, 325

Corporal. See Stefan.

Cowrie. RAF officer who shares Bridesman's hut.
97, 98, 115

Davies, Rhys. RFC hero.
88, 120

De Marchi. RAF officer.
99, 117, 323

Demont. French farmer who married Marthe and who provided a home for her and her sister and their half brother. Sorrow over the destruction of his farm by artillery for the second time kills him.
423

Demont, Marthe. Half sister of the Corporal. She cares for him and her older sister after her mother dies in bearing the boy who was to be the Corporal. At Beirut she marries Demont, a Frenchman,

so that he may be the passport for the three into France, where the boy's destiny awaits him. (She is known as Magda until she crosses half of Europe to face the French general who holds the refusal of her half brother's life.)
214, 217–223, 285, 390, 392–394, 396–401, 427–430, 432

De Montigny. French army officer.
282

Gargne, M. A French *patron* of the Runner's garret home.
149

Gargne, Mme. Wife of M. Gargne.
149

Gragnon, General. French division commander who is chosen to sacrifice his reputation and a regiment in an attack intended to fail. When his men refuse to fight he requests permission to shoot them all. Later he is himself killed by two American soldiers who are supposed to shoot him in front with a German pistol to make it appear as if he has been killed by the Germans, in this way concealing the fact that his men failed to attack the enemy. As the pistol is fired, Gragnon spins around and so is hit in the back of the head. The bullet hole is filled with wax, and he is then shot in the front of the head.
12, 26, 28–30, 34, 38, 39, 43, 54, 230, 362, 366

Hanley. Member of the RAF.
323

Harry, Mr. (Pronounced "Mistairy" by the old Negro groom.) An English groom, the only man whom a certain great race horse will obey. When Harry is transporting the horse out of New Orleans by train, a flood-weakened trestle gives way and the van plunges into the flood with him, the horse, and a Negro groom. Though the men save the horse's life, the animal is permanently lame in one leg. Rather than see him sent to a stud farm, they steal him and race him, using the Negro groom's grandson as jockey, in various obscure Southern towns. The horse, though

running on only three legs, beats the best of competition and apparently is winning large sums for the two grooms. But the men, interested only in the horse's excellence, do not bet. All this time they are being pursued by agents of the horse's wealthy owner, but the country people protect the men despite a big reward offered for their capture. At last Harry is obliged to shoot the horse to save him from the owner. It is then only a matter of time before Harry leaves his companions to join the British army, eventually becoming the member of a combat unit, where he engages in a lucrative practice of betting his fellow soldiers that they will not survive the many battles in which they participate. In his frantic efforts to bury his past along with memories of the horse he loved, Harry refuses to see his faithful Negro friend even when the latter comes all the way to France to find him. They finally die together, however, when a heavy barrage of artillery fire from both the British and the German sides wipes out large numbers of British and German enlisted men who are seeking to stop hostilities by joining hands in that area between battle lines which the Americans call "No-Man's Land." (The narrative of the stolen horse occurs on pages 151–204.)
150, 151, 201

Henri. French army commander.
34

Horn. British soldier whom the military Runner knocks out and whose uniform he appropriates for Tooleyman to wear.
316, 317, 319

Irey. A turnkey who has the Negro groom in his custody for a time.
170

James, Lt. Colonel. British officer in command of the group to which the Runner is transferred.
64

Jean. One of the Corporal's men. He comments about Polchek's not drinking wine at the last supper of the group.
338

Lallemont. French corps commander who assigns Gragnon to the attack that is intended to fail.
    22, 23, 26, 230

Landry. Sergeant in charge of the group of men whose orders read as follows: "Proceed to Verdun and thence . . . to the catacombs beneath the Fort of Valaumont and extricate therefrom one complete cadaver of one French soldier unidentified and unidentifiable . . . and return with it."
    417, 418

Lapin. French criminal. He and his companion in crime, Casse-tête, are executed with the Corporal.
    357–361, 384, 385

Levine, David. Young British second lieutenant, who feels that a door has been closed on glory because two days before his commission comes through, the old RFC, with its catalogue of heroes and its famed uniform, has been superseded by the RAF. Worse still, perhaps, just as he has finished his apprenticeship in the air, the French obtain an armistice. Believing that the British are still fighting, Levine, with two other RAF men, pursues and fires upon a German plane, which remains unharmed, as do their planes, although they are apparently hit by anti-aircraft fire. Later, after a German general has landed in the British field in the German plane and walked safely away with Allied officers, Levine, by allowing himself to be fired upon by a gun of one of the planes that took part in the strange pursuit, proves what he has suspected—the ammunition is blank.
    89, 92, 93, 95, 96, 103

Luluque. A Midian, one of the Corporal's followers. He asks that someone say grace before the last supper.
    336

McCudden. Hero of the RFC.
    88, 89, 91, 112, 119, 120

Mannock. RFC hero.
    88, 91, 112

Martel, General. French army officer. Just as he was about to sign a citation for meritorious action, he saw the document blown off his desk by a mysterious wind and into the fireplace, where it was destroyed.

269

Marya. Older sister of Marthe Demont and half sister of the Corporal. Although mentally deficient by ordinary standards, she has surpassing insight into the actions of people.

284–291, 294, 296, 390–392, 394, 396, 398, 425–433

Middleton, Captain. American army officer. He calls the Corporal "Brzewski" because he looks exactly like an American soldier of that name who died of influenza aboard ship and, under Middleton's supervision, was buried in mid-ocean.

279, 280

Milhaud, Madame. Operator of a French restaurant where the British flyers sometimes dine.

116

Monaghan. An American flyer in the RAF.

93, 99, 104, 108–110, 120, 323

Morache. One of the soldiers on the Fort Valaumont detail (*see* Landry). He is the owner of the watch that was given in exchange for a second body (that of the Corporal) to replace the one from Fort Valaumont which the soldiers have exchanged for some wine money with an old French woman who believes it to be the body of her son. (*See* Theodule.)

413, 414, 417, 421–424

Osgood. Flyer in the RAF.

99

Paul. The Breton, second in command to the Corporal.

340

Picklock. Soldier so called because of his civilian occupation. As a member of the Fort Valaumont detail (*see* Landry) he picks the lock of Sergeant Landry's suitcase and steals some brandy that the Sergeant is withholding until their job has been completed. Later, Picklock makes arrangements for the procuring of a second body to replace the one that the soldiers have traded for money with which to buy wine.

413–424

Polchek. One of the Corporal's twelve followers. He informs on his own friends.

330, 337–339, 346, 347, 355

Runner. A former British officer who gives up his commission to become a messenger. It is he who attempts to prolong the armistice into a permanent peace.

64–67, 69, 72–78, 80–82, 85, 141–145, 147, 150, 151, 191, 197–207, 310–315, 318, 320, 321

Sibleigh. Flyer in the RAF.

91

Smith, Lt. British officer whom the Runner knocks out. (*See* Bledsoe.)

317–319

Stefan ("the" Corporal). Illegitimate son of the Supreme Commander of the Allied Armies (who represents God), his life in many ways resembles that of Christ. He and his twelve followers are so influential among the common soldiers, both French and German, that they persuade a regiment of French soldiers to refuse to carry out an attack and the German soldiers opposite to refuse to take advantage of the situation. As a result, the French officials call for an armistice to work out a plan with all of the authorities (both friend and foe) to thwart this attempt to halt the war. Soon the Corporal and his men are betrayed into the hands of the Corporal's father, who tries to bribe his son into deserting his followers and fleeing to safety. This the Corporal will not do, because dying as a martyr will further his cause for peace, and so he is executed between two thieves. The Corporal's half sisters obtain his body and bury it on the Demont farm. Shortly, hostilities resume, and a barrage blasts the Corporal's body from its resting place; it is then lost forever to his family. Later it is found by a neighboring farmer, who, unaware of its identity, trades it to Picklock, who uses it to replace a body removed from Fort Valaumont—a soldier's body which he and his companions have given to an old woman in exchange for money with which to buy drinks. Stefan thus becomes France's celebrated Unknown Soldier. (Important references to the Corporal occur on pages 275–301, 333–370, 384–389, 397–401.)

399

Sutterfield, Reverend Tobe (*also see Tooleyman*). The Negro groom who is associated with Mr. Harry in saving the three-legged horse from oblivion (*see* Harry). Though he is not an ordained minister he "bears witness" and is morally justified in confirming Harry into the church. He is, in turn, made a Mason by Harry a short time before they part company. After Harry has gone to France, Tobe sets out to join him. In New York he meets a wealthy white widow who has been supporting a French air squadron as a retaliatory measure against the Germans because her son was one of the first airmen killed in the French service. Sutterfield, in his sorrow over the many lives being lost in the war, persuades the widow to seek peace through faith rather than force; and thus *Les Amis Myriades et Anonymes à la France de Tout le Monde* is organized, the association at whose expense Sutterfield is enabled to visit France in search of his friend "Mistairy." Though Harry refuses to acknowledge him when they meet in France the first time, Tobe later joins Harry in the front-line trenches at the request of the Runner, who needs Tobe for his campaign to prolong the armistice into a permanent peace. Tobe is to give the Masonic sign, which ritual the Runner believes will help him prevail on the soldiers because Harry has made every member of his company a Mason. As they, unarmed, march with others toward the enemy trenches, Tobe, Harry, and many of the troops of both sides are killed by artillery barrages from both the German and the Allied cannon. (The narrative of the stolen horse occurs on pages 151–204.)

141, 146, 149, 150

Theodule. Name of one of the unidentified soldiers killed in 1916 at Fort Valaumont. Insisting that the body removed from the Fort by Landry's detail is Theodule (though it surely is not), Theodule's mother gives Landry's men (without Landry's knowledge) 100 francs for the corpse.

> *404, 405, 415, 416*

Thorpe. Flyer in the RAF.

> *99, 108, 109, 114*

Tooleyman (from Tout le Monde). When Tobe Sutterfield becomes identified with the association *Les Amis Myriades et Anonymes à la France de Tout le Monde,* he changes his name to Tooleyman, "to make it easier for the folks from the Association." (*See* Sutterfield.)

> *149, 150*

Wilson, Sergeant. The best sergeant in the army, according to Buchwald's Iowa companion. The Iowan has overheard a remark about President Wilson and thinks the reference is to his favorite sergeant.

> *375*

Witt. Member of the RAF.

> *91*

* *Zsettlani, Piotr (Pierre Bouc).* One of the Corporal's men who denies his leader at the last supper by accepting the pseudonym Pierre Bouc. Later he tries to rejoin the Corporal and his men but is prevented by the guards. After the Corporal's death, it is apparently Zsettlani who visits the Corporal's half sisters and tries to pay them 30 coins for the soup they give him.

> *339, 346, 355, 356, 427*

THE TOWN (1957)

(*The Town* incorporates extensively revised versions of "Centaur in Brass" [in part i; originally published in *American Mercury*, February, 1932, 200–210] and "Mule in the Yard" [in part xvi; originally published in *Scribner's*, August, 1934], both in *Collected Stories of William Faulkner*. Pages 359–371 of *The Town* appeared in *Saturday Evening Post*, May 4, 1957, entitled "The Waifs.")

Adams. Predecessor of de Spain as mayor of Jefferson.
   11–13

Adams, Mrs. Fat wife of the former mayor. She is called "Miss Eve Adams" by the boys.
   11

Adams, Theron. Mr. Adams's youngest son, whom Manfred de Spain challenged to a fight with axes by way of refuting a charge that Mr. Adams, when he was mayor, made against Manfred.
   12, 13

* *Armstid, Henry.* One of the men Flem Snopes tricked into buying some worthless property. Henry lost his mind as a result of this trickery and is now locked up for life in a Jackson asylum.
   7, 8, 34, 228, 271, 292

Backus, Melisandre. Woman whom, according to Maggie Mallison, Gavin Stevens should have married.
   50, 63, 178–180

* *Beauchamp, Tomey's Turl.* Night fireman of the Jefferson Power Plant, one of two Negro men exploited by Flem Snopes, the superintendent, to help him appropriate all movable brass parts in the plant.
   15–30, 83, 85, 142

Best, Henry. Jefferson alderman present at the investigation of the disappearance of brass from the Jefferson Power Plant.
85–87

Binford, Mrs. Deewit's wife.
366, 367

Binford, Deewit. Man married to a Snopes girl. He takes Byron Snopes's wild children to raise on contract, the various Snopeses each paying him "a dollar a head a week." Afraid for his life, he quickly breaks his contract.
365–367, 369

Bird, Tom Tom. Negro day fireman at the Jefferson Power Plant. After he and Tomey's Turl [Beauchamp] compare notes, they realize they are being victimized by Flem Snopes, and so they join forces and save themselves at Flem's expense.
15–30, 83, 85, 109, 142

Birdsong, Preacher. Countryman who learns to box in World War I well enough to give Matt Levitt a good contest.
183

Bookwright, Cal. Father of Letty. He reluctantly permitted her to marry Zack Houston.
78, 79

Buffaloe. Electrician who made the first auto ever to appear in Jefferson (1904). Later he is appointed city electrician by Mayor de Spain.
12, 13, 16, 18, 30

Christian, Walter. Negro janitor of Uncle Willy Christian's drugstore. His grandfather had been a slave of Uncle Willy's grandfather. Whenever Uncle Willy carelessly puts down the key to the medicinal alcohol chest, Walter goes into it and samples the contents.
155, 159, 160

Christian, Uncle Willy. Drugstore owner, a bachelor of sixty, who needs a little morphine daily to change him from an unfriendly person to a benevolent one. When his drugstore is burglarized, the theft of his morphine, therefore, is a catastrophe.

60, 154–160, 162, 179, 180, 188, 194, 195, 202, 204, 205, 211, 212

Clefus. Negro man who cleans Gavin Stevens' office.

357

Compson, General. Brigadier general in the Confederate army and governor of Mississippi for two days.

69, 231

Compson, Mrs. Wife of General Compson. She gave old Het the purple toque that Het is still wearing fifty years later.

231

Compson, Jason. Jefferson man. He collects rent from Montgomery Snopes for his mother, who owns the building that houses Montgomery's studio.

151

Connors, Buck. Marshal of Jefferson. (It is possible that the reference on page 54 is to his son.)

23, 54, 60, 61, 68, 69, 116, 124, 125, 157, 158, 161, 162, 195, 196, 319, 361–363

Crenshaw, Jack. Revenue field agent in Jefferson district.

172, 174

de Spain, Major. Manfred's father, a major of Confederate cavalry during the Civil War, who afterward established his annual hunting camp. It is his bank stock that makes it possible for Manfred to become president of the Sartoris Bank.

43, 58, 117, 362

* **de Spain, Manfred.** Man of action, West Pointer, and veteran of the Spanish American War. He becomes mayor of Jefferson on the wave of the new automobile age. He takes Mrs. Flem (Eula Varner) Snopes as mistress, and though Flem is supposed to be ignorant of their association, de Spain rewards him just the same by creating a sinecure for him—the superintendency of the power plant. During this period, Manfred triumphs decisively over his rival for Eula, the idealistic Gavin Stevens. When old Bayard Sartoris dies, Manfred becomes president of the Sartoris Bank and remains so until Flem informs Will Varner of the relationship between de Spain and Will's daughter Eula, at which time Manfred is obliged to sell his bank stock to Flem. De Spain's plan to leave Jefferson with Eula is altered when she commits suicide. However, he owes it to Jefferson to leave town forever, and so he does, "for business reasons and health."

10–15, 24, 29, 30, 36, 43, 44, 47, 49, 52, 56–64, 66–70, 72–77, 83–85, 92–95, 97–101, 108, 110, 111, 116–119, 133–135, 137–140, 142, 147, 150, 151, 166, 186, 194, 233, 265–267, 272–275, 277–279, 281, 282, 290, 293–295, 298, 302–304, 308, 309, 311–314, 318, 319, 328–332, 334, 337–342, 344, 346–348, 360, 362

Dukinfield, Judge. The judge who is delegated to hear the investigation of the affair of the missing brass but who later disqualifies himself and designates Judge Stevens, Gavin's father.

87, 97

* *Du Pre, Mrs. Virginia (Jenny).* Colonel Bayard Sartoris' kinswoman who superintends his household.

117, 118, 139, 140, 244, 310

* *Edmonds, McCaslin.* Father of Roth and a member of the hunting camp that Boon Hogganbeck had served long ago.

58

* *Edmonds, Roth.* One of the men who sign a note for Lucius Hogganbeck to buy a Model-T Ford.

58

Elma, Miss. Office deputy for Sheriff Hampton and widow of Hampton's predecessor.

174

Garraway. Inflexible puritan, keeper of a small grocery store, the first person to move his account from the Sartoris Bank as a protest against de Spain's liaison with Mrs. Flem Snopes. Knowing Flem, however, Garraway has no pity for him.
312, 313

Gatewood, Jabbo. Son of Uncle Noon. Like his father, Jabbo intends to be a blacksmith, but when he sees de Spain's red auto he decides to be a mechanic.
68, 69

Gatewood, Uncle Noon. Jabbo's father, the Negro blacksmith whose grindstone Gowan Stevens and Little Top Sander use to sharpen the rake with which they puncture de Spain's tires. "Unk" Noon helps Ratliff convert his Model-T Ford into an early type of pickup truck.
65, 66, 68, 113

Gombault. A U.S. marshal.
165, 174

Gowrie. Man who delivers Gavin Stevens' liquor.
357

Grenier, Louis. One of the founders of Jefferson.
323

Habersham, Doctor. One of the founders of Jefferson.
323

Habersham, Emily. Lady who phones the Travelers' Aid in El Paso to solicit their help in delivering Byron Snopes's children to the Mexican police. [In the Vintage edition (1961) Eunice Habersham performs the acts attributed to Emily.]
370, 371

Habersham, Eunice. Peddler of vegetables in a homemade truck which she uses to haul orchids for Mrs. Rouncewell, the florist, when

Mrs. Rouncewell is deluged with orders. She is a stockholder in the Sartoris Bank.
71, 118

Hait, Lonzo. Agent of I. O. Snopes. They coöperated in a plan whereby they would arrange to have a number of mules at a spot on the railroad tracks at just the right time for a train to kill the animals, thus making it possible for the partners to collect handsome damages. Three years before the events in *The Town*, Lonzo himself had been killed along with five mules, for which misfortune Mrs. Hait was awarded $8,500, part of which I. O. feels he is entitled to but has never received.
232–235, 241, 243, 248, 249, 251, 255

Hait, Mrs. Mannie. Man-charactered, man-tongued widow of Lonzo. She lives alone and does her own plowing and can hold her own with even the Snopes world, for she outmaneuvers I. O. Snopes at every turn and receives the mortgage on her home as a gift from Flem.
231–257

* *Hampton, Hub.* Sheriff of Yoknapatawpha County. He is aware that Flem Snopes has successfully switched Montgomery Ward Snopes's offense from maintaining an obscene picture gallery to bootlegging, a much less odious offense.
104, 130, 158–166, 172–175, 192, 196, 197, 257, 361–363, 367

Handy, Professor. Negro musician from Memphis, whose band plays for the Christmas ball in Jefferson.
72

Harker. Old sawmill engineer who operates the boilers and engines for the pump and dynamo at the Jefferson Power Plant.
9, 15–17, 19, 21, 23–26, 28, 30, 109, 110

Harker, Otis. Relative of Mr. Harker. He sometimes substitutes for Mr. Harker when the latter wants a night off. Otis succeeds Winbush as night marshal of Jefferson.
25, 195, 196, 318, 319, 321, 333, 361

Het (old Het). Old Negro woman, officially a resident of the poor-house, who "finds" many a meal elsewhere, using Mrs. Hait's house as a base of operations.
231, 232, 234, 237–245, 247, 248, 250–252, 254–256

Hogganbeck, Boon. Father of Lucius and former handyman at Major de Spain's famous hunting camp.
58

Hogganbeck, Lucius. Owner of Jefferson's first Model-T Ford, which he buys by having several Jefferson men sign his note.
58, 59, 71, 101

Hogganbeck, Miss Melissa. History teacher at the Academy in Jefferson, who still teaches that history has not reached Christmas Day, 1865, because the next ten years are to show that the Southern surrenders were mistakes that will be rectified.
288

Holcomb, Ashley. Young boy, friend of Chick Mallison.
54

Holston, Alexander. One of the founders of Jefferson, for whom Holston House or Holston Hotel is named.
60, 62, 83, 323

Houston, Letty Bookwright. Cal Bookwright's youngest daughter, a schoolteacher, who married Zack Houston, a man with little schooling, and was killed within a year by Zack's blooded stallion.
78, 79

* *Houston, Zack*. Farmer who threw I. O. Snopes into a cooling tub of water because I. O. bungled the job of shoeing Zack's horse. One year after Houston's marriage to Letty Bookwright, she was killed by his stallion and Zack was later shot to death by Mink Snopes.
36, 37, 78–80, 82

Hovis. Cashier of the Sartoris Bank.
309

* *Ikkemotubbe* (*Doom*). Son of Issetibbeha's sister. Using poison as a persuader, he forced his way to the chieftainship of the Chickasaw Tribe.
307, 316

* *Issetibbeha.* Chickasaw chief, uncle of Ikkemotubbe.
307, 316

Job. Judge Dukinfield's janitor.
97

Killebrew, Miss. Teller at the Sartoris Bank.
309

Kneeland. Owner of the tailor shop where many of the Jefferson men rent dress suits for the Christmas ball.
70

Ledbetter, Mrs. Woman at Rockyford who buys a sewing machine from Ratliff.
295, 296, 298, 299

Levitt, Matt. Linda Snopes's beau, an expert boxer, who beats up Gavin Stevens because he thinks Gavin is trying to take Linda from him. He loses his job as mechanic, makes a general nuisance of himself by driving his racer about town with the cutout valve of his exhaust pipe open, and is finally ordered out of town by Sheriff Hampton.
183–186, 188–191, 194–197, 204, 212, 325, 364

Littlejohn, Mrs. Keeper of a boardinghouse at Frenchman's Bend.
34, 35

Long, Judge. Federal judge in Jefferson who sends a whisky maker (Provine) to the penitentiary, not because he is violating the liquor law, but because he allows his wife to carry water a mile and a half from the spring.
165, 168, 169, 171, 174

McCallum, Anse. Son of Buddy. He is put in jail by the sheriff for assaulting Matt Levitt with a fence rail. Later, though he fights valiantly, he loses to Matt, a Golden Gloves boxer.
196, 197

McCallum, Buddy. One-legged father of Anse. He orders his son to fight Levitt fairly, and when Anse is thoroughly beaten, halts the fight and suggests that Matt move on.
196, 197

McCarron. Eula Varner Snopes's first lover and the father of Linda Snopes.
100, 101, 135, 136, 192, 204, 221, 272, 273

McCaslin, Ike. Owner of a hardware store in Jefferson. He is the uncle of Roth Edmonds and was one of the men who years before went to Major de Spain's hunting camp.
12, 58

* *McGowan, Skeets*. Uncle Willy Christian's clerk and soda-jerker.
156, 160, 162, 180, 207, 361

McLendon, Jackson. Jefferson man who organizes a company of soldiers for World War I and finally becomes a captain.
104, 116

Mallison, Charles, Jr. (Chick). Young nephew of Gavin Stevens. Gavin, with the aid of Ratliff, is trying to make Chick an opponent of Snopesism. (Chick is the narrator in parts 1, 3, 7, 10, 12, 14, 16, 19, and 24.)
111, 170, 171, 190, 191, 200, 205, 207, 208, 212, 215, 310, 320, 345, 346, 353, 354

Mallison, Charles, Sr. Father of Chick. He likes to tease his brother-in-law Gavin Stevens about the latter's romances.
49, 61, 63, 67, 186, 187, 200

Mallison, Margaret (Maggie). Twin of Gavin Stevens and mother of Chick.

46, 47, 56, 67, 69, 89, 111, 133, 182, 186, 187, 200, 214, 220, 319, 334, 346

Nunnery, Mrs. Cedric's mother.
108, 109

Nunnery, Cedric. Five-year-old boy for whom Eck Snopes is searching when an oil tank explodes and kills Eck.
108–110

* *Peabody, Dr.* Old Jefferson doctor.
117, 156, 161, 366

Priest, Maurice. Sally's husband, who gives Grenier Weddel a black eye for sending Sally a corsage and Sally a black eye for accepting it.
77

Priest, Sally Hampton. Girl who returns Grenier Weddel's ring and marries Maurice, and who proudly wears the black eye her husband gives her because he is jealous of Grenier.
70, 77

Provine, Wilbur. Maker of illicit whisky, and, according to Ratliff, a "Snopes" type. He is sentenced to the penitentiary, not for making whisky, but for allowing his wife to walk a mile and a half to get water.
168, 171, 172

Quistenberry, Dink. Man who marries into the Snopes family and runs the Jefferson Hotel, formerly called the Snopes Hotel. Dink takes Byron Snopes's children into his car when they arrive at the Jefferson depot.
360, 361

Ratliff, Vladimir Kyrilytch. Shrewd itinerant sewing-machine sales-man, who sees much of what goes on about Yoknapatawpha County and quickly learns most of the rest. With Gavin Stevens, Ratliff is a dedicated enemy of Snopesism. (He is the narrator of parts 4, 6, 9, 11, 18, and 23.)

3–9, 15, 29, 31–37, 39, 40, 43–46, 88, 94, 103–107, 111–113,
115, 116, 118–121, 123, 124, 126, 129, 134, 135, 138–143, 149,
150, 154–158, 162, 166–171, 174–176, 177, 178, 189, 192, 195,
206, 219, 220, 223–225, 227–229, 231–237, 241–244, 248, 256–
261, 264, 265, 271, 276, 278, 292, 295, 298, 308, 318, 320, 322,
331, 335, 339, 342, 343, 346, 356–358, 364–366, 368, 370, 371

Renfrow. Owner of the oil tank that Eck Snopes is hired to watch.
   33

Riddell. Family name of the little boy whose polio sickness causes the
   schools in Jefferson to close for a day.
   310, 311, 337, 362

Roebuck, John Wesley. Young boy, friend of Chick Mallison. John
   is the boy Ab Snopes shoots with a load of squirrel-shot for stealing watermelons.
   54, 55

Rouncewell, Mrs. Jefferson florist. She is deluged with orders for orchids
   just before the Christmas ball.
   70, 71, 73, 77, 122, 199

Rouncewell, Whit. Probably Mrs. Rouncewell's son. He sees the two
   burglars in Christian's drugstore. Whit is one of the boys often
   seen with Linda Snopes and her girl friend.
   160, 212

Samson. Hotel porter.
   97

Sander, Aleck. Negro, son of Big Top and Guster. He is approximately
   the same age as Chick Mallison, his constant companion.
   45, 52–55, 63, 111, 181, 244, 310, 337–342, 362

Sander, Big Top. Negro, Guster's husband and father of Little Top and
   Aleck.
   52

Sander, Guster. Negro cook for the Stevens and Mallison families and wife of Big Top.
    48, 52, 63, 64, 336–338, 340–342

Sander, Little Top. Aleck Sander's older brother. Little Top helps Gowan Stevens puncture Manfred de Spain's tires.
    52, 64–68

Sartoris, Colonel Bayard (old Bayard). Son of Colonel John, from whom he inherited his title. Bayard, after having his team of horses frightened by the first auto in Jefferson, caused to be passed an edict that no gasoline-propelled vehicle should ever appear on the streets of Jefferson. Much later old Bayard dies of heart failure in young Bayard's auto. He was a passenger at the time because he thought his presence might help curb his grandson's reckless driving.
    11, 13, 41–43, 104, 106, 116–119, 136, 137, 139, 140, 147, 151, 169, 265–267, 274, 302, 312

Sartoris, young Bayard. Grandson of Colonel Bayard. Unaware of his grandfather's heart condition, young Bayard, by his reckless driving, causes old Bayard's death.
    116–118, 120, 140

Sartoris, Benbow. Son of young Bayard and Narcissa.
    244

Sartoris, Colonel John. Father of old Bayard and commander of the cavalry group of which Ab Snopes was a member when Ab was reportedly hanged for stealing Confederate horses.
    4, 41, 42

Sartoris, Narcissa Benbow. Young Bayard's second wife and mother of young Benbow.
    117

Snopes (the "actual Snopes schoolmaster"). Father of Byron and Virgil Snopes. He is described as ". . . a tall gaunt man in a soiled frock coat and a string tie and a wide politician's hat. . . . [with] a

demagogue's capacity for using people to serve his own appetites, all clouded over with a veneer of culture and religion. . . ." His stay in Jefferson is short; after being caught in an empty cotton house with a fourteen-year-old girl, he is tarred and feathered "out of the country." [The same character is identified as Wesley Snopes in *The Mansion*.]
    40

Snopes, *Ab*. Flem's father. He lives a mile out of Jefferson beside his watermelon patch, which attracts small boys, whom Ab furiously chases off. Once he shoots a boy in the back with squirrel shot; after that he is reduced to throwing rocks at the invaders. (He is probably the "original" Ab Snopes, reported hanged in the Civil War by his own men for stealing Confederate horses.)
    5, 41, 42, 55, 79, 129, 130

Snopes, *Admiral Dewey*. Eck's younger son.
    40, 127, 128, 146

Snopes, *Bilbo*. One of the twins that I. O. Snopes has by his "second" wife (he is apparently not divorced from his first spouse). Vardaman is his twin.
    37, 39, 129–131

* Snopes, *Byron*. Son of the "actual Snopes schoolmaster" and brother of Virgil. Backed by old Bayard Sartoris, he goes to business college and becomes an employee of the Sartoris Bank. After being drafted during World War I, Byron, by taping a plug of tobacco under his left armpit to speed up his heartbeat, procures a medical discharge. In time Byron absconds with a small sum from the bank. Years later he sends four children of his to Jefferson for Flem Snopes to take care of. The Snopes people try to look after the children, but the waifs are too wild and are finally returned to Byron.
    41–43, 106, 107, 117–119, 138, 140, 141, 262, 264–267, 275, 277, 278, 347, 359, 361, 364, 370

Snopes, *Clarence*. Oldest son of I. O. by his "second" wife (*see* Snopes, Bilbo). He torments Byron Snopes's four children, and eventually they are almost successful in burning him at the stake. [In the

Vintage edition (1961) Clarence encourages a younger brother, Doris, to tease the children; it is Doris, then, who is almost burned at the stake. This version is recounted in *The Mansion*.]
    37, 39, 365, 368, 369

Snopes, Eck. Flem Snopes's immediate successor in Jefferson. Eck comes to the Snopes restaurant wearing a brace on his neck which he broke saving a Negro from a falling log. Because he is too innocent and honest to replace Flem in the restaurant, he is fired and made night watchman of an oil tank. On this job he is blown to bits when he lowers a lighted lantern into an oil tank not yet emptied of its gas, while searching for the lost Nunnery boy.
    31–36, 39, 40, 79, 107–110, 127, 143, 150, 168

Snopes, Mrs. Eck. Landlady at the Snopes Hotel for a time. She later buys half interest in a grocery store with the $1,000 the oil company gives her for Eck's death. At length she nominally becomes sole owner of the store, though it really belongs to her son Wall-street.
    40, 110, 128, 129

Snopes, Eula Varner. Flem's wife. Shortly after coming to Jefferson with her husband and Linda, her baby by another man (McCarron), she becomes the mistress of Manfred de Spain. During the investigation of the stolen brass she, sent by Flem, visits Gavin Stevens' office to give herself to him if he will call off the proceedings that will incriminate Flem. When Gavin refuses, she departs, unabashed, as is her nature. Years later, when Flem has tricked Linda into loving him as a father and, with the aid of Will Varner —who is now aware of Eula's double life—has forced de Spain out of the bank, Eula, seeing Linda's marriage to Gavin as the only solution for her daughter, begs Gavin to marry Linda. The best she can get from Gavin is his oath that he will marry Linda later if there is no other way. Shortly after this incident, Eula commits suicide.
    4, 6–9, 14–16, 24, 46, 47, 49, 50, 52, 53, 55–57, 70, 73–75, 119, 132–134, 136, 179, 189, 194, 205, 214, 219, 227, 228, 259, 261, 293, 294, 298, 300, 304, 308, 309, 311, 326, 336, 340, 342, 343, 348, 351, 354, 355

Snopes, Flem. Chief of the Snopeses. For eighteen years, pretending not to know, he allows his wife Eula and Manfred de Spain to carry on their affair. At first he is satisfied with certain petty material rewards such as the empty superintendent's job created for him at the power plant. After he virtually falls into the vice-presidency of the Sartoris Bank, however, his ambitions gradually rise. Though his basic ethics remain unchanged, he now dreams of respectability and position, and he goes about attaining them in any way that to his primitive but shrewd mind seems effective. Starting humbly, he exchanges his country cloth cap for a large black hat, acquires modern furniture in his home, learns all he needs to know of the banking business. Then, regardless of cost, he consolidates his progress by removing the objectionable Snopeses such as Montgomery Ward and I. O. from Jefferson. By now he secretly aspires to the bank presidency, and Will Varner's bank stock becomes important enough to Flem for him to try to win Linda Snopes's affection so that she may be influenced to sign over her inheritance to him (Linda is Eula's illegitimate daughter). He is successful in this, and now two great ambitions fuse: to avenge himself on Manfred de Spain (and probably on Eula also) and to become president of the Sartoris Bank. He can achieve both by showing Linda's will to Will Varner and by informing Will about Eula and Manfred. Again Flem is successful; nor does he cease at this point. In the role of martyred husband he gazes, at the last, upon his monument to Eula, the elaborate tombstone on which he has caused to be placed the words "A Virtuous Wife is a Crown to Her Husband."

3, 5–9, 15–20, 22–26, 28–34, 38, 48, 50, 52, 53, 56, 70, 73, 75, 77–84, 92, 94, 95, 99, 118, 119, 120, 124, 126, 128, 129, 131, 134–142, 146–151, 166–171, 174–178, 188, 205, 214, 221–224, 227, 228, 245–247, 251–254, 257, 260, 261, 268, 269, 271, 273, 274, 276, 277, 279, 281–287, 290, 294, 295, 297, 299, 300, 308, 309, 312, 319, 320, 323, 327–331, 333, 338, 339, 342, 343, 346–349, 351–354, 358–360, 364–367, 369

Snopes, I. O. A failure as a blacksmith and as a schoolmaster. This mouther of "worn saws and proverbs" also fails in the Snopes restaurant, where he succeeds Flem Snopes as manager. Only at breeding does he seem to be a success, for he has fathered several children by at least two women, only one of whom he is legally married to. His most audacious business venture is a curious partnership with Mr. Hait (*see* Hait, Lonzo) which causes him much misery in the form of lost money when Mrs. Hait completely outwits him. He does finally salvage some cash at the hands of Flem but with the proviso that he, I. O., leave Jefferson forever.

36–40, 79, 104, 129, 150, 196, 232–240, 242–244, 247, 248, 250–253, 255–258, 347, 360, 365

Snopes, Mrs. I. O. I. O.'s second "wife," to whom he is illegally married. She is the mother of Clarence and the twins Vardaman and Bilbo. She cries "Them Indians! Them Indians!" by way of attracting help for her son Clarence, whom Byron Snopes's children are attempting to burn at the stake.

367, 369

Snopes, Linda. Eula's illegitimate daughter by McCarron. She merely tolerates Flem Snopes, who she thinks is her father, until he refuses to let her go away to college. Then she becomes his enemy, but his thoughtful, generous acts begin to win her over; and his admission that he is wrong in keeping her at the Jefferson Academy completes the job. Through tears she calls him "Daddy" for the first time, even though she has begun to doubt that he is her true father; and later, in Oxford, she signs over her inheritance to him, as he had hoped she would do. After her mother's suicide she commands Jefferson's complete sympathy as she looks, with Flem— who Gavin Stevens has made her believe again is really her father —upon her mother's tomb and departs for New York, alone.

50, 131, 179–181, 183–192, 194, 195, 198–200, 203, 210, 213– 215, 221–223, 259–261, 291, 298, 300, 310, 320, 321, 325, 328, 330, 331, 336, 339–341, 343–349, 351, 352, 354

Snopes, Mink. The only Snopes who, in Ratliff's words, is "mean without no profit consideration or hope at all." He killed Zack Houston when Flem Snopes was on his Texas honeymoon, and waited in vain for Flem, the chief Snopes, to come to his aid. He spends two and a half months in the Jefferson Jail before being sent to serve a life sentence in the penitentiary in Parchman.

78, 79, 81, 82

* Snopes, Montgomery Ward. Son of I. O. He goes to France with Gavin Stevens as a YMCA worker, and while running an army canteen, he imports a French girl to entertain the boys in the backroom. Gavin, his superior officer, saves him from disgrace because his family name is the same as Eula's, with whom Gavin, perhaps unconsciously, is in love. Back in Jefferson after the war, Montgomery opens an arty photography shop which is a front for a peep show featuring obscene photographs. When he is found out, he is prosecuted for the much less odious offense of bootlegging, thanks to the expert manipulation of Flem Snopes, who is now concerned with dignifying the family name in Jefferson.

    39, 104, 105, 107, 112–116, 120–126, 150, 151, 154, 156, 161–171, 176, 177, 257, 347

Snopes, Vardaman. Son of I. O. by his second "wife." Vardaman is the twin of Bilbo.

    37, 39, 129–131

Snopes, Virgil. Son of the "actual Snopes schoolmaster" and brother of Byron.

    41

Snopes, Wallstreet Panic (Wall). Eck's son and, like his father, an untypical Snopes. He is honest. At the age of twelve he enters kindergarten and labors earnestly as a student and as a janitor and newsboy. By the time he has completed his schooling he, through his mother, is the owner of a grocery store. The girl he marries is equally ambitious, and they make a success of their store, though they nearly lose it once when "Wall" overbuys. Flem Snopes essays to get a share of the store by forcing a loan on him. The plan fails, however, and Wall, backed by his Snopes-hating wife, finds the necessary money elsewhere and is saved. He subsequently builds a successful wholesale grocery business.

    34, 40, 110, 127–129, 143, 144, 146–148, 150, 167, 279, 282, 362

Spilner. Man behind whose house Mrs. Hait ties and kills I. O. Snopes's mule.

    253

* **Stevens, Gavin.** Acting city attorney who shares with Ratliff the burden of combating Snopesism in Jefferson. Probably equal to his hatred of this unethical force is his complex but, in the final analysis, boyish love for Eula Snopes. It is a love that he is probably unaware of as such, a love that irrationally sets Eula on a pedestal to which he will not allow himself to reach even when she, to save Flem Snopes, is willing to give herself to him. As Eula's daughter Linda approaches womanhood, Gavin attempts to protect her from Snopesism by giving her good books to read and by trying to get her to a college away from Jefferson. He misses the supreme chance to save Linda, however, when he refuses Eula's plea that he marry Linda. His idealism cannot come close enough to reality to allow this. Courageous and loyal to the end, nevertheless, he sees that Eula, though a suicide, gets a decent burial and even procures the elaborate tombstone for which Flem is to get the entire credit. (He is the narrator of parts 2, 5, 8, 13, 15, 17, 20, and 22.)

3–8, 11, 13, 15, 16, 19, 20, 27, 29, 45–63, 65, 68–77, 81, 84–86, 94, 98, 100, 103–107, 110–112, 115, 116, 120–127, 129, 131, 134–136, 154, 156, 161–176, 178–192, 194, 195, 198–201, 208, 214, 215, 219, 231, 233, 244–248, 250–257, 260, 261, 296, 298, 302–305, 309, 311, 318, 320, 321, 332, 335–338, 340–345, 348, 356–358, 362, 364–366

* *Stevens, Gowan.* Young cousin of Gavin Stevens who lives in the Stevens–Mallison home while his parents are abroad. Being several years older than Chick Mallison, Gowan knows many things that occur before Chick is born, and he becomes a sort of narrator through Chick, since the latter learns about many of the events in *The Town* from Gowan.

3, 11, 16, 22, 24–28, 45–53, 55–57, 59–69, 71–77, 105–107, 110–112, 114, 116, 133, 134, 186

Stevens, Judge Lemuel. Father of the twins Gavin and Margaret [Mallison].

48, 49, 97–99.

Stone. Oxford lawyer who draws up for Linda Snopes the papers that surrender her inheritance to Flem Snopes.

326–328

Thorndyke. Episcopal minister, one of the four ministers sent by the women of Jefferson to "forgive" Eula Snopes by conducting her funeral services jointly. Gavin Stevens, aware of the implication, forbids them to officiate.
342

Tom. Customer in the Sartoris Bank who cannot read the note old Bayard Sartoris has written out for him. Neither can Bayard, so he tears it up and writes out another.
139

Trumbull. Man who ran Will Varner's blacksmith shop for fifty years until the Snopeses took over. Later Flem Snopes "sold" Trumbull back to Varner when Flem's man, I. O. Snopes, fled from Frenchman's Bend.
36, 38

Tull, Mrs. Vernon's wife. Her sister's niece by marriage is the illegal wife of I. O. Snopes.
38

Tull, Vernon. Farmer near Frenchman's Bend.
39, 365–367

Varner, Mrs. Wife of Will, mother of Jody and of Eula [Snopes].
227, 292–295, 297, 299, 300, 343, 344

Varner, Jody. Will's son, brother of Eula [Snopes].
5, 6, 32, 227, 228, 273, 294, 295, 299, 328, 343, 344, 369

Varner, Will (Uncle Billy). Fire-eating father of Eula [Snopes] and owner of most of Frenchman's Bend. He has never forgiven Flem Snopes for outsmarting him in connection with the old Frenchman's place; consequently he arranges his will so that Flem will never have any of the Varner wealth in his own name; hence, when Will is informed in the same instant that his granddaughter Linda Snopes has signed over her heritage to Flem and that his daughter Eula [Snopes] has been living in sin with Manfred de Spain for eighteen years, his anger knows no limits. He storms into Jefferson at 4 a.m., intent on throwing both de Spain and

Flem out of the country, but a different plan virtually forms itself out of the circumstances, whereby de Spain and Eula will leave town together, and Flem will get the Sartoris Bank. This arrangement leaves Varner not happy but mollified, for the time at least.

5–8, 32, 36–38, 79, 81, 82, 117–119, 137, 147, 151, 224, 227, 228, 260, 261, 263, 265, 271, 273–278, 283, 286, 288–295, 297–300, 303, 304, 308, 309, 311, 313, 319, 320, 334, 338, 339, 343, 351, 365

Weddel, Grenier. Young bachelor whom Sally Hampton turned down to marry Maurice Priest. After the fight between Gavin Stevens and Manfred de Spain at the Christmas ball, Grenier and Maurice do battle because Weddel has sent Mrs. Priest an orchid, a triple-sized one.

70, 73, 77

Widrington, Mrs. Wealthy woman, a newcomer to Jefferson. She is owner of the Pekinese [*sic*] that Byron Snopes's children steal.

362, 364

Wildermark. Owner of a Jefferson dry-goods store where Gavin Stevens and his sister purchase a traveling case for Linda Snopes. Mrs. Hait buys her archaic shoes from Mr. Wildermark, who orders them especially for her once a year.

198, 200, 234

Wildermark (the senior). Good chess player. He may be the father of the dry-goods store owner.

306

Winbush, Grover Cleveland. Flem Snopes's partner in the restaurant until he is eased out. He then becomes night marshal in Jefferson. He loses this job after a time because he is more interested in visiting Montgomery Ward Snopes's pornographic peep show than he is in preserving law and order.

4, 43, 88, 93, 124–126, 154, 156–163, 166, 167, 174, 195, 297

Wyott, Doctor. Atheistic president emeritus of the Jefferson Academy and grandson of its founder. He can read Greek, Hebrew, and

Sanskrit and has even beaten the senior Mr. Wildermark at chess.
306

Wyott, Miss Vaiden. Second-grade teacher to whom Wallstreet Panic
Snopes finally proposes marriage in gratitude for her help. Deeply
touched, she introduces him instead to the girl he does marry, and
she, Miss Vaiden, goes to teach in another town.
127, 128, 145, 146

THE MANSION (1959)

(*The Mansion* incorporates a revised version of "By the People" [in part 13], which appeared originally in *Mademoiselle*, October, 1955.)

Albert. Ex-Marine and member of Goodyhay's congregation, who explains to Mink Snopes why a Negro woman and an ex-prostitute are allowed to attend Goodyhay's religious meetings: they both lost men in World War II. Albert drives the truck that leaves used lumber for Goodyhay's chapel. When he and Mink arrive with a second load at the proposed site, they learn that someone of authority has forbidden Goodyhay to build there.
> 274, 275, 277

Allanovna, Myra. Proprietress of an expensive New York tie shop for which she designs the ties that bear her name. She gives Ratliff an Allanovna worth $150.
> 167, 169, 170, 172, 231, 320

Allison, Miss. Manfred de Spain's cousin, retired principal of a Los Angeles grammar school. She and her mother return to Jefferson from California to live in the old de Spain house, which Linda Snopes Kohl gives back to them after Flem Snopes's death.
> 429

* *Armstid, Henry.* Frenchman's Bend farmer. Armstid, Ratliff, and Odum Bookwright were tricked by Flem Snopes into buying the Old Frenchman's place.
> 127, 138, 142

Backus, Mr. Father of Melisandre [Stevens]. He died shortly after her marriage to Harriss.
> 195, 196, 357

Baddrington, Harold (*Plex*). Pilot of the plane in which Charles Mallison is shot down; called Plex [from Plexiglass] because he is

obsessed with thoughts of "cellophane," even has a plan for winning the war with it.
294

Barron, Jake. Convict at Parchman who was killed in an effort to
escape. (See Stillwell.)
97

Benbow, Narcissa. Maiden name of the girl who married Bayard Sartoris,
aviator in World War I.
189

Biglin, Mrs. Luther's wife. Each evening after attending the movies,
she awakens Luther so he can take his post under Flem Snopes's
window.
428

Biglin, Luther. Young farmer and dog trainer and considered one of
the best bird shots in the county. After service in World War II,
he becomes Jefferson jailer. When Mink Snopes is released from
Parchman, Luther, unknown to Flem Snopes, acts as Flem's body-
guard, sitting under the banker's window each night to guard
him against vengeance from Mink. He visualizes himself dra-
matically saving Flem and being handsomely rewarded. Two jobs,
however, are more than he can handle, and he often sleeps at his
post.
206, 408, 409, 411, 428

Binford, Lucius. Once Miss Reba Rivers' pimp, he later settled down
with her in her bawdyhouse. After his death she gets two white
dogs that she calls Miss Reba and Mr. Binford. On occasions when
she begins grieving over Mr. Binford, she gets uproariously drunk
on gin.
72, 79

Bishop, Ephriam (Eef). Sheriff who amicably alternated terms with
old Hub Hampton and now has the same relationship with Hub,
Jr.
370, 381, 408, 409, 428, 429

Bookwright, Calvin. Maker of excellent bootleg whisky. In his old age he sells his product to only a chosen few, Ratliff among them.
170, 171, 231, 372

Bookwright, Herman. One of the local rivals for Eula Varner's [Snopes] affections. He was one of the young men who suddenly left Frenchman's Bend when it was known that Eula was pregnant.
126

Bookwright, Homer. Man in Jefferson who said that Mrs. Tubbs, "being human even if she is a woman," was curious about what Montgomery Ward Snopes's pornographic pictures were like.
63

Bookwright, Odum. Farmer at Frenchman's Bend. Odum, Henry Armstid, and V. K. Ratliff were tricked by Flem Snopes into buying the Old Frenchman's place.
127, 138, 142

Brummage, Judge. Judge who sentenced Mink Snopes to prison for life.
43

Buffaloe. Electrician in Jefferson who made an automobile that frightened Colonel Bayard Sartoris' matched team into running away.
34

Burden, Joanna. Jefferson resident. Her mailbox was used as a point of reference when some of the local boys were teasing Tug Nightingale.
185

Christian, Uncle Willy. Owner of the drugstore that was robbed when Grover Cleveland Winbush, night watchman, was attending Montgomery Ward Snopes's peep show. It is in this drugstore that Gavin Stevens, years later, entertains Linda Snopes [Kohl].
55–57, 59, 69, 134, 135, 137, 187, 201

* *Compson, Benjy.* Idiot who set himself and the Compson house on fire and burned to death in it.
322, 328

Compson, Candace. The Compsons' only daughter. When her marriage failed, she disappeared, leaving her daughter Quentin with the infant's grandparents.

322

Compson, Jason. Second son of the Compsons. In charge of the Mc-Caslin Hardware Company, he is now a man of some means. Claiming to have advance information that the government plans to put an air-training field on the old Compson pasture, which Jason's father sold in 1909 and Jason bought back twenty years later, Jason sells all of the Compson property to Flem Snopes. Later, the government designates another location for the airfield and Jason openly exults. When he realizes, however, that the property will have permanent value for housing the rapidly expanding population, he regrets his deal with Flem and looks in vain for a flaw in the title of the property.

322–327, 330, 332, 334

* *Compson, Quentin.* The Compson to whom Mohataha had granted some land in 1821.

334

Compson, Miss Quentin. Candace's daughter. She climbed down the rain pipe one night and ran off with a carnival.

322

Crack. A member of the Sartoris Rifles.

184

Dad. Man in charge of tearing down an old building for Goodyhay. While Mink Snopes is sleeping, Dad steals $10 from him and disappears.

266, 270, 271

de Spain, Major. Father of Manfred.

153, 154, 215, 328, 358, 422

* *de Spain, Manfred.* Mayor of Jefferson and later the successor to Bayard Sartoris as president of the Sartoris Bank. When Flem

Snopes made it known that Manfred and Eula Varner Snopes had been lovers for eighteen years, Manfred had to give everything up and leave Jefferson.

34, 56, 62, 86, 125, 127–130, 135, 137–146, 148, 152, 153, 155, 193, 211, 212, 245, 358, 360, 401, 422

Devries, Colonel. Opponent of Clarence Snopes for Congress. Hero of World War II, he, though white, commanded Negro infantry in battle. When Devries came out of the ether after having his war-injured leg amputated, he pinned his current medal on the Negro sergeant who, at the risk of his own life, had saved him. He is elected to Congress after Clarence has been eliminated from the race. (*See* Snopes, Clarence Eggleston.)
308–315, 317, 318, 320

Dilazuck. Owner of the livery stable in front of an auction lot where Tug Nightingale spent most of his time.
181

Dukinfield, Judge. Judge who disqualified himself and appointed Judge Stevens to hear impeachment proceedings against Mayor de Spain. (*See* Stevens, Judge.)
130

* *Du Pre, Mrs. (Jenny).* Young Bayard Sartoris' great-aunt, who, it was believed, maneuvered Bayard into marrying Narcissa Benbow.
189

Ewell, Walter. One of the hunting party organized to kill the bear seen near Varner's mill dam.
31

Gihon. Federal officer who informs Gavin Stevens that Linda Snopes Kohl carries a Communist card and asks him, her closest friend, to persuade Linda to exchange names of Communists for immunity. His request is refused by Gavin.
233, 242, 243

Goodyhay, Brother Joe C. A former Marine sergeant turned preacher to a group of ex-service men and their families. His sermons,

larded with profanity, have an almost hypnotic effect on his people, especially when he tells in military terms of the Lord restoring him to life and ordering him to carry a dying "mama's boy" to safety. After Dad steals $10 from Mink Snopes, who is working on Goodyhay's chapel, Goodyhay collects enough money from his congregation to make up for Mink's loss.
    265, 267, 270, 271, 273–277, 279, 282

Gowrie, Nub. Farmer in Beat Nine to whom Mink Snopes said he sold his cow. He may have been the bootlegger from whom Flem Snopes bought the whisky he put into the bottles in Montgomery Ward Snopes's studio.
    14, 61

Grier, Res. Farmer who swapped a dog to Solon Quick for half a day's work shingling a church.
    316

Hait, Lonzo. Local horse-and-mule trader with whom Tug Nightingale was associated for a time.
    181, 182

* *Hampton, Hubert (Hub).* Sheriff when Montgomery Ward Snopes was arrested for conducting an obscene peep show in his photography shop.
    52, 53, 55–61, 63, 102, 367, 369, 370

Hampton, Hubert, Jr. (Little Hub). Hub's son, who has inherited "not only his father's four-year alternation as sheriff, but also his father's capacity to stay on the best of political terms with his alternating opposite member, Ephriam Bishop."
    103, 171, 370

Harriss. Wealthy underworld figure who married Melisandre Backus [Stevens] and, after her father's death, converted the old Backus home into an imposing "Virginia or Long Island" horse farm.
    195, 196

Henry. Negro man who looked after Houston's livestock.
    14

Hogganbeck, Lucius. Operator of an automobile jitney in Jefferson.
35

Holcomb, Sister Beth. Member of Goodyhay's group. After Mink Snopes
has done some work for her, she directs him to Goodyhay's house.
265, 268–270, 277

Holland. President of the Bank of Jefferson. He installs a bathroom in
the Meadowfill home despite Meadowfill's objections and gives
Essie Meadowfill [Smith] a job for life in his bank.
329

Holston, Alexander. One of the county's three original settlers who
built the log ordinary [a tavern] that the present edifice has long
since swallowed. Operated by two maiden sisters, the last descendants of Alexander, the Holston House still clings to its old
traditional ways.
34, 362, 382, 383

* *Houston, Jack.* Wealthy farmer, arrogant and proud, who spent his
time sulking all alone in his big house after a stallion killed his
wife. Mounted on a new stallion, he nearly rode Mink Snopes down
and then abused him for not getting off the road. When Mink's
cow strayed into his pasture, Houston penned it up and finally
had Mink work off the debt of $18.75 at 50 cents a day. After
Mink had discharged this debt, Houston added a dollar pound-
fee and for this lost his life to Mink, who shot him from ambush.
3, 5–27, 29, 30, 35, 37–39, 41, 42, 44, 64, 67, 82, 90, 99–101,
378, 381

Jabbo, Captain. Guard at Parchman who shot Jake Barron when Jake
tried to escape.
97

Killegrew, Hunter. Deputy who conducted Montgomery Ward Snopes
to the penitentiary at Parchman.
64

Kohl, Barton (Bart). Communistic Greenwich Village sculptor. After
living with Linda Snopes for several years, he marries her just

before they leave for active duty in the Spanish Civil War. Soon afterward, in an outmoded airplane, he is shot down by Hitler's Luftwaffe.

110, 161, 172, 174, 178, 200, 201, 217–219, 229, 232, 233, 237, 238, 248

Kohl, Linda Snopes. Eula Varner Snopes's daughter by Hoake McCarron. After her husband has been shot down in Europe, Linda, deaf from "being blown up" while driving an ambulance for the Spanish Loyalists, returns to Jefferson, where she lives with Flem Snopes, her nominal father, in the old de Spain mansion. But for Gavin Stevens, to whom she says, "You're all I have now," her life is empty, without point. At first many think she and Gavin will marry; but he marries someone else—and with Linda's blessing. She has known the fullness of marriage and she wants Gavin to know it too. Perhaps, as Gavin says, "She is doomed to love only once." She makes many fruitless attempts to do something that has meaning: for a time she works with the Negroes, trying to improve their schools, until even they beg her to leave them alone. During the war she works as a riveter in the Pascagoula shipyards. Later, back in Jefferson, she walks tirelessly, and alone, and drinks bootleg whisky regularly. Finally she is instrumental in getting Mink Snopes pardoned; and when he shoots Flem she helps him escape. After Flem's funeral, she returns the de Spain house to Manfred's only living relatives, kisses her Gavin goodbye, and departs in a new British Jaguar which she had ordered the moment she knew Gavin could get Mink the pardon.

86, 102, 109, 112–114, 119, 124, 137, 138, 140, 142, 143, 145–149, 157, 158, 161, 171–174, 179, 192, 194, 197, 198, 206, 211–219, 221, 226, 228, 231, 232, 240, 253, 254, 320, 350, 351, 354, 357–359, 365, 369, 371–374, 378, 381, 389, 394, 420–423

Ledbetter, Mrs. Customer of Ratliff's. When he delivered her a new sewing machine he earned an extra 50 cents by taking Flem Snopes to Will Varner's house, which was on the way to Mrs. Ledbetter's.
142

Long, Judge. Judge who sentenced Montgomery Ward Snopes to prison.
63, 369, 373

Ludus. Minnie's lazy husband, a persuasive Negro who takes money from his wife and gives it to other women. When Minnie asks him to stop he nearly tears her ear off with a flatiron.
80

McCallum, Raphael (Rafe). Owner of the wild stallion that Melisandre Harriss' son used in an attempt to kill the Argentine steeplechaser. Rafe, on a tip from Gavin Stevens, got to the stallion in time to save the Argentine's life.
255

McCarron, Hoake. Linda Snopes Kohl's natural father. At Gavin Stevens' request he attends Linda's wedding in New York, where he introduces himself as an old friend of the family and adds, "Her grandfather and my father may have been distantly related." Linda, of course, knows who he is; and she goes for a ride in the park with him, after which he departs.
4, 116, 117, 119, 120, 122, 124–127, 135, 136, 139, 141, 169, 170, 172–175, 177

McCaslin, Isaac (Uncle Ike). Hunter who went with Ewell to hunt the bear seen at Varner's mill dam. McCaslin refused to sell Mink Snopes buckshot shells just before Mink killed Houston. Now an old man, he spends most of his time hunting and fishing, while Triplett runs the McCaslin Hardware Company, a function later taken over by Jason Compson.
31, 32, 323, 370

* *McGowan, Skeets.* Uncle Willy Christian's soda-jerker. A smooth young man who teased Tug Nightingale too much and was beaten so badly that he was taken to the hospital.
187, 188

McLendon, Captain (Mack). Cotton buyer. During World War I he organized the Jefferson company to be known as the Sartoris Rifles in honor of the original Colonel Sartoris, holding his men together by means of simple instinctive humanity. After Tug Nightingale had been disowned by his father, Mack let Tug live

with him until the company was formed, and protected him from those who loved to tease him.
183–187

Mallison, Charles, Jr. (Chick). Nephew and trusted companion of Gavin Stevens. When Linda Snopes Kohl returns from Spain, Chick remembers her as the girl to whom he used to take messages from Gavin; and he even toys with the idea of becoming her lover. After studying law at Harvard and at the University of Mississippi and visiting Europe to please Gavin, he joins the U.S. Air Force. When his plane is damaged and the pilot makes a one-engine landing in enemy territory, Chick is taken captive and remains until the war's end in a POW camp at Limbourg, which is bombed regularly by low-flying RAF planes. He returns to Jefferson in time to rejoice over Clarence Snopes's defeat, and he later helps Gavin check the Snopes–Meadowfill feud. (He is the narrator of parts 8, 9, and 11.)
109–113, 148, 149, 192, 199, 238, 244, 294, 295, 300–309, 311, 312, 314–316, 319–323, 325, 327, 330–335, 337–339, 341–348, 350, 353, 354, 356–359, 361, 383

Mallison, Maggie. Gavin Stevens' twin, mother of Charles, Jr.
206, 383

Meadowfill. Essie Meadowfill Smith's father. A fierce, niggardly old man, he has alienated most of his neighbors and is hostile toward his most recent one, Res Snopes, whose hog pen adjoins Meadowfill's orchard. When Essie is old enough to contribute to the family support, her father gives up foraging for food in the cheap stores and perversely retires to a secondhand wheelchair, which he seldom leaves. He spends his time guarding his property against trespassers, especially against Snopes's hog, which he joys to pepper daily with small shot from his .22 rifle. When Meadowfill refuses to sell his lot to an oil company because 13 feet of land that morally belongs to him is legally Snopes's, he prevents Snopes from selling his lot, since the oil company must have both lots or none. As a result, Meadowfill nearly suffers serious consequences (*see* Snopes, Orestes). Through the intervention of Gavin Stevens,

however, the Meadowfill family emerges from the difficulty victorious.
327–347, 361

Meadowfill, Mrs. Meadowfill's gray drudge of a wife; she is Essie's mother.
346, 348

Meeks, Doc. Itinerant vendor of patent medicine.
154

Minnie. Maid at Miss Reba Rivers' bawdyhouse. Since her husband Ludus nearly tore her ear off with a flatiron, she had to wear her hat all of the time.
72, 73, 75, 77, 79–82

Mohataha. Chickasaw matriarch who granted the Compson land to Quentin Compson in 1821.
334

Nightingale, Mr. Tug's father, a Hard-Shell Baptist who believed the earth was flat and that Lee had betrayed the whole South when he surrendered. Mr. Nightingale thought of McLendon's company as being part of a Yankee army, and when he heard that Tug had joined it, he put Tug out of his home and disinherited him.
181–188

Nightingale, Tug. Only surviving child of his widower father. Tug did not do well in school, and at his principal's suggestion, quit in the third grade. Tug had a gift with mules and horses and spent most of his time around the auction lot near Dilazuck's livery stable. When he was past thirty, he joined McLendon's company to help "make the Germans quit mistreating folks," and his father disowned him for joining a "Yankee army." For a while he lived with McLendon, who protected the simple fellow from his tormentors. When Mack's company was sent to Texas, Tug was detached and sent overseas as a cook, the first Yoknapatawpha soldier to go overseas and the last to return (1919). After his return he worked as a barn and fence painter, harmless and gentle;

but he could be dangerous if pressed, as Skeets McGowan found out.
181–188

* *Quick, Solon (Lon).* Constable under Will Varner at Frenchman's Bend during the time that Mink Snopes and Houston had the trouble over Mink's cow. (Also *see* Grier, Res.)
17, 18, 20, 23, 24, 26, 29, 31, 37, 316

Quick, Theron. One of Hoake McCarron's rivals who attacked Hoake. During the fight Eula Varner [Snopes] knocked Theron unconscious with the loaded handle of a buggy whip. Later, when Eula's pregnancy became known, Theron was one of the youths who suddenly left Frenchman's Bend.
123, 124, 126

Ratcliffe (Ratliff), Nelly. Woman who found the first Vladimir Kyrilytch in the U.S. hiding in her hayloft. She fed him and kept him concealed until it was safe for him to come out of hiding. By then, Nelly being pregnant, she and V. K. were married; and he took her name Ratcliffe (later spelled Ratliff). (*See* Vladimir Kyrilytch.)
162, 165

Ratliff, Vladimir Kyrilytch (V. K.). Bland, itinerant sewing-machine agent, who has now added radios and television sets to his stock in trade. A bachelor, he makes his own shirts and does his own cooking in a house spotlessly clean. Long Gavin Stevens' confederate against the gross, unethical Snopes world, Ratliff, who sees, hears, and remembers most of what goes on in the county, is a perfect complement for Stevens, his farmer's wisdom serving as a check on the idealistic excesses of Gavin. Always ready, he enters wholeheartedly into any conflict that involves Gavin, not through blind loyalty but because their basic beliefs are the same. And when a crisis, particularly one involving Eula Snopes or Linda Kohl, has passed, leaving Gavin at the mercy of his second thoughts, it is Ratliff who understands and ministers to him gently, without seeming to be gentle. No mere shadow of Gavin, Ratliff often acts independently, as in the Clarence Snopes incident: Gavin thinks Snopes cannot be defeated for Congress; Ratliff thinks he can be, and does it by the primitive expedient of having some boys brush Clarence's trousers with switches taken from a nearby dog thicket. And when numerous dogs begin to swarm over Clarence, his political life is at an end. Humorous, imaginative countryman, Ratliff is Faulkner's principal observer and commentator in *The Mansion,* the summation of the Snopes saga. (He is the narrator of parts 3, 6, and 7.)

32, 103, 150, 157, 158, 167, 170, 176, 187, 192–194, 196, 197, 200, 203–206, 211, 218–220, 222, 227, 228, 230–232, 242, 254, 256, 295, 296, 298, 302, 304–307, 309, 312, 313, 315, 316, 318–322, 332, 333, 344, 349, 351, 356, 359–361, 366, 368–373, 376–378, 381–383, 385–393, 395, 417–419, 421, 425–433

Rivers, Reba. Madam of a Memphis brothel. Loquacious, hard-bitten, yet noisily sentimental when drunk, Miss Reba led a busy, eventful life in her establishment, which she ran with a firm hand. Just before Montgomery Ward Snopes went to the penitentiary at Parchman, he had the unwitting Miss Reba anonymously send $40 to Mink Snopes at Parchman.

72, 73, 75–77, 79–81, 85

Rouncewell, Mrs. Owner of the Commercial Hotel until Flem Snopes took it over.

128

Rouncewell, Whit. Boy who saw burglars in Uncle Willy Christian's drugstore.

59

Sartoris, Bayard (Colonel). First president of the Merchants and Farmers Bank. After an auto frightened his horses, he had a law passed banning motor-driven vehicles in Jefferson. Finally he died of heart failure riding in the auto of his grandson, whose reckless driving the Colonel was trying to curb.

34, 128, 135, 142, 145, 152, 153, 156, 189, 379

Sartoris, Bayard (young). Flyer in the RFC in World War I. According to Maggie Mallison, he returned to Jefferson bearing a double

burden: anguish over being ashamed that he had thought having a twin (John) in the RFC doubled his, Bayard's, chances of survival; and anguish over having to meet John in the hereafter ashamed of being ashamed that he had entertained the idea of somehow usurping John's superior record and coming home an ace. And so Bayard returned to Jefferson, hunting death. After the auto incident that caused his grandfather's death, Bayard abandoned his pregnant wife, wandered away, and finally got himself killed in an experimental plane in Dayton.
    183, 188–191, 209

Sartoris, Benbow. Son of Narcissa [Benbow] and young Bayard. At seventeen he was considered one of the best bird shots in the county, second only to Luther Biglin.
    206

Sartoris, John. Young flyer in the RFC in World War I. He was shot down by the Germans. (*See* Sartoris, Bayard [young].)
    183, 189–191, 209

Sartoris, Colonel John. Colonel in the Civil War and later a railroad builder. If he had had them, he would not have been ashamed of any of the thoughts that burdened his great-grandson Bayard.
    183, 191, 406

Smith, Essie Meadowfill. Meadowfill's daughter, a quiet, mousy girl. With the highest grades ever made in her high school, she wins a scholarship, which she turns down. She asks the donor, president of the Bank of Jefferson, to lend her the $500 instead so she can have a bathroom installed in her home. After working in the bank for some time she marries McKinley Smith and soon becomes a mother, a wealthy one, since, at Gavin Stevens' instigation, Res Snopes has given her the deed to his land that the oil company wants to buy.
    329, 330, 335, 336, 338–340, 342–344, 346–348, 361

Smith, McKinley. A former Marine corporal, who builds a house in Eula Acres close to Meadowfill's home. He does the heavy work on the house himself and while so engaged is a possible target for

Meadowfill's rifle, since McKinley, engaged to Meadowfill's daughter Essie, is a threat to the "system of peonage" by which the old man lives. Just about the time his house is completed, however, McKinley does marry Essie, and in two months Essie is pregnant. Thus the Smiths have qualified for Gavin Stevens' christening present, Meadowfill's old wheelchair, symbolic of his hostility, which Gavin has taken in lieu of a legal fee.

339–341, 343–349, 361

Snopes, Ab. Old man living 2 miles outside of Jefferson, whom Will Varner had evicted from his house years before, because Ab owed Will two years' rent on it. (He is probably Flem's father.)

87, 123, 152

Snopes, Admiral Dewey. Son of Eck; younger brother of Wallstreet. Montgomery Ward Snopes said Admiral Dewey was never a Snopes.

83, 153, 420

Snopes, Bilbo. A true Snopes.

87

* *Snopes, Byron.* Once Bayard Sartoris' bank clerk, he stole some of the bank's money and went to Mexico. In the 1920's he sent, C.O.D., his four half-Apache children to the Snopeses in Jefferson. Since the children were too wild to handle, the Snopes clan soon sent them back, prepaid, to Mexico.

87, 152, 298

Snopes, Clarence Eggleston. Mississippi Senator. Formerly a notorious brawler, he was made constable of Frenchman's Bend by Will Varner. Though his energies were then devoted to preserving the peace, his strong-arm proclivities persisted, and Will, to get him out of the way, put him in the state legislature. Utterly without principle, he soon became a shrewd opportunist. His "soak-the-rich" battle cry (after Huey Long) increased his power. He could have been elected governor; but he had his eye on Washington. And now, after twenty years in politics, he finds his road to Congress obstructed by Colonel Devries, a war hero. Seeming to praise Devries' accomplishments, Clarence subtly damns him for his sympathy with Negroes. Only Ratliff's country strategy prevents Clarence, apparently a sure winner, from being elected. After the dog episode, Snopes, utterly humiliated, withdraws from the race because Varner will not back a man that the dogs "can't tell from a fence post." (*See* Ratliff, V. K.)

 61–63, 70, 71, 73, 74, 82, 83, 87, 102, 161, 295–315, 317–320, 322

Snopes, Doris. Clarence's youngest brother. He has the mentality of a child and the moral principles of a wolverine. He perpetrated Clarence's jokes on Byron Snopes's children until they tied him to a stake for burning. Only Doris' screams saved him.

 298

Snopes, Eck. Father of Wallstreet and Admiral Dewey. According to Montgomery Ward Snopes, Eck and his boys aren't true Snopeses: "They are only our shame."

 83, 102, 153

Snopes, Eula Varner. Mother of Linda [Kohl] by Hoake McCarron. Ratliff believes that McCarron would have married Eula after the pregnancy if she had been willing. When she came to Jefferson, Ratliff says that she took one look at Gavin Stevens and "adopted" him for the rest of his life for her and for her daughter, who could inherit her generosity but not her beauty. "It was a physical and spiritual beauty so great that she had no right to destroy it," says Gavin. Then he underscores Ratliff's suggestion that she committed suicide because she was bored—bored because she tried to find somebody strong and brave enough to accept her love and failed both times.

 4, 86, 114–120, 123–129, 131, 133, 135–139, 141–143, 145, 147, 148, 151, 155, 158, 163, 211, 232, 332, 340, 430, 434

Snopes, Flem. President of Bayard Sartoris' bank. He lives—at first alone, later with Linda [Kohl]—in de Spain's ancestral home, now made over to resemble Mount Vernon, on a small scale. As Flem, friendless, spends his days at the bank and his nights in the mansion, he has to think about Mink Snopes, who will one day leave prison and try to kill him. Years before, Flem had bought

a stay of possible execution with a most ingenious plan: By sub-
stituting whisky for developing fluid in bottles Montgomery Ward
Snopes used in his picture salon, he had made it possible for his
kinsman to be sent to the penitentiary at Parchman for possession
of illegal liquor instead of to Atlanta for exhibiting pornographic
pictures. Once in Parchman, Montgomery, because he was still in
Flem's power, persuaded Mink to try to escape. As Flem had intended, Mink did try and failed; and his original sentence was
doubled. In 1946, when Mink is finally pardoned, through the
offices of Linda, Gavin Stevens, Ratliff, and others, Flem seems
strangely unconcerned. Probably he does not think that Mink,
sixty-three years old and a stranger in the new world with only
a few dollars, can make his way to Jefferson, or perhaps he has
resigned himself to whatever may happen, or perhaps, like Eula
Snopes before him, he is bored. At any rate, when he faces his
desperate, armed kinsman, Flem appears immobile and even detached, too, until the blast sounds that ends his life.
   *3, 4, 6, 17, 26, 27, 32, 35, 37, 40, 42, 51–61, 63, 71, 74, 83,
85–87, 89, 92–94, 98, 103, 115, 116, 123, 126–129, 135, 137–
139, 141–149, 152, 153, 155, 156, 162, 164, 192, 197, 198, 202,
213, 215, 219–222, 227, 242, 243, 259, 322–330, 332, 333, 335,
348, 355, 356, 358, 364, 365, 367–370, 372–374, 377–382, 386,
387, 389, 390, 393, 394, 396, 401, 408–413, 415, 421, 428, 430,
431*

Snopes, I. O. Father of Clarence and Montgomery Ward by "simul-
   taneous bigamy." (Clarence and Montgomery Ward had different
   mothers, the second of whom I. O. had married without the
   formality of a divorce from the first one.)
   83, 87, 152

Snopes, Lump. The clerk Flem Snopes had work for him in Varner's
   store when Flem went to Texas on his honeymoon.
   27, 28

Snopes, Mink (M. C.) Farmer near Frenchman's Bend. Utterly poor,
   he gave up religion early. His closest approach to God or *Old
   Moster* was a belief that *they* (*them, it*) allowed a sort of justice
   to prevail so that a man could not be forever harried by life

without getting in his return licks at the opposition. When he had stood as much as he could bear, it was his turn, his "lief." And so Mink, with a desperate patience, took all of the outrage that Houston could heap upon him until he added that dollar pound-fee for the pasturage of Mink's cow; and then Mink killed him. To the very last day of his trial Mink looked for Flem, the most powerful of the Snopeses, to save him; but Flem stayed away. And when, in 1908, Mink went to the penitentiary at Parchman, both men knew that he had a debt to settle. As the years passed, Mink might have forgiven Flem enough to let him live, but Montgomery Ward Snopes's plan of escape, with Mink dressed in women's clothes, spelled Flem's doom. In 1946, when Mink is pardoned, he finds himself in a world he scarcely recognizes; but having turned down Gavin Stevens' $250, the acceptance of which would have pledged him to stay away from Jefferson, he is free at least. And a timeless animal-like shrewdness, born in part of his great need, helps save him for his revenge. With about $12 he reaches Memphis, where he buys an ancient pistol and three bullets for $11. By now Mink's belief in *them* giving a man his lief after he has suffered to the limit has merged with a sense of *Old Moster*, "who jest punishes; He dont play jokes." Mink will get to Jefferson and his old "cooter"-like pistol will fire. And so it happens. Five and a half days after leaving Parchman, Mink faces his old kinsman and kills him. The next evening Stevens and Ratliff find Mink resting in a cavelike cellar under the ruins of his old cabin. Gavin gives him money from Linda Kohl and asks him where he can be reached in the future. Mink gives him, with something of pride, the initials he adopted in prison long ago. He is not just Mink any more: he is M. C. Snopes.

3–5, 7–15, 17–23, 25, 27–29, 31, 32, 35–39, 41, 43, 45–48, 50, 64, 67, 70, 82, 83, 87, 88, 91, 94, 95, 152, 261, 262, 266–277, 279, 281, 282, 291, 292, 366, 369, 372–374, 379–382, 384–386, 388, 392, 393, 399, 401, 402, 404, 406, 409, 411–416, 425, 428, 430, 431, 433, 435

* Snopes, Montgomery Ward. A true Snopes. In 1923, through Flem Snopes's machinations, Montgomery Ward went to the penitentiary at Parchman instead of Atlanta, where he really belonged. There he persuaded Mink Snopes to try to escape in woman's

clothing. Afterward Montgomery knew he was safe from Mink's vengeance. Mink was concerned solely with Flem, the mastermind behind the abortive escape plan. After his release from prison at the end of two years, Montgomery went to Los Angeles, where he is now "engaged in some quite lucrative adjunct or correlative to the motion-picture industry or anyway colony." (He is the narrator of part 4.)

52–64, 89, 92, 97, 152, 259, 367, 368

Snopes, Orestes (*Res*). Cattle-and-hog dealer. When Res moves into the old Compson carriage house, he and his neighbor Meadowfill begin to feud because Snopes's hogs get into the old man's orchard and he peppers them with shot. When an oil company wants to buy Meadowfill's lot and part of Snopes's, Meadowfill, peeved because a 13-foot strip of land that is morally his belongs legally to Flem Snopes, refuses to sell his lot, thus blocking the sale of Snopes's property too, since the oil company wants all or nothing. Res, now working in earnest for Flem, who owns the Compson land, encourages his hogs to go into Meadowfill's orchard, hoping that the old man will fire a solid shot and kill a hog. Then Res can invoke the ordinance against firing a gun inside the city limits and perhaps blackmail Meadowfill into selling. But Meadowfill does not oblige. After McKinley Smith and Essie Meadowfill become engaged, Res, knowing about Meadowfill's hatred for McKinley, gives his hog to McKinley and sets a booby trap triggered in such a way that when Meadowfill raises his window he will be fired upon. Shortly, McKinley Smith's gift hog does invade the old man's orchard. Meadowfill, opening his window to shoot the hog, is himself blasted with buckshot. Just as Res has figured, Meadowfill, thinking Smith has fired on him, is ready to shoot Smith with a solid shot from the .22. Fortunately Gavin Stevens and Chick Mallison, who have been on watch, rush into Meadowfill's house in time to prevent a catastrophe. A little later, Gavin "sells" the booby trap to Res in return for a deed made out to Essie for the 13-foot strip and that part of Snopes's property which the oil company wishes to buy.

322, 328, 330, 331, 333–344, 346–348

Snopes, Vardaman. A true Snopes.

87

Snopes, Virgil. Son of Wesley; cousin of Montgomery Ward Snopes. When he went to barber college at Memphis, he took a room at Miss Reba Rivers' place, thinking it was a hotel and Miss Reba a mature Christian woman. Later, when Virgil met his cousin Clarence Snopes in the red-light district, Clarence discovered that Virgil had remarkable prowess with women and he earned a great deal of money betting on him.
   71–74, 83, 87

Snopes, Wallstreet Panic. Eck's son, he never acted like a Snopes nor even looked like one. He began as a delivery boy in a small grocery store to put himself and his younger brother through school. Finally he became owner of a chain of wholesale grocery establishments blanketing half of Mississippi, Tennessee, and Arkansas. He is present at Flem Snopes's funeral.
   83, 102, 153, 213, 214, 420

Snopes, Watkins Products (Wat). The carpenter in charge of renovating Flem Snopes's house. About a year after the house is finished, Wat, having noticed how Flem's propped-up feet defaced the ornate fireplace in his room, fastens a little unpainted wooden ledge at just the right height. Ever after, when Flem was at home he propped his feet upon that ledge just as Wat hoped he would.
   154, 156, 328, 333

Snopes, Wesley. Father of Virgil. A revival song leader, he was tarred and feathered and put out of the country when he was caught after church with a fourteen-year-old girl in an empty cotton storehouse.
   71, 83, 87

Snopes, Yettie. Mink's wife, who sent a letter to Mink at the penitentiary in Parchman asking when she could visit and if she should bring their daughters. Mink said there was no use in her coming because he would be home soon. He did go home about thirty-five years later, but Yettie was dead and the daughters gone. (One becomes a madam in a Memphis brothel, but Mink never

knows it although he passes near it the night he spends in Memphis en route from Parchman to Jefferson to kill Flem Snopes.)
50

Spoade. Son of the man who had been at Harvard with Gavin Stevens in 1909. Spoade, the younger, invites Charles Mallison to Charleston to see what a Saint Cecilia ball looks like from the inside.
206

Stamper, Pat. Master horse-and-mule trader with whom Tug Nightingale had some association, and who recognized in Tug his genius for handling mules and horses.
181, 186

Stevens, Judge. Gavin's father, appointed by Judge Dukinfield to try Gavin's suit against Mayor de Spain in connection with the missing brass.
130

Stevens, Gavin. Jefferson lawyer, "meddlesome," tireless, idealistic, heroic. His is a character that can best be understood through his interaction with other people. Surely Ratliff comes close to explaining Gavin's relationship to Eula Snopes, and to Linda Kohl later, when he says that Gavin would have nothing left if he did not exercise the "right and privilege and opportunity to dedicate forever his capacity for responsibility to something that wouldn't have no end to its appetite and wouldn't never threaten to give him even a bone back in recompense." Linda would have married Gavin or gladly given herself to him without marriage, but he could not accept her gratitude in any form. To serve was his role. Perhaps his marriage to Melisandre was a sort of service to Linda; for she, knowing a part of herself was buried with Barton Kohl, wanted Gavin to have more than she could give him. That Gavin can give better than he can receive may also be seen in his relationships with his friends and relatives. At times this "giving" irritates even his friend Ratliff, for it keeps Gavin "too busy," makes him appear meddlesome; but, finally, this quality may be a positive one. His nephew Chick Mallison says of him: "But he is a good man. Maybe I was wrong sometimes to trust and follow him but I was never wrong to love him." (He is the narrator of part 10.)

53, 55, 58–60, 62, 63, 77, 125, 140, 163, 170, 180, 181, 187, 189, 190, 192–201, 203, 205–213, 215–226, 229–232, 236, 238, 239, 241, 252–255, 295, 296, 299, 300, 304–306, 311, 314, 315, 321, 322, 324–327, 332–334, 341–343, 350, 351, 355, 356, 362–365, 368–382, 384–395, 409, 417–420, 423, 428–433

Stevens, Melisandre Backus Harriss. Gavin's wife. She had been Linda Snopes's [Kohl] predecessor as the object of Gavin's zeal to educate young women. While Gavin was away at college, she married Harriss, a bootlegging czar, and bore two children. After Harriss is murdered, she marries Gavin.

194–196, 198, 254, 255, 352, 356, 357, 359, 362–364

Stillwell, Shuford H. Fellow prisoner of Mink Snopes's who escaped from the penitentiary at Parchman. Jake Barron, another convict who tried to escape at the same time, was killed by a guard. Because Mink had not coöperated with the others in their plan to escape, Stillwell held him responsible for Barron's death and sent him threatening notes every holiday. Mink then put God to work on Stillwell, and since Mink's need to be free was so great, he was not surprised to learn that Stillwell had been killed near San Diego when a deconsecrated church collapsed on him.

96, 97, 100, 101

Strutterbuck, Captain. Man of about fifty, supposedly a veteran of two wars, who loved to talk about his military life. Montgomery Ward Snopes met Strutterbuck at Miss Reba Rivers', where the captain had business with Thelma. When halted by Miss Reba as he tried to leave without paying, he gave her a money order for $2.

75, 80, 81

Strutterbuck, Q'Milla. Name signed to Strutterbuck's money order. Minnie, a maid at Miss Reba's, said it must be the name of his wife because "Wouldn't nobody but his wife sent two dollars."

81

Thelma. Girl who entertained Captain Strutterbuck at Miss Reba's. She was new there and nearly let him get away without paying. *75–77, 80, 81*

Triplett, Earl. Man who gently eliminated Uncle Ike McCaslin from the McCaslin Hardware store just as he himself was later eliminated by Jason Compson. *323*

Tubbs, Mrs. Wife of Euphus. It was said that she pampered Montgomery Ward Snopes when he was a prisoner because she was curious about his obscene pictures. Certainly he spent much of his time doing light work in her kitchen and garden. *63*

Tubbs, Euphus. Mercenary jailer in Jefferson when Montgomery Ward Snopes was a prisoner there. By way of consoling Montgomery, Tubbs told him it was better to go to the Parchman penitentiary than to Atlanta because it was closer and because the money and food for Montgomery's keep would remain in the state family so to speak. When Montgomery was let out on bond, Tubbs wanted to release him before the bond went into effect so he could pocket Montgomery's supper money. *60, 63, 65, 71*

Tull, Mrs. Woman who Mink Snopes thought wrote the letter that Yettie Snopes sent to him in the penitentiary at Parchman, because, as Mink said, "Yettie cant even read reading, let alone write writing." *50*

Tull, Vernon. Farmer at Frenchman's Bend who may have seen the bear when it ran across Varner's mill dam and into a thicket. *31*

Turpin. Draft-evader whom Gavin Stevens and Ratliff found hiding in Mink Snopes's cabin three years previous to Mink's final trip there. *418*

Varner, Jody. Linda Snopes Kohl's uncle, who tells her about Montgomery Ward Snopes's sentence to Parchman and of Mink Snopes's abortive attempt to escape a short time after Montgomery's arrival.
    4, 27, 367, 420

Varner, Will (Uncle Billy). Virtual owner of Frenchman's Bend. Father of Eula, he arranged her marriage to Flem Snopes. To pay Flem for fathering another man's child, Will gave him the old Frenchman's place, believing it to be worthless, and when Flem sold the worthless property for a good profit, Will never forgave him. Eighteen years later Flem used his father-in-law once again when Will was practically forced into helping Flem into the presidency of de Spain's bank. Seldom, however, does anyone best Varner. He remains all-powerful in his country empire, politically as well as economically. He privately appointed Clarence Snopes as constable of Frenchman's Bend, later placed him in the state legislature, and would have made him national Congressman. Dogs at Varner's political picnic, however, swarm over Clarence's trousers, making him look ridiculous (*see* Ratliff, V. K.); and so Varner breaks Clarence by withdrawing his support.
    4, 7, 10, 16–24, 26–32, 37–40, 62, 65, 66, 89, 93, 115, 117–120, 123–127, 135, 138, 139, 142, 144–147, 152, 155, 197, 284, 295–299, 301, 302, 306, 310, 311, 313–317, 319, 320, 355, 394, 408, 413, 417, 427

Vladimir Kyrilytch. Member of a Hessian troop in Burgoyne's army whose last name is unknown. After the surrender at Saratoga, the terms of which Congress refused to honor, Vladimir Kyrilytch and his comrades were banished to straggle for six years in Virginia without food, money, or (in V. K.'s case) knowledge of the language. V. K. found harbor with Nell Ratcliffe, whom he finally married and whose name he adopted. Ever since that time the successive V. K. Ratcliffes' oldest sons have been named Vladimir Kyrilytch Ratcliffe (later spelled Ratliff).
    162, 164–166

Wattman, Jakeleg. Linda Snopes Kohl's bootlegger.
    220, 221, 355, 356

Winbush, Mrs. Woman who, Montgomery Ward Snopes thought, told Fonzo Winbush and Virgil Snopes never to rent a room to live in unless the woman of the house looked mature and Christian, but most of all motherly. This advice sent them to Miss Reba Rivers' brothel in Memphis. (*See* Snopes, Virgil.)
71

Winbush, Fonzo. Nephew of Grover Cleveland Winbush. He went to barber college with Virgil Snopes. (*See* Snopes, Virgil.)
71–73

Winbush, Grover Cleveland. Night watchman who was fired the night Christian's drugstore was robbed, because, instead of being on duty, he was attending Montgomery Ward Snopes's obscene peep show.
52–57, 59, 68, 69, 73, 115, 117, 127, 128, 138

THE REIVERS (1962)

Acheron. Colonel Linscomb's racehorse, involved in a series of races with Coppermine (Lightning).

Alice. Miss Ballenbaugh's Negro cook.
  77, 79, 175

Avant, Jim. Hound specialist from Hickory Flat, Mississippi.
  194

Ballenbaugh, I. "Ancestryless giant" who took over Wyott's place when mule- and ox-drawn wagons plying between Memphis and Wyott's ferry superseded the riverboats from Vicksburg as carriers of freight and cotton. Ballenbaugh converted Wyott's "wilderness-cradled hermitage" into "a roaring place indeed: it became dormitory, grubbing station and saloon" for the transient freighters and tough mule-skinners who passed that way.
  69, 72, 73–76

Ballenbaugh, II. Ballenbaugh Sr.'s son, another giant, who in 1865 succeeded his father as proprietor of the establishment at Ballenbaugh's Ferry. After Colonel Sartoris' railroad ruined Ballenbaugh Sr.'s place as a stopover for merely tough customers, the son, making whisky now instead of simply selling it as his father had done, turned the establishment into a rendezvous for lawbreakers, male and female, a place where successive sheriffs feared to go. These conditions persisted until Hightower put a stop to them in the summer of 1886.
  74, 75

Ballenbaugh, Miss. Daughter of Ballenbaugh, Sr. A prim, iron-gray woman of fifty, she operates a good farm and a small store with sleeping accommodations in the attic for guests. On their way to

Memphis, Boon Hogganbeck and young Lucius Priest stop overnight at her place.

76–81, 93, 175, 212, 303

Ballott. Foreman of Maury Priest's livery stable.

10–14, 37, 56, 64, 65, 67, 299

Beauchamp, Bobo. Mr. Van Tosch's groom, a young country-bred
Negro who gets "mixed up" with a white man to whom he must
pay $128. Unable to borrow from his employer, Bobo is desperate
under the pressure of the white man to settle the debt by Monday.
Late Sunday afternoon Bobo meets Ned McCaslin in a Memphis
blind tiger and confides in him, mentioning Mr. Van Tosch's
horse, Coppermine [later called Lightning], which the white man
wishes Bobo to steal so that he (the white man) can sell it and
thus cancel Bobo's debt. After one look at the horse, Ned conceives an elaborate plan, whereupon Bobo, leaving the Priest auto
instead for the white man, borrows Coppermine without the
owner's knowledge and surrenders him to Ned.

229, 230, 285, 287–293, 298

Beauchamp, Lucas Quintus Carothers McCaslin. Negro; Bobo Beauchamp's cousin. Sarah Priest, whose mother had described the
white man, old Lucius Quintus Carothers McCaslin, to her, says
that Lucas is just like him: he looks (except for his color) and
behaves like him: "just as arrogant, just as iron-headed, just as
intolerant."

229

Binford, Mr. "Landlord" of Miss Reba's establishment and for five
years her relatively faithful lover. Small, but dominant, meticulous
in dress and manner, direct in speech, he runs a strict house for
Miss Reba. He is the front man, "the single frail power wearing
the shape of respectability." His is the duty to handle the money,
bills, police, and tradesmen; and he is utterly reliable except in
one respect—he has a weakness for horse races. When Otis, whom
he has ostensibly taken to the zoo, reveals that they have been to
the horse races, where Mr. Binford lost nearly $40 betting, Miss
Reba's anger causes him to leave her. Once before he had done

this and had returned only when Miss Reba had begged him to, "on her bended knee."

99, 101, 106, 108–111, 113, 114, 133, 160, 164, 278

Bookwright, Calvin (Uncle Cal). Maker of whisky.

13

Briggins, Lycurgus. Uncle Parsham Hood's grandson, a dependable, intelligent young Negro, who is an invaluable assistant to Ned McCaslin in preparing for the horse race. He further proves his worth by tying Otis astride a bareback jumping mule and thus forcing the boy to give up Minnie's gold tooth.

168, 171, 172, 174–176, 178, 180, 181, 185, 186, 189, 203, 221, 223–228, 230, 232–235, 245, 247–252, 258, 267, 269, 270, 271, 282, 283

Briggins, Mary. Daughter of Uncle Parsham Hood and mother of Lycurgus.

248, 250, 251, 254

Buffaloe, Mr. The "mechanical wizard" who keeps Jefferson's steam-driven electric plant running. His auto, which he himself has made, is the one that frightens Colonel Sartoris' matched carriage horses into bolting and practically destroying the Colonel's surrey, which was fortunately unoccupied at the time.

25–27, 29, 39, 49, 50, 57

Caldwell, Sam. Customer and admirer of Everbe Hogganbeck. Flagman and relative of a high official on the railroad out of Memphis, Sam, at Everbe's request, illicitly provides special rail transportation from Memphis to Parsham for Ned McCaslin and the horse. From then on he shares the troubles of all those involved with Lightning (Coppermine), his aid being so resourceful and thorough that Ned early says of him, "I could be wishing that you and me was frequent enough to be permanent."

131, 135–139, 141, 143–152, 162–165, 167, 171, 172, 198, 199, 204, 205, 217–220, 233, 235–237, 241–244, 250, 256, 258, 261, 274–276, 278, 279, 281, 303

Callie, "Aunt." Negro woman who has nursed each successive child of the Priests, beginning with Maury, Sr., when he was an infant.
34, 36, 41, 43, 45, 47–50, 52–57, 59, 60, 62, 63, 66, 300, 301

Charley. Employee of the railroad who helps Boon Hogganbeck and Sam Caldwell move the boxcar so that Ned McCaslin can get the racehorse into it.
148, 151, 152

Christian. Owner of a Jefferson drugstore situated below Dr. Peabody's office.
15

Clapp, Walter. Mr. Van Tosch's horse trainer.
226–228, 231–233, 241, 253, 290

Compson, General. One of Boon Hogganbeck's three "proprietors." It was, indeed, as a sort of nurse for General Compson, who was growing deaf, that eleven-year-old Boon made his first connection with the hunters at Major de Spain's camp.
18, 19, 21–23, 82

Coppermine. The racehorse stolen by Bobo Beauchamp and raced by Ned McCaslin. Later called Lightning.

de Spain, Major. Father of Manfred and one of Boon Hogganbeck's three "proprietors." He was also proprietor of De Spain's camp (later called "McCaslin's Camp"), that vast section of land less than 20 miles from Jefferson, where each fall men the Major selected hunted wild game.
18–20, 22, 72, 73, 78, 82

de Spain, Manfred. Banker son of Major de Spain and, for a time, mayor of Jefferson. He is mentioned as having sold the camp that had once belonged to his father and as having owned the first automobile in Jefferson.
21, 25

Doom. A Chickasaw king. He is mentioned as "the regicide-usurper."
   73

Ed. Official judge at the race between Coppermine (Lightning) and Acheron.
   266

Edmonds, Louisa (Cousin Louisa). Wife of Zachary.
   47, 54, 61, 66, 226

* *Edmonds, McCaslin.* Father of Zachary and also a sort of foster father to young Isaac McCaslin and Boon Hogganbeck. One of the early hunters at De Spain's camp, he is mentioned as the one to whom young Ike had abdicated the McCaslin plantation on his twenty-first birthday. The Edmondses, McCaslins, and Priests together hold a one-third interest in the corporation that is Boon Hogganbeck, with the remaining two-thirds being held by Major de Spain and General Compson.
   18, 21–24

Edmonds, Zachary (Cousin Zachary). Current holder of the old McCaslin place 17 miles out of Jefferson. While their parents attend Grandfather Lessep's funeral in Bay St. Louis, the Priest children are supposed to stay with the Edmondses, and all of them do except young Lucius, who steals away to Memphis with Boon Hogganbeck in Grandfather Priest's auto. With others of his family Zachary shares a one-third "proprietorship" in Boon Hogganbeck.
   18, 24, 45, 53, 59, 61–63, 89, 169, 171, 183, 226, 246

Ephum. Negro man who probably works for Miss Ballenbaugh and is apparently interested in Alice, her cook, though Alice disclaims any desire to marry him. At Boon Hogganbeck's invitation Ephum gets his first automobile ride in the Priest car along with Miss Ballenbaugh and Alice. It is at Ephum's house that Ned McCaslin spends the night en route to Memphis.
   77, 79, 175

Ewell, Walter. One of the regular hunters at De Spain's camp. Though an expert shot himself, he could do nothing to improve Boon

Hogganbeck's marksmanship. Ewell told one of the camp's favorite stories about how Boon fired upon a buck five times at ten paces without hitting him.

21, 23

* *Fathers, Sam.* Part Negro and half Chickasaw Indian woodsman. It was he who tracked down General Compson and camped with him all night when the General got lost in the woods at De Spain's camp.

21, 22

Fittie, Aunt. Owner, apparently, of a brothel where Everbe Corinthia [Hogganbeck] worked before coming to Miss Reba's. After Everbe's mother died, Aunt Fittie took her to raise and "started her out soon as she got big enough."

143, 154, 156, 157

Gabe. Maury Priest Sr.'s blacksmith (a Negro, probably). Though short, he is "bigger" than Boon Hogganbeck and has a leg "terrifically twisted" from an injury sustained while shoeing a horse.

6, 9, 10

Grenier, Louis. Huguenot who came to Mississippi in the 1790's and established Jefferson and named it.

8

Grinnup, old Dan (Grenier, Dan). Employee without title of the Priest livery stable. A descendant of Louis Grenier, he is dirty, drunken, homeless, and without family except for one idiot relative. At times, when in his cups, he scornfully says that once Greniers led Yoknapatawpha society; now Grinnups drive it. He holds his job because of sentiment on the part of his employers: perhaps because Mr. Ballott's first wife had been Dan's daughter; perhaps because Maury Priest, Sr., had, when a boy, hunted with old Dan's father.

8

Hampton. Jefferson sheriff who takes charge when Boon Hogganbeck, in an effort to shoot Ludus, succeeds only in creasing a Negro

girl and in shattering a window in the McCaslin hardware store. Hampton disarms Boon, holds him in brief custody, sees that the girl has medical attention, and that Boon's "proprietors" make a satisfactory settlement with the girl and her family.
10, 14, 15

* *Hampton, Hub* (*Little Hub*). Grandson of the Jefferson sheriff in 1905, when the story *The Reivers* takes place. "Little Hub," says the narrator in 1961, "is sheriff now, or will be again next year."
14

Hightower, Hiram. A giant Baptist minister who served during the Civil War with General Forrest as chaplain on Sunday and as one of his "hardest and most outrageous troopers" on the other days of the week. In the summer of 1886, armed only with a Bible, he rode into the lawless stronghold of Ballenbaugh II and converted the entire settlement with his bare fists.
75

Hogganbeck, Boon. Assistant to Mr. Ballott at the Priest livery stable. Beyond the fact that Boon's grandmother was a Chickasaw Indian who married a white whisky-trader, Boon's origin is uncertain. All Ike McCaslin remembers about his first glimpse of Boon is that he was already a giant when eleven or twelve and that Boon was present on the McCaslin place, where Ike himself was raised, and that Boon soon attached himself to the De Spain camp as a sort of nurse for General Compson. Then began the McCaslin–De Spain–Compson Corporation, a holding company in which all members of the three families "had [forever after] mutually equal but completely undefined shares of responsibility" where Boon was concerned. When *The Reivers* begins Boon is about forty-one, "tough, faithful, brave and completely unreliable, . . . six feet four inches tall . . . [weighs] two hundred forty pounds and . . . [has] the mentality of a child." When Lucius "Boss" Priest buys the Winton Flyer auto, Boon's livery-stable duties become secondary, for the car has become his "soul's lily maid." He is accordingly made night foreman at the livery stables and thereafter he spends most of his free time washing the car and driving it whenever he can. When the adult Priests go to

Grandfather Lessep's funeral in Bay St. Louis, young Lucius Priest and Boon tacitly agree to take a trip in the auto that Boss Priest thinks is locked safely in his carriage house. Late on a Saturday afternoon they set out, each ready to turn back at a word from the other, and at length they reach Memphis, 80 miles away, having discovered en route that Ned McCaslin is a stowaway. Boon, eager to see Miss Corrie, a prostitute of whom he is very fond, takes the innocent Lucius to Miss Reba's place, where Everbe Corinthia, known as Miss Corrie [Hogganbeck], works. The simple Boon is hoping to keep Lucius in the dark as to the nature of Miss Reba's establishment. Shortly Boon is involved in Ned's horse-racing plan, and because he is responsible for the Winton Flyer, which Ned has made a sort of pawn for the horse, he is bound to see Ned's elaborate plan through. In the days that follow, Boon's life is one of nearly total frustration. He is torn between the need to function as one of Ned's chief aides and his need to vent his jealousy of Everbe, first on Sam Caldwell, whose offices are necessary to the success of Ned's scheme, and later, on Butch Lovemaiden, whose enmity might ruin all chances of Ned's racing the horse Lightning (Coppermine). As if this burden were not enough for one even as strong as Boon to bear, Everbe informs him that she will have no more of their illicit love. When, after the first heat has been run at Parsham, Butch succeeds in getting Boon, Ned, and the horse taken into custody and then has Everbe bail them out by practicing her former profession with him, Boon can no longer restrain himself. He beats Butch. In Ned's words, "He nigh . . . [ruins] him." But before this Boon also "whups" Everbe and thus alienates young Lucius for a time. This double violence lands him in jail again, along with Butch. Again Boon is released seconds after Butch is freed, and because Butch has called Everbe "whore," Boon again attacks Butch and is a third time put in jail, where he remains until the next day, when Boss Priest secures his release. Seven days after their departure for Memphis, Boon, Lucius, and Ned return to Jefferson, with Boss Priest, to resume their customary lives. Boon later varies the pattern of his former life, however; for he marries Everbe and moves with her to a "doll-sized" house, where they have a baby and name it after young Lucius.

3–7, 9–24, 26–29, 31–44, 46–72, 76–102, 104–108, 112, 114–

Hogganbeck, Everbe Corinthia (Miss Corrie). One of Miss Reba's girls, whom Boon Hogganbeck comes to visit. She has previously worked in Arkansas in a call house run by "Aunt" Fittie, who took Everbe to raise after her mother died and who, according to Otis, started the girl working as a prostitute when she was only eleven or twelve years old. When Everbe comes to the more lucrative job at Miss Reba's she changes her name to Corrie because she thinks "Everbe Corinthia" sounds too "old timey" and "countrified" for her type of work; and when her nephew Otis comes to visit her at Miss Reba's, Everbe pays him 5 cents a day to keep her real name secret. Despite her background, she is a gentle, sensitive person who objects to the use of coarse language, especially in the presence of young Lucius Priest, whom she is drawn to from the first. When Lucius fights Otis because he objects to the things Otis has said about Everbe, she is so touched that she promises Lucius to give up her present way of life. Her importunate lover Boon makes this promise difficult for her to keep even though she says that her love for him is one of the reasons for her wanting to reform. Soon Everbe, too, is caught in the web of Ned McCaslin's horse-race scheme, and she does much to help, at first by securing the aid of Sam Caldwell and later by going back on her promise to Lucius in order to gratify Butch Lovemaiden so that he will secure the release from custody of Ned and the horse Coppermine (Lightning). To Lucius, hurt by her defection, the big girl pathetically explains her act by saying, "I thought I had to. I didn't know no other way." During her stay in Parsham Everbe has more problems than the formidable one of pacifying Boon and fighting off Butch. She also feels responsible for Otis' theft of Minnie's gold tooth, and she expresses a willingness to buy Minnie another tooth even while she sobs over Otis, who, as she says, "Is only a child." When the races are over and Miss Reba and Minnie return to Memphis, Everbe, true to the promise she made Lucius, does not go with them but accepts a job for Mr. Poleymus taking care of his invalid wife. Some time later she and Boon marry and move to Jefferson, where they have a son whom she names after young Lucius.

99, 100, 102, 106–108, 112, 113, 115, 118, 124–127, 130–136, 138, 139, 143–145, 149–151, 153–160, 162–165, 171–181, 188–192, 194, 199, 201–203, 205–209, 211, 212, 214, 215, 217, 218, 233, 253, 255, 261, 275, 276, 278, 279, 304

Hogganbeck, Lucius Priest. Infant son of Boon and Everbe.
305

Hood, Uncle Parsham ("Possum"). An old Negro with white mustache and goatee, named, as are the town and countryside, after the man Parsham. Quiet and dignified, he commands the respect even of the white people of the town. Having seen the first two races between Acheron and Coppermine (Lightning), he is able to give Ned McCaslin important information about the two horses. His tidy home becomes the headquarters of Ned's group, and his position in the community provides them a degree of protection. Young Lucius Priest says "yes, sir" to him, and before Boss Priest arrives in town, he eats and, one night, sleeps with the old man rather than stay with those of his own race. Uncle Parsham's quiet word is law to his family and friends, even to Ned, who at Uncle Parsham's command tells young Lucius the sordid details about Everbe's [Hogganbeck] submission to Butch Lovemaiden and Boon Hogganbeck's whipping of them both. He is, as Faulkner has his narrator say, "the aristocrat of us all and judge of us all."

168, 170, 171, 173, 174, 176, 178, 181, 185, 190, 203, 220, 222–225, 228–234, 239, 243–247, 249, 250, 252, 254–258, 262, 263, 267, 271, 281, 282, 303

* *Issetibbeha.* Chickasaw chieftain. The daughter of one of his tribesmen was Boon Hogganbeck's grandmother.
19, 73

Jackie. One of Miss Reba's girls.
201

Legate, Bob. One of the regular hunters at De Spain's famed camp.
21

Lessep, "Grandfather." Young Lucius Priest's maternal grandfather, whose funeral all the adult Priests of Jefferson attend in Bay St. Louis, 300 miles away.
43, 44, 50, 133

Lessep, "Grandmother." Maternal grandmother of young Lucius Priest.
44

Lessep, Alexander. Great-uncle of young Lucius Priest and probably the brother of Grandfather Lessep, who died in Bay St. Louis.
43

Lightning. See Coppermine.

Linscomb, Colonel. Owner of Acheron, the horse that races Coppermine (Lightning). The Colonel, a lawyer, also owns the half-mile track on which the races are run and, apparently, a good deal of the surrounding property. He is Grandpa Priest's host when that gentleman comes to Parsham and sends his chauffeur-driven auto to Hardwick with Sam Caldwell and Minnie to secure Boon Hogganbeck's second release from jail. It is in the Colonel's office, "the finest room" young Lucius Priest has ever seen, that Ned McCaslin tells Bobo Beauchamp's tangled story. In the same room Boss Priest and Mr. Van Tosch make arrangements for the fourth and final heat to be run the next day between Acheron and Coppermine (Lightning).
181, 191, 194, 219, 223, 225, 234, 241, 262, 268, 269, 275, 277, 278, 281, 284–286, 293, 294, 296, 298

Lovemaiden, Butch. A deputy for Hardwick, the county seat, 13 miles from Parsham. Drawn to Parsham by news of the race, no doubt, he shows up at Uncle Parsham Hood's on the day Boon Hogganbeck, Ned McCaslin, and the others arrive from Memphis with the horse. Instantly attracted to Everbe [Hogganbeck], Butch, his sweaty bulk smelling of whisky, forces his attentions on her, at the same time taunting Boon, who does not know that Butch,

despite badge and pistol, is only a guest in Parsham. After seeing
Lightning (Coppermine) run a practice heat, Butch suspects that
Ned has used dope on the horse; but it is plain that Butch does not
care if only Coppermine can score an upset victory next day.
Later Butch gets a scare when Miss Reba arrives in Parsham. She
realizes immediately Butch's situation in the town and is able to
keep him away from Everbe—but only for the moment. Next
day, after the first heat, he is attacked by Boon, perhaps on general principles or perhaps because Butch has presented a document
that, in his own words, has to do with "a little legal difficulty
about who owns the horse [Coppermine]." At any rate, he succeeds in getting Boon, Ned, and Coppermine taken into custody,
all a part of his design to have his way with Everbe, who, as he
has suspected, will do anything to see the horse free to run. After
she has submitted to him he probably withdraws his question of
Coppermine's ownership. Ned suggests that Mr. Poleymus, the
Parsham constable, suspecting that Butch has used him, might
have released the prisoners anyway. Whatever the cause, they are
liberated and Butch is again attacked by Boon and badly whipped
this time. When several men pull Boon away and hold him, Butch
tries to beat him with his pistol; then Mr. Poleymus comes on
the scene, strips Butch of badge and pistol, and has him and Boon
taken to the Hardwick Jail. Butch, locked up in a cell near Boon's,
calls Everbe "whore" and when, a short time later, the two men
are released, Boon instantly falls upon Butch for the third time.
    *172–178, 181, 184, 185, 188–192, 194, 195, 203, 206–209,
215, 229, 233, 239–244, 255–257, 259, 275–277*

Ludus. Negro employee of Priest's livery stable. To visit a new girl
    friend 6 miles out of town, Ludus keeps a wagon and team of
    mules out all night without proper authority. Boon Hogganbeck,
    the night foreman, does not even hear Ludus' lie about losing a
    tire off one of the wagon wheels and leaving wagon and team at
    Maury Priest's. What concerns Boon is that Ludus has brought
    some cheap liquor instead of the $2 worth of Bookwright whisky
    that Boon gave him the money for. Soon after the complete story
    of Ludus' trickery comes out, Ludus tells Son Thomas that Boon
    is "norrer-headed." Boon, thinking he said "norrer-asted" (the
    fact that "son of a bitch" was included seems unimportant to

either of the men), gets a pistol and chases Ludus through the main square of town, where Boon fires five shots at him, all of them missing. Ludus' only official punishment is that he is given a week off work without pay.

    5, 9–15, 17, 18, 42

Luster. Negro employee of the Priest livery stable. He accompanies Maury Priest and his son Lucius to the town square in pursuit of Boon Hogganbeck and Ludus, and later helps carry the wounded Negro girl to Dr. Peabody's office. After Boss Priest has acquired an auto, Luster is deputized by Boon to take the Priest hack in Boon's stead to meet the afternoon train.

    6, 10, 14, 15, 32

Lytle, Horace. An important bird-dog specialist who comes to Parsham each year during the hunting season.

    166, 194

McCaslin, Cousin. Uncle of Zachary Edmonds and owner of the mare that Ned McCaslin, without authorization, bred to the farm jack and thus produced the mule that, aided by Ned's use of a sardine as bait, could outrun any mule in the country. At twenty-two the mule died unbeaten, and was buried at McCaslin.

    120, 121

McCaslin, Delphine. Ned's fourth and last wife. She is Sarah Priest's cook.

    30, 33, 34, 36, 54, 55, 65, 299, 302

McCaslin, Isaac (Cousin Ike). Relative of young Lucius Priest and owner of the hardware store whose window Boon Hogganbeck shatters with a bullet intended for Ludus. Though young, Ike is already the best woodsman and hunter the country ever had (after De Spain's death the camp is called McCaslin's camp); consequently he is enraged at Boon, not for breaking his window, but for being such a poor shot. Ike is one of Boon's "proprietors" and will, of course, pay for the window himself. It is Ike who furnishes most of the information that is known about Boon's early years in Yoknapatawpha, for he and Boon were raised together at McCaslin from the time Boon was around ten or eleven years old. It is also Ike who figures as an unwitting agent in young Lucius' getaway to Memphis with Boon: Lucius, his parents out of town at a funeral, sets up the story that on Sunday he wants to try a certain fishing hole near Jefferson and will not, therefore, spend Saturday night with Zachary Edmonds at McCaslin, where he is supposed to stay; he then tells Ned McCaslin that he will spend the night with cousin Ike; he next tells Ike that he will stay with Ned and Delphine; and finally, the innocent Ike simply tells Zachary Edmonds that Lucius is staying in town Saturday night. Lucius' way is now clear.

14, 15, 18–20, 22, 54, 55, 61–63, 65, 96

McCaslin, Lancaster. "Time-honored" father of Lucius Quintus and grandfather of Ned, according to Ned's story.

31

McCaslin, Lucius Quintus Carothers (Old L. Q. C.). First of the McCaslins to come to Mississippi. In 1813 he crossed the mountains from Carolina with slaves and foxhounds and settled on the place that is still occupied by his descendants and still bears his name. Even the original two-room, mud-chinked hut remains, though it is buried under the additions that the wives of the successive Edmondses have made.

61, 69, 82, 89, 285

McCaslin, Ned William. Grandfather Priest's Negro coachman, born in the "McCaslin backyard" in 1860. According to Ned, his mother was a daughter of old Lucius Quintus Carothers McCaslin by a Negro slave. And Ned never lets the people in his life, white or black, forget this fact, or legend. Audacious a little beyond the bounds of prudence, using "Mr." and "Sir" sparingly, he is, even so, intelligent enough and sensitive enough to manipulate the white man's world about him pretty much to his liking. Ned is no selfish opportunist, however. At bottom, he is capable of a deep loyalty. Strong, too, in Ned's makeup is the ability to discern merit in people and to appreciate it to the fullest. Of Sam Caldwell, and later of Mr. Poleymus, the constable, Ned says, "He's a man, mon"; and he is immediately aware of and apprecia-

tive of Miss Reba's insight into reality. With such people shrewd
Ned knows that he need not play Uncle Remus in order to prosper.
Ned, of course, is not deceived by the smokescreen that Boon
Hogganbeck and young Lucius Priest throw around the prepara-
tions for their trip to Memphis, and the Winton Flyer is not far
out of Jefferson before he is discovered aboard, a stowaway. Once
in Memphis he runs across his cousin Bobo Beauchamp, learns
about Bobo's trouble, and after taking a look at a certain horse
that Bobo is expected to steal to liquidate his debt to a white
man, he conceives an elaborate plan to rescue Bobo. Though the
horse, Coppermine (later called Lightning), a trained racehorse,
will not normally run to win, Ned has reason to believe he can
make a winner of him by using the same method he had used on
a racing mule years before. Without Boon's knowledge, Ned
exchanges the Priest auto for the horse, and, the deed done, he
persuades the confused Boon and others to help him get Coppermine to Parsham, there to run against a horse that has previously
beaten him twice. Established at last in Parsham, Ned, certain
he can make Coppermine win one heat and hoping he can make
him win a second one, intentionally lets him lose the first heat.
Then pending the settlement of a question raised by Butch Lovemaiden concerning the legal ownership of Lightning, Ned and the
horse are held in custody. When Butch, thanks to Everbe [Hog-
ganbeck], withdraws his protest, Ned and the horse are freed
next day to run the last two heats. The second heat is ruled a
tie because, though Acheron outspeeds Coppermine, Acheron
breaks through the railing and runs outside the track; consequently Coppermine is the only one to cross the legal finish line.
At the suggestion of a friend of Colonel Linscomb, Acheron's
owner, it is agreed that the winner of the next heat will be
declared victorious in both heats two and three. In heat three, as
the two horses head into the homestretch with Coppermine slightly
behind, young Lucius, the rider, following Ned's instructions, pulls
his mount far enough to the side for him to see Ned only, standing just beyond the finish line. Coppermine can then think of
only one thing—to reach Ned as soon as possible. He does just
that and wins the race, as well as considerable money for Ned—
and enough for Bobo. By this time Boss Priest has arrived at the
track, and Ned is requested to appear at Colonel Linscomb's, where

Boss is staying, and there to explain the whole matter of the auto and horse exchange. That evening on Colonel Linscomb's gallery, Ned explains privately to Boss how he made the horse, as well as the mule of long ago, run: he used a "sourdean" (sardine) for a reward at the finish line. Then, Boss and Ned having rejoined Mr. Van Tosch and Colonel Linscomb in the Colonel's office, Ned unfolds the story of Bobo's entanglement with the white man and of Ned's first plan to save Bobo. They had planned to have the white man watch the first heat, which Coppermine would be sure to lose. On the second heat the white man would, of course, bet against Coppermine, pledging the stolen auto (which Ned knew that he could not sell anyway) against the horse, which was, for the purpose of Ned and Bobo, their property. But this heat Coppermine would win; thus the auto and the horse would revert to him and Bobo. Ned's first plan was changed, however, when the white owners of the two horses appeared on the scene. Then ". . . yawl come and ruint it," Ned said to the white men. Thus, to save Bobo, Ned had to bet and win money, which, of course, he did. After Ned ends his story, Mr. Van Tosch and Boss Priest arrange for one more heat to be run the next day, the particulars of their bet to be as follows: if Coppermine beats Acheron, Boss will win Coppermine and Mr. Van Tosch will be told Ned's racing secret; if Acheron wins, Boss will keep Ned's secret but must pay $495 for the choice of taking or leaving Coppermine. Next day this special heat is run. Maybe Ned does not want his secret known; perhaps he is tired of straining for victory now that Bobo is safe; or, perhaps he wants to make McWillie, Acheron's rider, feel good. At any rate he does not appear at the finish line with his promise of a sardine, and so Coppermine loses. Without apparent regret Ned turns Coppermine over to Bobo, and late the following day, Friday, the travelers are back in Jefferson. The following Monday Ned informs young Lucius that he bet on Acheron to win that last heat—and that Uncle Parsham Hood now has $20 for his church.

30–37, 54–56, 58, 59, 61, 65, 69–72, 76, 77, 79–90, 92, 93, 95–97, 115–121, 123–131, 133, 134, 136, 137, 139–152, 158, 162–173, 175–186, 189, 191, 192, 197, 203–205, 211, 213, 214, 216–226, 228–244, 250–259, 261–263, 267–274, 278–282, 284–299, 302–304

McCaslin, Theophilus. Cousin Ike's father. Since Theophilus had been a member of the party of horsemen that legend said almost captured a Yankee general when General Forrest led them into the lobby of the Gayoso Hotel, members of the McCaslin–Edmonds–Priest family always stop at that hotel when they are in Memphis.
  96

McDiarmid. One of the judges of the horse race, also operator of the depot eating-room in Parsham. According to "legend" he can slice a ham so thin that his entire family makes a summer trip to Chicago on the profits from one ham.
  235

McWillie. Negro youth who rides Acheron in the races against Coppermine. McWillie's father is chauffeur and houseman for Colonel Linscomb.
  225–227, 231, 232, 236–238, 253, 263–266, 271–273, 275, 278, 283, 284, 295–297

Minnie. Miss Reba's trusted Negro maid, possessor of a large removable gold tooth. She had one of her natural ones pulled to make room for this prize, which she takes out when she eats so she can enjoy looking at it and so it won't get "all messed up with no spit-mixed something to eat." Minnie is desolate when she and Miss Reba arrive in Parsham, because the tooth she scrimped for three years to buy has been stolen some time during the early hours of that morning while she was sleeping. She and Miss Reba suspect Otis from the first, and their suspicions are justified when Lycurgus Briggins forces Otis to give up the tooth of which Minnie is so proud.
  100–102, 107–109, 112–116, 118, 124, 126, 133–135, 139, 141, 152, 153, 158, 199, 200–202, 205, 216, 218, 220, 221, 229, 259, 261, 274, 275, 278, 279

* *Moketubbe.* One of "our own petty Chickasaw kings," mentioned by the narrator.
  73

Otis. Miss Corrie's [Hogganbeck] nephew. A runt nearly fifteen who passes for ten, he is visiting Corrie at Miss Reba's because, in

Corrie's words, "he never had no chance" on the farm in Arkansas. Even more impressive than Otis' foul-mouthed conversation is the fact that he seems to see everything in terms of money. Merely because Mr. Binford has taken a few cents (including Otis' "hush" money) from him, vindictive Otis reveals to Miss Reba the fact that Mr. Binford has been betting on a horse race. He even charges his Aunt 5 cents a day to keep her name, Everbe Corinthia, a secret, and is regretful that he did not ask for a dime instead. Inadvertently he gives the secret away to young Lucius Priest and then suggests that perhaps he too can capitalize on the information. As the two boys talk, Otis laments the fact that he cannot have a peephole in Miss Reba's attic floor so he can charge men to let them watch Miss Reba's girls entertain their customers just as he had charged men—and boys—at Aunt Fittie's place for the same sort of privilege when Everbe (Miss Corrie) worked there. At this point, Lucius, outraged by Otis' remarks about Everbe, attacks him, and Otis cuts Lucius' hand with a pocketknife. Only a short time later, just before leaving Miss Reba's for good, Otis steals Minnie's gold tooth while she sleeps. The next afternoon, in Parsham, Otis, who is supposed to ride Coppermine, insists upon being paid in advance and, impervious to his Aunt's pleas, asks $20, more than twice Ned's fortune, as Otis well knows. When Otis, still in possession of the gold tooth, learns that Minnie and Miss Reba have arrived in Parsham, he goes into hiding but is located and treed by Uncle Parsham Hood's dogs and Lycurgus Briggins, who forces him to give up the tooth.

101, 106, 109–113, 125, 135, 138–145, 151–154, 157, 158, 163, 165, 171, 172, 174, 176, 178–181, 190, 192, 194, 195, 198, 203, 212, 217, 218, 220, 225, 234, 249, 250, 261

Parsham. The man after whom the town and countryside were named. Colonel Linscomb occupies what remains of the old Parsham place, by which name it is still known.
281

❋ *Peabody, Dr.* Jefferson doctor who treats the Negro girl whom Boon Hogganbeck creases when he is trying to shoot Ludus.
15

Peyton, George. A famous bird-dog specialist who comes to Parsham each year during the quail season.
   194

Poleymus. The constable of Beat Four, which includes the town of Parsham and vicinity. Though old, Mr. Poleymus is able, and after he begins to suspect that Butch Lovemaiden has been using him to get at Everbe [Hogganbeck], he strips the roving deputy of his badge and pistol and puts him into jail along with Boon Hogganbeck, whom Mr. Poleymus is obliged to jail on three separate occasions: first because Butch questions Boon's ownership of "Lightning," and twice for attacking Butch. After the troublesome races are over in Parsham, Mr. Poleymus hires Everbe to take care of his invalid wife.
   254, 257–262

Powell, John. Head hostler of the Priest livery stable and owner of the revolver with which Boon Hogganbeck attempts to shoot Ludus. The revolver, which John bought from his father on the day he was twenty-one years old, is a symbol of his manhood; and he would give up his job rather than come to work without it. Maury Priest knows this, and being a gentleman, refuses to acknowledge the presence of the firearm on his premises, even though all firearms are forbidden there except the one in his office. John Powell, likewise a gentleman, would never compel Maury to make such acknowledgement and consequently keeps the revolver in a discreetly placed pocket in his jumper, which he keeps on his private nail in the harness room. Boon, like everyone else in Maury's employ, knows about the revolver, and in the heat of his compulsion to shoot Ludus, takes it from John's secret pocket. Thus John Powell's silence about the revolver is made a larger moral issue than loyalty to his race; consequently he tells the truth about Ludus' keeping a team of mules and a wagon out overnight.
   4–12, 14, 15, 37, 38

Priest, Alexander. The narrator's baby brother.
   30, 34, 47, 50, 53, 54, 56, 59, 60, 246, 300

Priest, Alison Lessep. Wife of Maury and mother of the narrator and his brothers.
   34, 40, 62, 301

Priest, Lessep. One of the narrator's younger brothers.
   53, 56, 59

Priest, Lucius (Grandfather; Boss). Father of Maury, Sr., and President of the Bank of Jefferson. When Colonel Sartoris, president of the Merchants and Farmers Bank, gets an ordinance passed banning mechanically propelled vehicles on the streets of Jefferson, Lucius Priest, though he, too, disapproves of such vehicles, buys a Winton Flyer in defiance of the ordinance because he will not be dictated to by the president of a younger bank than his. It is his intention to keep the car locked in his carriage house, perhaps using it just often enough to fulfill his need to abrogate the ordinance of Colonel Sartoris; but the crafty, car-smitten Boon Hogganbeck maneuvers Boss Priest and his family into taking occasional short rides and soon these little excursions become standard procedure. When Boss Priest shows up in Parsham, he sits as an unofficial judge of the three runaways and apparently decides that their defection is not great. Caught in the spirit of competition, he bets on Coppermine to win a special fourth heat and loses $495 but gets to keep Ned McCaslin's secret. After he has returned to Jefferson with the three other travelers and the time comes for Maury, Sr., to have a reckoning with his son young Lucius, Grandfather takes over, but does not physically punish Lucius. Rather, he points out that living with his lie (or network of lies wrapped about his trip to Memphis) will be Lucius' punishment, for he can live with it and "through" it: "A gentleman always does. . . . A gentleman accepts the responsibility of his actions and bears the burden of their consequences even when he did not himself instigate them but only acquiesced to them, didn't say no though he knew he should." At the very last we hear from Boss Priest again, this time through Boon's new family, who are buying their small house from him at the rate of 50 cents a week.
   18, 23, 25, 28–33, 36–39, 41, 45–49, 51, 54, 56, 65, 66, 77, 82, 86, 93, 96, 97, 104, 105, 107, 116–118, 120, 126, 143, 166,

Priest, Lucius (Loosh). Narrator of *The Reivers*, who, in 1961, tells his grandson the story as it happened to him when he, Lucius Priest, was a boy of eleven.

When the parents of the young Lucius go to Bay St. Louis to attend the funeral of his mother's father, Lucius' conscience loses its first round against Non Virtue when he not only acquiesces in Boon Hogganbeck's unmentioned plan to go to Memphis in Boss Priest's auto but becomes a positive agent in furthering their getaway scheme. Once at Miss Reba's in Memphis, where he impresses the grownups with his manners, the innocent boy begins to learn many things about adult life too quickly. His principal instructor is Otis, who tells Lucius what sort of house Miss Reba's is as he explains the term "pugnuckling" to the shocked eleven-year-old boy. In this connection Otis goes on to say things about Everbe [Hogganbeck] which provoke Lucius, who has already begun to like her, into attacking him and taking away his pocket-knife, but only after Otis has succeeded in cutting the fingers of Lucius' right hand. Everbe soon learns the details of the fight from Otis and, deeply touched by Lucius' defense of her, promises him to give up the kind of life she has been living at Miss Reba's. The next day, in Parsham, Lucius, "anguished with homesickness" and burdened with the knowledge that at a word from him Boon and Ned McCaslin would drop the whole idea of the race and take him home, gets in ever deeper when he agrees to replace Otis as Coppermine's rider. Now he has not only the responsibility of guarding Everbe's new virtue against Boon and Butch Lovemaiden but also that of winning the race, not for money but to somehow justify what he and Boon and Ned have already done. He realizes now that there is no turning back: he "was a child no longer now; innocence and childhood were forever lost, forever gone." After the first heat has been run, an unwilling Ned tells him the details of Boon's whipping Everbe; whereupon he faces Boon and flails at him with his fists, then goes for solace to Uncle Parsham Hood, with whom he sleeps that night. After the second heat, ruled a tie, Lucius rides Coppermine to victory in the all-important third heat but refuses to accept the money

Miss Reba has won for him, telling Ned to give it to Uncle
Parsham. After forgiving Everbe for her "lapse" with Butch, he
goes with his grandfather to Colonel Linscomb's, where he learns
how Ned made Coppermine win. And the next day he rides in the
special race, losing this time. When he returns to Jefferson very
different from the little boy who left there a week ago, he is surprised to find that the town has not changed too. As he has expected, his father takes him into the cellar dutifully to whip him
with the razor strop. But somehow this punishment seems inade-
quate to Lucius, not worthy of his father or of him. Grandfather
Priest takes over and solves the problem by telling Lucius that
he must provide his own punishment by living with the knowledge of his deceit, assuring him that, as a gentleman, he can live
with and "through" it. Grandfather's wise handling brings on, it
would seem, Lucius' redemption, which begins in the flood of tears
that he has for so long needed to shed. Some time later he visits
Everbe Hogganbeck in her Jefferson home and there meets her
first-born, whom she has named Lucius Priest Hogganbeck.
*34, 47, 71, 77, 82, 96, 100–102, 107, 125, 127, 128, 151, 156,
163, 173, 177, 181, 196, 203, 205, 217, 219, 220, 259, 260, 286,
300*

Priest, Maury, Jr. One of the narrator's younger brothers.
53, 54, 56, 59, 246

Priest, Maury, Sr. Father of Lucius, the narrator. He is owner of the
Priest livery stable and was once a sort of agent for Ned McCaslin
and his famous racing mule, although Maury did not know the
secret of how Ned made the mule run.
5, 10, 12–14, 41, 82, 96, 117, 120, 197, 286, 300

Priest, Sarah Edmonds. Grandmother of the narrator.
30, 32, 34, 35, 40, 65

Rainey, Paul. Hound specialist from just a few miles down Colonel
Sartoris' railroad who comes to Parsham each winter for two
weeks. He uses Wall Street money to buy enough Mississippi land
for him and his friends to hunt bear, deer, and panther in. He

once took his pack of bear hounds to Africa to see what they would do to a lion.
166, 194

Reba, Miss (Mrs. Binford). Operator of what is apparently one of the better call houses in Memphis. "A young woman . . . with a kind hard handsome face and hair that was too red." Though rough in speech, she is apparently generous and loyal to her friends, and Ned McCaslin is quick to perceive her shrewd intelligence and her sense of reality. She probably supplies most of the money that Ned bets on Coppermine, and she places a bet for Lucius Priest without his knowing it until after the race. She is the first one to give the troublesome Butch Lovemaiden a scare, when she tells him that unless he leaves Everbe [Hogganbeck] alone, she will tell the real "law" in Parsham that Butch has registered a couple of whores at the hotel. Especially considerate of Minnie's feelings, she makes the clerk allow Minnie to stay in the white hotel, and she does not rest until Minnie has recovered her stolen tooth.
98, 100–103, 106–116, 118–120, 124–136, 138, 139, 152–154, 196, 199–202, 204, 210, 215–218, 222, 233, 254, 256, 261, 275– 278, 280, 281, 290

Rhodes, Miss. Young Lucius Priest's schoolteacher, who lets him make up the work he misses while he is in Memphis.
303

Rouncewell. Oil company agent in Jefferson who supplies gasoline for Boss Priest's automobile.
47, 50

Rouncewell, Mrs. Owner of a boardinghouse in Jefferson in 1961.
24

Sartoris, Colonel. President of the Merchants and Farmers Bank, who, when his carriage horses are frightened by Mr. Buffaloe's home-made auto, causes an ordinance to be passed banning all mechanically propelled vehicles on the streets of Jefferson. Simply to abro-

gate this ordinance, Lucius Priest, president of the older bank in Jefferson, buys an automobile.
25, 29, 30, 38, 50, 57

Sartoris, Colonel John. Father of the banker. He was a "soldier, states-man, politician, duelist." The railroad he built superseded the ferry at Ballenbaugh's.
74

Snopes, Flem. Jefferson banker murdered by a mad kinsman. He is mentioned as being a hotel keeper in Jefferson about 1905 when he began to bring other Snopeses into Jefferson from Frenchman's Bend.
24

Stevens, Judge. Jefferson judge, whose office is located "just down the gallery" from Dr. Peabody's office. He advises Maury Priest after the Boon Hogganbeck shooting incident.
15–17

Sutpen, Thomas. Once a large landholder in northeastern Mississippi. The narrator (in 1961) says that all of "that stretch of river bottom which was a part of Thomas Sutpen's doomed baronial dream . . . is now a drainage district."
72, 78

Tennie's Jim. Grandfather of Bobo Beauchamp and one of the workers at De Spain's camp.
22

Thomas, Son. Maury Priest's youngest Negro driver. According to Boon Hogganbeck, Ludus tells Son Thomas that Boon is a "narrow-asted son of a bitch." Ludus insists that he said "norrer-headed." Either way Son Thomas seems to be in a vulnerable position himself and Boon regrets that if he had another pistol he would probably miss Son Thomas just as he has already missed Ludus.
4, 15–17, 47, 56

Van Tosch. Legal owner of Coppermine (Lightning). Originally from Chicago, he now lives in Memphis, where he breeds, races, and trains racehorses. Because Coppermine will not run to win, he puts him up for sale in a stable, where he is available for Bobo Beauchamp, Mr. Van Tosch's employee, to steal. Mr. Van Tosch is present in Parsham when Acheron and Coppermine run the second heat, and, as Coppermine's acknowledged owner, agrees to let the third and last heat count for both heats two and three. That evening, he is a guest at Colonel Linscomb's when Ned McCaslin tells his story, and he is so interested in obtaining the secret of how Ned made Coppermine win the third heat that he proposes a special fourth heat with Ned's secret at stake. That same evening, Mr. Van Tosch, impressed by Ned's account of Bobo's trouble, probably realizes he should have been more sympathetic when Bobo first approached him for a loan; and when Ned suggests that he retain Bobo in his employ, he readily assents.

Vera. One of the girls at Miss Reba's place. Boon Hogganbeck uses her room to change clothes in.

Virgil. Clerk at the hotel in Parsham.

Watts, Birdie. Keeper of a brothel, which, according to Mr. Binford, is across the street from Miss Reba's place.

Winbush, Mac. Owner of the property 8 miles out of Jefferson where Calvin Bookwright sells whisky.

Wordwin. Cashier of the Bank of Jefferson and the one who first brings Boss Priest's automobile from Memphis to Jefferson.

Wyott. A friend of the Priest family. En route to Memphis, Boon Hogganbeck and Lucius Priest are just passing Wyott's, 8 miles out of Jefferson, when they discover Ned McCaslin is a stowaway aboard the Winton Flyer they are driving.

Wyott, I. Man who in "the old days" built a store at the river crossing that the Indians pointed out to him, and named it Wyott's Crossing. He also built a ferry for use at this point, which was the only crossing within miles and the head of navigation too. When mule- and ox-drawn wagons began to replace the boats as transportation, Wyott moved away and became a farmer, giving place to the first Ballenbaugh in the country. Wyott's Crossing then came to be called Ballenbaugh's Ferry.

72, 73, 78

Short Stories and Sketches

SOURCES AND EDITIONS USED
IN THE PREPARATION OF THE GUIDE

"Thrift," *Saturday Evening Post*, CCIII (September 6, 1930), *16–17, 76, 82.*
Idyll in the Desert. New York: Random House, 1931. (A limited, signed edition of 400 copies.) *17 pp.*
"Once Aboard the Lugger," *Contempo*, I (February 1, 1932), *pp. 1 and 4.*
Miss Zilphia Gant. Dallas, Texas: Book Club of Texas, 1932. *xi + 29 pp.*
Go Down, Moses. New York: Modern Library, 1955. *383 pp.* The 1942 Random House edition, *Go Down, Moses and Other Stories*, has the same pagination.
"Afternoon of a Cow" (under the pseudonym Ernest V. Trueblood), *Furioso*, II (Summer 1947), *pp. 5–17.*
Collected Stories of William Faulkner. New York: Random House, 1950. *900 pp.* The 1951 Chatto and Windus (London) edition has the same pagination.
Big Woods. New York: Random House, 1955. *198 pp.*
New Orleans Sketches. Introduction by Carvel Collins. New York: Grove Press, 1961 (an Evergreen Books paperback edition). 223 pp. The 1958 Rutgers University Press (New Brunswick, N.J.) edition and the 1958 Sidgwick and Jackson (London) edition have the same pagination.

The following short stories and sketches by Faulkner were incorporated in his novels or in other collections, usually after extensive revision.

"Wash" (from *Doctor Martino*), "Centaur in Brass," "Mule in the Yard," and "A Bear Hunt," which are included in the *Collected Stories of William Faulkner*, were later revised extensively and incorporated in other works: "Wash" was incorporated in chapter vii of *Absalom, Absalom!*; "Centaur in Braass" and "Mule in the Yard," in part i and part xvi respectively of *The Town*; and "A Bear Hunt," in *Big Woods*. The prelude to the story "Race at Morning" in *Big Woods* is a revised part of "Mississippi," originally published in *Holiday*, April, 1954. "By the People," which appeared originally in *Mademoiselle*, October, 1955, was revised and incorporated in part xiii of *The Mansion*. "The Waifs," which appeared originally in *Saturday Evening Post*, May 4, 1957, was incorporated in *The Town* on pages 359–371. *The Hamlet* includes extensively revised versions of "Fool about a Horse" (pp. 33–53; from *Scribner's*, August, 1936), "The Hound" (pp. 250–296; from *Doctor Martino*), "Spotted Horses" (pp. 309–379; from *Scribner's*, June, 1931), and "Lizards in Jamshyd's Courtyard" (pp. 383–421; from *Saturday Evening Post*, February 27, 1932). "Notes on a Horse-thief," originally published separately in a limited, signed edition (Greenville, Mississippi: Levee Press, 1951), was revised and incorporated in *A Fable* on pages 151–189. The first five sections of *Knight's Gambit*, previously published separately as short stories ("Smoke," *Harper's*, April, 1932 [also in *Dr. Martino*]; "Monk," *Scribner's*, May, 1937; "Hand Upon the Waters," *Saturday Evening Post*, November 4, 1939; "Tomorrow," *Saturday Evening Post*, November 23, 1940; and "An Error in Chemistry," *Ellery Queen's Mystery Magazine*, June, 1946), are reprinted in the novel without revision. The first six chapters of *The Unvanquished*, previously published separately as short stories ("Ambuscade," *Saturday Evening Post*, September 29, 1934; "Retreat," *Saturday Evening Post*, October 13, 1934; "Raid," *Saturday Evening Post*, November 3, 1934; "Skirmish at Sartoris," *Scribner's*, April 1935; "The Unvanquished" *Saturday Evening Post*, November 14, 1936; and "Vendée," *Saturday Evening Post*, December 5, 1936), were revised and incorporated in the novel, with all except "The Unvanquished" (called "Riposte in Tertio" in the novel) retaining their titles as chapter titles. "A Point of Law" (originally published in *Collier's*, June 22, 1941) and "Gold Is Not Always" (originally published in *Atlantic*, November, 1940) were extensively revised and incorporated in "The Fire and the Hearth" in *Go Down, Moses*. The story "Lion" (originally published in *Harper's*, December, 1935) was also extensively revised and incorporated in "The Bear" in *Go Down, Moses*.

THRIFT
(*Saturday Evening Post,* September 6, 1930)

Ffollansbye. First officer to recommend Mac for promotion. Before the
war ends, he is killed.
   16, 17, 78, 82

MacWyrglinchbeath (*Mac*). A Highland Scot in the British Army.
His entire military career is devoted to making enough money to
pay his neighbor in Scotland for the care of his horse and cow and
have some left over besides. To this end he cripples himself so that
he may be transferred from the infantry to the flying corps and
thus become eligible for flight pay, and he accepts well-earned
promotions until he is offered a second lieutenancy. He refuses
this promotion because uniforms and social responsibilities will
nullify the increased pay. After the war he is faced with a difficult
decision: shall he pay for the keep not only of his horse and cow
but also of the two-year-old calf of his cow, or shall he let his
neighbor keep the calf? After figuring carefully and consulting a
lawyer, he, as his neighbor well knows he will do, takes the horse
and cow only. The calf will not fetch enough on the market to
justify Mac's paying for its keep.
   16, 17, 78, 82

Robinson. Gunner in Mac's plane. He is killed in action.
   78

Whiteley. British Army officer who interrogates Mac about his desertion.
   17

IDYLL IN THE DESERT
(New York: Random House, 1931; a limited, signed edition of 400 copies)

Crump, Lucas. Mail rider. Discursive yarn-spinner, he finally tells the
story of the two consumptives. He does much to help, first, the

man, and later, the woman. He sends the woman money, which she thinks comes from her husband, and he finally takes an eight-month leave of absence from his job so he can watch over her.

10

Howes (or *House*), *Darrel* (*Dorry*). Young consumptive. After a two-year stay at Siugut, a camp for consumptives, he is cured and departs, abandoning his mistress, a married woman, who has joined him at the camp and, unknown to him, become infected herself. Many years later Dorry, with his bride, sees his former mistress without recognizing her. She is on a stretcher at the depot in Blizzard, Arizona, waiting for the train on which she dies en route to Los Angeles. She recognizes Dorry, the man she has thought through the years would come back to her.

8, 11–16

Hughes, Manny. Postmaster in Blizzard, Arizona. He makes the letters containing money which Crump sends to the woman at Siugut look as if they come from her husband.

13, 14

Lewis, Matt. Owner of a livery stable. He assists Crump in looking after the consumptives at Siugut.

4, 10, 15, 17

Painter. Grocer. At the request of Crump he gives Howes groceries on credit.

10

ONCE ABOARD THE LUGGER
(*Contempo*, I [Feb. 1, 1932], pp. 1 and 4)

Joe. Pete's older brother.

1

Pete. One of the four men on the boat. He is seasick for the entire trip and becomes so surly that he refuses even to drink any of the whisky he has stolen from his brother Joe. When the lugger lands on the island across the sound, Pete at first refuses to debark, but later helps the narrator, the "Nigger," and the Captain load the mysterious cargo on the boat before the four of them bed down to rest before the return trip.

1, 4

MISS ZILPHIA GANT

(Dallas, Texas: Book Club of Texas, 1932)

Gant, Mrs. Jim's abandoned wife. After killing Jim and his mistress, she moves to Jefferson, where she opens a dressmaking shop. Her hatred of men is by now an obsession, and she will not allow Zilphia to be in their company. The day Zilphia and a painter marry, Mrs. Gant, who has become more and more masculine in manner and appearance since Jim left her, sends the bridegroom away at the point of a shotgun. Three days later, when the painter has gone for good, Mrs. Gant dies in her chair, erect and fully dressed.

3–5, 7–17, 21, 22

Gant, Jim. A stock trader. He leaves his wife and two-year-old daughter to go away with Mrs. Vinson. Both he and Mrs. Vinson are hunted down by Gant's outraged wife and shot to death.

1–8

Gant, Zilphia. Only child of Jim Gant and his wife. Because Mrs. Gant hates men, she keeps Zilphia a virtual prisoner. Some time after her husband of a few hours has left Jefferson, Zilphia reads in a newspaper of his marriage to another woman. Thereafter, through a detective agency, she keeps in touch with the couple's affairs. When the wife dies after giving birth to a daughter and the husband is killed by an auto en route to the hospital where his wife dies, Zilphia leaves Jefferson for three years. When she returns she is wearing a wedding ring, and she has a little girl, who she says is her daughter and whom she begins to guard just as Mrs. Gant had once guarded Zilphia.

7–17, 20, 21, 23, 25, 28, 29

Vinson, Mrs. Proprietress of a primitive inn. She runs away with Jim
   Gant to Memphis, where she, as well as Jim, is shot to death by
   Mrs. Gant.
   3

GO DOWN, MOSES (1942)

(See the genealogical chart of the McCaslin–Edmonds–Beauchamp family on page 316.)

WAS

Beauchamp, Hubert. Owner of a large estate half-a-day's ride from the home of the McCaslins. Hubert wants to get his sister, Miss Sophonsiba, married off. When Uncle Buck (Theophilus McCaslin) creeps into Sophonsiba's bed by mistake, Hubert insists that they become engaged. This decision is reaffirmed when Hubert beats Uncle Buck in a poker game in which the stakes are $500 against Sophonsiba—low hand to get Sophonsiba and also buy, at $300, a troublesome slave (i.e., Hubert to buy Tomey's Turl, or Uncle Buck to buy Tennie Beauchamp so that Tomey's Turl will no longer have to run off to see Tennie). When Uncle Buddy (Amodeus McCaslin) arrives, he induces Hubert to play another hand and wins his brother's freedom from the betrothal and also gets the slave girl Tennie without payment (by using Tennie to "raise" his stake during the game).
5, 6, 8–18, 20–29

Beauchamp, Miss Sophonsiba. Hubert's sister. She plainly wants to marry Theophilus McCaslin.
5, 6, 9–15, 21, 22, 24–28

* *Edmonds, Carothers McCaslin (Cass).* Nine-year-old great-nephew of Buck and Buddy McCaslin. He accompanies Uncle Buck to the home of the Beauchamps, where he sees all, and is therefore the narrator of this story.
3–5, 7, 10, 15, 21, 26

Jonas. Negro worker for uncles Buck and Buddy McCaslin.
7

McCaslin, Amodeus (Uncle Buddy). A better card player than his twin brother, he bests Hubert Beauchamp in a game of stud poker, thus winning the slave girl Tennie and his brother's freedom from a forced betrothal with Miss Sophonsiba Beauchamp.
  4–8, 10–12, 21, 25–30

McCaslin, Isaac (Uncle Ike). Son of Theophilus. The story of "Was" is told to him by McCaslin Edmonds, since all of the events therein occurred before Isaac was born.
  3

McCaslin, Theophilus (Uncle Buck). The twin brother of Amodeus and the father of Ike McCaslin. When he creeps into Miss Sophonsiba Beauchamp's bed by mistake one night, her brother Hubert considers them engaged. His attempt to win his freedom through poker fails, and it remains for his brother Amodeus, a better card player, to best Hubert and win Theophilus' freedom (though he later marries Sophonsiba anyway).
  4–30

Tennie. A young Negro girl, the property of Hubert Beauchamp. She is acquired by the McCaslins in the same card game that releases Theophilus McCaslin from his betrothal.
  5, 15, 17, 18, 23, 24, 26, 28, 29

* *Tomey's Turl*. Negro boy more than half white, property of the McCaslins. He likes the girl Tennie, slave of the neighboring Beauchamps, and frequently runs away from the McCaslins to visit her. After the card game between Hubert Beauchamp and Uncle Buddy McCaslin, Tomey's Turl is enabled to have Tennie with him.
  4–9, 12–15, 17–19, 25, 27–29

THE FIRE AND THE HEARTH

Beauchamp, Henry. Son of Lucas and Molly.
  111–114

* *Beauchamp, James* (*Tennie's Jim*). Oldest son of Tomey's Turl and Tennie Beauchamp. He ran away from home.
    104, 106

Beauchamp, Lucas (*Uncle Luke*). Youngest child of Tomey's Turl and Tennie Beauchamp. He stays on the old McCaslin place, finally becoming the oldest living descendant on the hereditary land. As a young man, he and Zack Edmonds battle because Lucas is suspicious, probably unjustly, of the relationship between Zack and Lucas' wife. Lucas is triumphant. Years later he makes illegal whisky on the McCaslin property. During this period his old wife nearly divorces him because he spends most of his time seeking buried treasure, using a divining machine that he has acquired through shrewd trading. Finally, he is prevailed upon to give up his futile search for gold.
    39, 43–47, 51, 53–57, 59, 60, 62, 63, 65–74, 76–82, 85–98, 100, 101, 103–105, 107–109, 112–126, 128–131

Beauchamp, Molly. Lucas' wife, who nursed her son Henry and the motherless white boy Carothers Edmonds as if they were brothers. After the death of Zack Edmonds' wife, she lives at Zack's house longer than Lucas thinks is necessary. After Lucas and Zack have a showdown, she returns to her own home.
    45–47, 60, 70, 75, 98, 113, 115, 120, 121, 124–131

Beauchamp, Sophonsiba (*Fonsiba*). Daughter of Tomey's Turl and Tennie Beauchamp. She marries and goes off to live in Arkansas.
    105, 107

Beauchamp, Tennie. Negro, wife of Tomey's Turl and mother of James, Fonsiba, and Lucas.
    105

Dan. Negro lotman on Edmonds' place.
    83–85, 88, 96, 123–125

* *Edmonds, Carothers* (*Roth*). Grandson of Cass, son of Zack. He is now owner of the old McCaslin estate. He supplies old Isaac Mc-Caslin, who should be the owner of the estate, with the bare

necessities of life. Roth Edmonds does what he can to manage his property, not an easy task with such tenants as Lucas Beauchamp and George Wilkins on it; and Roth manifests great concern for Molly Beauchamp when Lucas neglects her in his search for buried treasure.

 33–36, 40, 42–45, 59–62, 64–68, 70–73, 76–80, 83, 85–87, 96–99, 101–106, 109, 116–131

* *Edmonds, McCaslin (old Cass).* Grandson of Ike McCaslin's aunt and grandfather of Carothers Edmonds.

 35, 43–46, 49, 56, 59, 73, 104, 106, 110, 126

Edmonds, Zack. Carothers' father. He kept Molly Beauchamp on at his house several months after Mrs. Zack's death and faced the suspicious and jealous husband, Lucas, in a showdown. Zack lost, though bravely, and sent Molly back to Lucas.

 35, 39, 43, 44, 46–48, 50, 53, 59, 73, 104, 106, 109, 114, 116, 122

Gowan, Judge. The judge who tries Lucas Beauchamp and George Wilkins for making whisky illegally.

 71, 72

Henry. Assistant to Judge Gowan.

 74

Hulett. Court clerk.

 129

McCaslin, Amodeus (Buddy). Carothers (Roth) Edmonds' great-great-great-uncle and twin brother of Theophilus, both sons of old Carothers McCaslin.

 36, 39, 40, 45, 105, 106, 114, 115

McCaslin, Carothers. The white man who received from the Indians the patent for the land that became the McCaslin estate. Carothers fathered Tomey's Turl incestuously by one of his Negro slaves who was his own daughter; thus he is grandfather of Lucas Beauchamp.

 36, 44–46, 51–53, 104, 105, 108, 114, 116, 118, 126

McCaslin, Isaac. Son of Buck. He repudiated his patrimony, and Mc-Caslin Edmonds succeeded to it. Isaac now lives near Jefferson in a cheap frame house, which he and his partner built on his father-in-law's land with materials provided by his father-in-law. There he is the recipient of Roth Edmonds' occasional donations.

> *36, 39, 52, 56, 57, 106–108, 114, 115, 118*

McCaslin, Theophilus (Buck). Twin brother of Amodeus. These two sons of old Carothers McCaslin, Buck and Buddy, first put into operation in the early 1850's their plan for the manumission of their father's slaves.

> *36, 39, 40, 45, 105, 106, 114, 115*

Oscar. Negro lotman on Edmonds' place.

> *83–85, 119, 120, 124, 125*

Rideout, Dr. The doctor Roth Edmonds summons to attend Aunt Molly Beauchamp.

> *125*

Thisbe, Aunt. Old Negro woman.

> *50*

Tom. Deputy from Jefferson.

> *65*

Tomey, Aunt. Mother of Tomey's Turl by old Carothers McCaslin. She is grandmother of Lucas Beauchamp.

> *57, 105*

∗ *Tomey's Turl.* Son of old Carothers McCaslin by a slave girl. He is the father of James (Tennie's Jim), Sophonsiba (Fonsiba), and Lucas Beauchamp.

> *106, 108*

Wilkins, George. Slow-witted husband of Nat, Lucas Beauchamp's daughter. Like his father-in-law, George makes whisky illegally on Roth Edmonds' land.

> *33–35, 39–45, 59, 60, 62–77, 80, 82, 83, 85, 86, 88–96, 98, 101, 102, 120, 122–127*

Wilkins, Nathalie (Nat) Beauchamp. Daughter of Lucas Beauchamp
and wife of George. She helps her husband protect himself against
Lucas when Lucas reports George for making whisky illegally, an
offense of which Lucas is equally guilty.
  34, 63, 66–68, 70–77, 101, 122, 124, 125, 127

PANTALOON IN BLACK

Acey. Negro member of the mill gang who tries to cheer Rider when
Rider is grieving over his wife's death.
  136

Alec, Uncle. Husband of Rider's aunt. This aunt took care of Rider
when he was a boy and wants him at her home during his time of
trouble.
  150

Beauchamp, Lucas. Oldest tenant on land of Carothers Edmonds.
  138

Birdsong. White night watchman of the mill where Rider works. Birdsong conducts a crooked dice game by which means he cheats the
mill hands out of their money. When his deceit is discovered, Birdsong attempts to draw his pistol, but is prevented from doing so
when Rider slashes his throat with a razor.
  155–157

* *Edmonds, Carothers.* Rider's landlord.
  137, 138

Ketcham. Jailer in whose custody Rider is placed after the Birdsong
killing.
  157–159

McAndrews. Foreman of the mill where Rider works.
  156

Mannie. Rider's wife. She dies only six months after their marriage.
135, 138–140, 145, 151

Maydew. Sheriff who arrests Rider after the Birdsong killing.
154, 156–158

Rider (Spoot). Negro sawmill worker whose bride of six months dies suddenly. Desperate, Rider gets very drunk and joins in a dice game at the mill. When Birdsong, the white night watchman, is caught cheating, he attempts to draw his pistol, and Rider slashes his throat with a razor. The following day Rider's body is found hanging from the bell-rope in a Negro schoolhouse, where he has been lynched by some of Birdsong's numerous relatives.
135, 136, 146, 151, 152

THE OLD PEOPLE

Ash, Uncle. Negro camp cook.
175, 176

Compson, General. One of the hunting party.
164, 169, 175, 177–179, 185

de Spain, Major. Host at the hunting camp.
164, 169, 170, 173, 175, 177–179, 185

de Vitry, Chevalier Soeur-Blonde. Ikkemotubbe's French companion, who returns from New Orleans with the Indian.
165

* *Edmonds, McCaslin.* Cousin of the boy narrator (who is really Ike McCaslin). Edmonds is Ike's senior by sixteen years and more like a father to Ike than a cousin. Edmonds is a regular member of the hunting party.
164, 165, 167–170, 173–175, 177, 179, 185–187

Ewell, Walter. Member of the hunting party. His gun never misses.
164, 169, 175–181, 183–185

de Spain, Major. Host of the hunting camp where Ike McCaslin went
as a boy sixty years ago.
344, 350, 354

* *Edmonds, Carothers (Roth).* Great-great-great grandson of Isaac
McCaslin's grandfather. He has a child by a woman who, unknown to him, has Negro blood and is also the great-great-great
granddaughter of Carothers McCaslin. Although she has previously
agreed to abide by Roth's private "code," which forbids marriage,
she comes to the hunting camp hoping that he will somehow accept her and their baby boy. Knowing that she will come to see
him, Edmonds makes a point of being absent from the camp
and tells Uncle Isaac McCaslin to simply say "No" to her and
give her some money. But she does not want the money, for she
really loves Edmonds.
336, 338–340, 344–349, 352, 355, 364

* *Edmonds, McCaslin.* Isaac McCaslin's cousin.
351, 359

Ewell. Member of de Spain's original hunting camp.
352

* *Fathers, Sam.* Son of a Negro slave and a Chickasaw chieftain. He
made a hunter of Isaac McCaslin when the latter was a boy of
twelve.
350, 354

Hogganbeck. Member of de Spain's original hunting camp.
352

Isham. Old Negro worker at the hunting camp.
348, 349, 354, 357, 361

Legate, Will. One of the hunting party whose father had once hunted
with Ike McCaslin. He teases Roth Edmonds about Edmonds'
interest in "does," obviously referring to Edmonds' mistress.
337–339, 343–347, 353, 354, 356, 364

McCaslin, Amodeus (Uncle Buddy). Isaac McCaslin's uncle. He died long ago.
359

McCaslin, Isaac (Uncle Ike). Young hunter of "The Bear." Now an old man, he still comes to the woods each November to hunt. It is his unpleasant duty to dismiss Roth Edmonds' mistress, since Roth lacks the heart. When he discovers that she is part Negro, he tells her to go North and marry a Negro—thinking to himself of the possibility of a well-born Southern white marrying a Negro: "Maybe in a thousand or two thousand years in America. . . . But not now! Not now!" In his hurt over what one person can do to another, he thinks: "No wonder the ruined woods I used to know dont cry for retribution! . . . The people who have destroyed it [the land] will accomplish its revenge."
336, 337, 345–347, 353, 355, 356, 358, 359, 361, 364, 365

* *Tomey's Terrel (Turl)*. Part Negro boy who married Tennie Beauchamp.
359

Wyatt, Henry. One of the hunting party.
347, 348

GO DOWN, MOSES

Beauchamp, Lucas (Luke). Husband of Aunt Mollie. He is a tenant on Edmonds' land.
377

Beauchamp, Aunt Mollie Worsham. Old Negro woman, wife of Lucas and grandmother of Samuel. Sensing that something has happened to Samuel, she asks Gavin Stevens to find him. She wants him home, dead or alive; and since he is dead, she wants him to come home right: there must be flowers, hearse, and a notice in the newspaper.
370, 373, 375, 379, 380

Beauchamp, Samuel Worsham (Butch). Grandson of Aunt Mollie. After a series of crimes in and about Jefferson and Chicago, he is executed in Chicago for killing a local policeman.
369, 372–374

* *Edmonds, Carothers (Roth).* Owner of the farm on which Lucas and Mollie Beauchamp live and where Samuel Beauchamp once lived. Edmonds sent Samuel away when he caught him robbing the farm commissary.
370, 371, 373, 375, 377, 380

Rouncewell. Owner of the Jefferson store that Samuel Beauchamp was caught burglarizing.
373

* *Stevens, Gavin.* County attorney. He has Samuel Beauchamp's body brought home for burial and pays all of the expenses, using some of his own money and collecting the rest from Jefferson businessmen.
370–383

Wilmoth. Editor of the Jefferson newspaper. He helps Gavin Stevens with his task of recovering Samuel Beauchamp's body.
375

Worsham, Miss Belle. Jefferson spinster. Her grandfather owned the parents of Mollie [Beauchamp] and Hamp; consequently Mollie is like a member of Miss Worsham's family. Miss Worsham regards it as her duty to get Samuel Beauchamp's body for a respectable burial. Even though she is very poor, she wants to bear all of the expense no matter how great it is.
374, 377–383

Worsham, Hamp. Mollie Beauchamp's brother. He and his wife live with Miss Worsham and help her eke out a living in Jefferson by selling chickens and vegetables.
371, 375, 376, 379, 380

Worsham, Samuel. Father of Miss Worsham. It was for him that Mollie Beauchamp named her grandson.
376

AFTERNOON OF A COW

(*Furioso* II [Summer, 1947], pp. 5–17; under the pseudonym Ernest V. Trueblood.)

Faulkner. A writer. He is short-tempered and irascible. When a brush fire forces the cow Beulah into a ravine, Faulkner, with the help of the Negro Oliver and Trueblood, attempts to push it up the steep side of the ravine. It slips back, falling on top of Faulkner, who "receives the full discharge of the creature's afternoon of anguish and despair." Faulkner at this point calmly leads the cow along the ravine until it rises level with the pasture.
5–6, 8–9, 11–17

Faulkner, Mrs. His wife.
8

Grover (Rover). Son of the Faulkners' Negro cook. He is one of the three boys who start the fire.
5, 16

James. Faulkner's nephew. One of the three boys who start the fire.
5, 10, 16

Malcolm. Faulkner's son. With his two friends, James and Grover, he is responsible for the fire in the haystack which spreads over the pasture.
5, 10, 16

Oliver. Negro field worker for Faulkner. He informs Faulkner and Trueblood of the fire and aids in the attempt to get the cow out of the ravine.
5–6, 8–9, 11–12, 14–17

Trueblood, Ernest V. (Ernest be Toogood). The narrator of the tale. He is the ghost writer of all of Mr. Faulkner's fiction. He requests and is granted permission to use the incident of the fire and the cow as the basis for a story using his own diction and style rather than Faulkner's.

5

COLLECTED STORIES OF
WILLIAM FAULKNER (1950)

(Four of the stories included in this collection were later revised extensively by Faulkner and incorporated in other works, where they are treated in the Guide: "A Bear Hunt" [in the collection *Big Woods*], "Centaur in Brass," "Mule in the Yard" [both in *The Town*], and "Wash" [in *Absalom, Absalom!*].)

BARN BURNING

* *de Spain, Major*. Ab Snopes's landlord after Mr. Harris. De Spain also loses a barn to Ab.
> *12, 18, 19, 23*

de Spain, Mrs. Lula. Wife of Major de Spain.
> *11, 16*

Harris, Mr. Owner of burned barn who brings Ab Snopes to trial.
> *3, 4, 5*

Lizzie. Sarty Snopes's aunt.
> *22*

Sartoris, Colonel John. Commander of the Mississippi regiment of which Ab Snopes claims to have been a member. Ab named one of his sons after John Sartoris.
> *4, 24*

Snopes, Abner (Ab). The barn-burner. During the Civil War he was wounded for stealing horses from his own men.
> *5, 9, 13, 14, 18, 20*

Snopes, Lennie. Wife of Abner.
> *22*

Snopes, Net. Abner's twin daughter, who fails to halt Sarty Snopes.
22

Snopes, Colonel Sartoris (Sarty). Ten-year-old son of Ab Snopes. He
runs away from home because his father is a barn-burner.
4, 13, 22

SHINGLES FOR THE LORD

* *Armstid.* Farmer who lives near Whitfield's church. He helps put
out the fire.
34, 38, 39, 41

Armstid, Mrs. Armstid's wife.
39

Bookwright, Homer. One of the early arrivals on the church-shingling
job.
27–31, 34–37, 41

Grier, Res (Pap). One of the volunteer workmen on Whitfield's church.
In an effort to beat Solon Quick out of half a dog, he accidentally
burns the church down.
27–43

Killegrew (Old Man). A seventy-year-old farmer from whom Pap
Grier borrows a froe and a maul.
27, 28, 38

Killegrew, Mrs. Wife of old man Killegrew.
28

* *Quick, Solon.* Owner of the school-bus truck. He helps with the
church and draws Grier into the bet that destroys the church.
27–38, 40, 41

Snopes. One of the volunteer workmen on the church.
31, 38, 41

Tull, Vernon. Church member who volunteers to help nail the shingles on the church roof. He is an equal partner with Pap Grier in the ownership of a dog.
    31–34, 36, 37, 41

Varner, Will. Man who gives Vernon Tull the puppy, half of which Vernon gives to Pap Grier for helping to raise the animal.
    32

Whitfield, Reverend. Preacher whose church is being roofed by members of the congregation.
    27, 28, 30, 38, 40–42

THE TALL MEN

Gombault. The marshal. He understands the McCallum family.
    47, 53

McCallum, Mrs. Wife of old Anse.
    60

McCallum, Anse. Son of Buddy.
    50, 52

* *McCallum, Anse, "old."* Father of Jackson, Stuart, Raphael, Lee, and Buddy. During the Civil War he walked from Mississippi to Virginia to enlist in Stonewall Jackson's army.
    54–57, 60

McCallum, Buddy. Youngest of old Anse's sons, he served in World War I. He catches his leg in a hammer mill and has to have the limb amputated.
    47–50, 54–57, 60

McCallum, Jackson. Oldest son of old Anse.
    50–52, 54, 55, 57, 60

McCallum, Lee. Son of old Anse. He phones for Dr. Schofield.
45, 52, 54, 55

McCallum, Lucius. Son of Buddy.
50, 52

McCallum, Raphael (Rafe). Son of old Anse.
47, 51, 52, 54–56

McCallum, Stuart. Son of old Anse.
50–52, 54, 55, 60

Pearson, Mr. Government investigator for the draft board. He brings
warrants for the McCallum boys because they have not registered
for military service.
47, 50

Schofield, Dr. Physician who amputates Buddy McCallum's leg.
45

* *Stevens, Gavin.* A lawyer Buddy consulted about selling cotton.
56

[For the story "A Bear Hunt" see the collection *Big Woods*.

TWO SOLDIERS

Foote. The policeman in Jefferson who apprehends Pete Grier's little
brother.
89, 90, 92

Grier, Pete. Young farmer who goes to Memphis to join the army the
day after the Japanese attack on Pearl Harbor.
81–90, 92–98

Habersham, Mrs. Woman who questions Pete's brother in Jefferson and
arranges for him to go to Memphis in search of Pete.
89, 91

Killegrew, "Old Man." Owner of the radio over which Pete and his little brother hear the news about Pearl Harbor.
    81, 82

McKellogg, Colonel. Army officer who provides a limousine and a military chauffeur to take the little Grier boy home.
    98

McKellogg, Mrs. The Colonel's wife, a kind Memphis lady who takes the little Grier boy to her home and then sends him back to his family in Frenchman's Bend.
    99

Marsh, Uncle. Brother of Pete's mother. Marsh was wounded in World War I.
    84, 85, 87

Tull. Father of the girls whom Pete courts.
    83

SHALL NOT PERISH

Bookwright, Homer. Owner of the cattle truck on which the father of the dead Pete Grier rides to town for supplies.
    102

* *de Spain, Major.* Bereaved father. He is saved from committing suicide by the understanding and courage of Mrs. Grier, who has also lost a son in World War II.
    103, 104, 106, 107, 109, 110

Grier, Pete. Young soldier killed in World War II.
    101–106, 108, 111–114

Killegrew, "Old Man." Owner of the radio over which Pete and his brother used to listen to the war news.
    103

✳ A ROSE FOR EMILY

HAIR

Bidwell. Storekeeper in Division, a town on the Mississippi–Alabama border, where the Starnes home is located.
    146, 147

Burchett. Man with whose family Susan Reed lives.
    131, 134–136

Burchett, Mrs. Wife of Burchett.
    131, 134–136, 141

Cowan, Mrs. Hawkshaw's landlady in Jefferson.
    136, 142

Ewing, Mitch. Depot freight agent in Jefferson.
    142, 143

Fox, Matt. Coarse, prying barber who works for Maxey.
    132–134, 136, 142–144

Hawkshaw. See Stribling.

Maxey. Owner of the barbershop where Hawkshaw works.
    131–133, 136, 137, 140–144

Reed, Susan. Orphan who lives with the Burchetts. Though of questionable morals, she finally marries Hawkshaw.
    131, 141, 143

Starnes, Sophie. Girl engaged to Hawkshaw. She dies before they ever get a chance to marry, but he pays off all her family's obligations.
    140, 146

Starnes, Will. Lazy father of Sophie, girl to whom Hawkshaw was engaged. Will died and left nothing but the mortgage on his house, which Hawkshaw pays off.
    138, 140

Starnes, Mrs. Will. Sophie's mother, who, because she is better born than Hawkshaw, lets him do her housework each April when he takes his vacation.
138–140, 146

* *Stevens, Gavin.* District attorney in Jefferson.
144, 145, 147, 148

Stribling, Henry (Hawkshaw). A close-mouthed barber who finally marries Susan Reed, the woman he has loved since she was a child.
131–135, 137–146, 148

[For the story "Centaur in Brass" see the novel *The Town.*]

DRY SEPTEMBER

Butch. Hot-headed youth, a member of the lynching party.
170–172, 176–178, 180

Cooper, Miss Minnie (Aunt Minnie). White woman about forty years old, said to have been attacked by Will Mayes, a Negro.
169, 174–176, 182

Hawkshaw (Hawk). Barber who insists that Will Mayes would not have harmed Miss Cooper. He even accompanies the lynching party in an effort to dissuade the leader. (Mayes calls him "Mr. Henry.")
171, 173, 176, 178, 179

McLendon. Leader of the lynching party. He had commanded troops in France and had been decorated for valor.
171–173, 176–180, 182

Mayes, Will. The Negro who is lynched because it has been rumored that he assaulted Miss Cooper.
169, 170, 172, 173, 176, 177

DEATH DRAG

Black. Driver of car that takes the strange aviators into town.
189

Ginsfarb (Demon Duncan). Owner of the unlicensed stunt plane who jumps from the airplane onto the top of a moving car and returns to the plane via a ladder suspended from it. He will risk his life to save a few cents' worth of gasoline.
194–198

Harris. Man who rents his car to aviators for their death drag.
205

Jake. Driver of the aviator's stunt car.
196

Jock. Pilot of Ginsfarb's stunt plane. Ginsfarb's economy measures have made Jock a nervous wreck.
193–197, 205

Jones. Secretary of the Fair Association.
190

Vernon. Restaurant man.
194, 196

Warren, Captain. Formerly a flyer in the Royal Flying Corps.
187, 192–194, 198, 200–205

ELLY

Ailanthia. Elly's grandmother, who knows about Paul's Negro blood and is outraged over her granddaughter's intimacy with him. Elly loathes the old woman, tries to get Paul to kill her, and is finally the cause of her death.
212

de Montigny, Paul. A young man, partly Negro, who enjoys intimacies with Elly but refuses to marry her. For this reason she causes him to lose control of the car he is driving and is thus responsible for his death and for that of her grandmother. Elly herself is miraculously saved.
207, 209–212, 214, 216, 217, 219–223

Elly (Ailanthia). Young girl who deserts Philip, her betrothed, and because Paul will not marry her, causes him to be killed as well as her grandmother, whom she loathes.
207, 209–219, 223

Philip. Assistant bank-cashier to whom Elly is engaged although she is in love with Paul de Montigny.
214, 215

UNCLE WILLY

Barbour. Uncle Willy Christian's Sunday-school teacher.
227

Barger, Sonny. Negro storekeeper.
234

Bean, Captain. Flyer at the Jefferson airport. He refuses to give Uncle Willy flying lessons because Uncle Willy needs a doctor's permit.
241

Bundren, Darl. Countryman who was taken to the insane asylum in Jackson.
228, 229

Callaghan, Miss. Schoolteacher.
228

Christian, Mrs. Uncle Willy's wife for a short time.
238

Christian, Uncle Willy. Old drugstore-owner, much beloved by the young boys. He has the dope habit, of which well-meaning

blunderers try to cure him. In an effort to escape them he is killed
in his own airplane.
225–247

Hovis, Mrs. One of the Jefferson ladies who try to break Uncle Willy
of the dope habit.
229

Merridew, Mrs. Most active of those who are trying to force Uncle
Willy Christian to give up his narcotics.
228–239, 241, 244, 245

Miller, Brother. Teacher of the men's Bible class that Uncle Willy is
forced to attend after reformers take charge of him.
227, 228, 230

Robert, Uncle. Uncle of the boy narrator of "Uncle Willy."
239

Schultz, Reverend. Preacher at Uncle Willy Christian's church. He
tries to force Uncle Willy into leading a pure life.
227–230, 232, 234, 237

Schultz, Sister. Wife or sister of Reverend Schultz.
229

Secretary. Negro chauffeur for Uncle Willy Christian.
235, 236, 239, 241–247

Wylie, Job (Old Job). Uncle Willy's handyman.
226, 232–234, 236, 239–247

[For the story "Mule in the Yard" see the novel *The Town.*

THAT WILL BE FINE

Church, Mrs. Jefferson lady who calls on Mrs. Pruitt because of Mr.
Pruitt's position. Mrs. Church never calls again because on the

occasion of this lone visit she finds Mrs. Pruitt without a corset on and smelling of liquor.
274

Emmeline. Louisa's baby's nurse.
274, 279

Fred, Cousin. Georgie's cousin.
267, 275, 276

Fred, Uncle. Husband of Georgie's Aunt Louisa.
267, 271, 275, 276, 278–280

George. Georgie's father.
271, 272

Georgie. The narrator, a seven-year-old boy from Jefferson. He sees his uncle's acts through the innocent eyes of childhood.
272, 274, 287

John Paul. Negro servant.
269, 270

Jordon, Mrs. Lady at whose house Georgie sleeps on the night of his Uncle Rodney's death.
287

Louisa, Aunt. Rodney's sister, who is Uncle Fred's wife and aunt of Georgie, the narrator.
267, 269–275, 278, 279, 287

Louisa, Cousin. Georgie's cousin.
267, 275, 276

Mandy. Negro cook in whose cabin Rodney is hidden for a time.
274–276, 284

Pruitt. President of the Compress Association, who, to please his wife, innocently gives Rodney a job with his company.
271, 273, 274, 278, 279

THAT EVENING SUN

Compson, Quentin. The Compsons' oldest son. He is the narrator.
292, 301, 304

Dilsey. The Compsons' cook.
290, 292, 295, 297–300, 305

Frony. Dilsey's daughter.
294, 298

Jesus. Nancy's husband, who Nancy fears will kill her with his razor.
290, 292–294, 296, 297, 299, 300, 309

Lovelady. White insurance agent for the Negroes.
308

Nancy. Negro woman who cooks for the Compsons when Dilsey is ill. She has been having sexual relations with various white men, notably Mr. Stovall, deacon in the Baptist church, who beats her when she asks him in public for her pay. She is now pregnant and fearful that her husband Jesus will kill her.
289–309

Rachel, Aunt. Old Negro woman. She is said to be Jesus' mother.
294, 306, 307

Stovall. Cashier in the bank and deacon in the Baptist church. He beats Nancy when she asks him in public to pay her for sexual intimacies.
291

T. P. Negro boy, probably Dilsey's son.
294

RED LEAVES

Berry, Louis. Indian.
322–327, 331, 337

de Vitry, Chevalier Soeur Blonde. A Frenchman who became Doom's patron and gave him ideas of chieftainship. He called him *du homme,* and hence "Doom."
317, 318, 320

* *Doom.* Born a subchief, he became The Man, The Chief, and acquired many slaves. When he died he was succeeded by Issetibbeha, his son.
316–319, 322, 324, 326, 327, 336

* *Had-Two-Fathers.* Indian attendant of Moketubbe.
336

* *Issetibbeha.* Son of Doom, and Chief until his death. Now that he is dead his personal Negro, who has fled, must be found and killed before the Chief's body can be interred.
313–321, 323–331, 333, 336–340

* *Moketubbe.* Son of Issetibbeha, and Chief now that his father is dead. It is his traditional duty to lead the chase for his father's personal Negro, who has fled. Moketubbe, fat and lazy, does not relish his task.
316, 317, 320, 321, 323, 325–327, 334–337, 339

Three Basket. Indian.
313, 315–317, 322, 323, 325–327, 336, 338–341

A JUSTICE

Basket, Herman. Indian, friend of Crawfishford, who told Sam Fathers the story that Sam passes on to the twelve-year-old Compson boy.
345–359

Callicoat, David. White man mentioned by Herman Basket as the one who used to tell the steamboat "where to swim" in the days when the big craft made four trips annually up the river alongside which Doom's people lived. (*See* Doom.)
346, 347

Compson, Caddy. Only daughter of the Compsons; Jason's sister.
343, 358, 360

Compson, Jason, Jr. Second son of the Compsons.
343, 358

Crawfishford (Craw-ford). Sam Fathers' father, an Indian who had
a son by a Negro man's wife, the son being Sam Fathers, whose
real name is Had-Two-Fathers.
347, 348, 352, 354, 355, 357, 359

* *Doom (Ikkemotubbe).* Nephew of Issetibbeha, The Man, and boy-
hood friend of Crawfishford and Herman Basket. When he went
to New Orleans he adopted the name of a steamboat man, David
Callicoat, because Ikkemotubbe planned some day to "own a
steamboat too." When he returned to his old home after seven
years, he called himself Doom (*du homme*—The Man) and used
poison to win his way to the chieftainship of his tribe.
345–355, 357–359

* *Fathers, Sam (Had-Two-Fathers).* Old workman, half-Indian, part
Negro, on the farm of the Compson children's grandfather. Sam
tells the oldest Compson boy (Quentin) the strange story of his
parentage.
343–345, 358, 360

Roskus. Negro servant of the Compsons.
343

Sometimes-Wakeup. Brother of the Chief whom Doom poisoned.
349

Stokes. Manager of the Compson farm.
343, 344, 358, 360

A COURTSHIP

Colbert, David. Chief Man of the Chickasaws in the Yoknapatawpha
section.
363, 365, 374, 379

de Vitry, Chevalier Soeur-Blonde. White man who accompanied Doom when the latter returned to the plantation from New Orleans.
363

Hogganbeck, David. Pilot of Captain Studenmare's riverboat and mighty rival of Ikkemotubbe for the affection of Herman Basket's sister.
361, 362, 365–380

* *Ikkemotubbe (Doom).* Son of Issetibbeha's sister. He vies with David Hogganbeck for the affection of Herman Basket's sister. When he succeeds to the chieftainship of his tribe he is called "Doom."
361–380

* *Issetibbeha.* Chickasaw chief, uncle of Ikkemotubbe.
361–363, 365, 370, 372, 378

Log-in-the-Creek. Lazy young Indian who spends most of his time sleeping and playing the harmonica. It is he who wins the hand of Herman Basket's sister.
363, 364, 366–371, 379, 380

* *Moketubbe.* Son of Issetibbeha. He resigns his succession to Ikkemotubbe.
363

Owl-by-Night. Young Indian who is interested in Herman Basket's sister until Ikkemotubbe looks favorably upon her.
363–365, 369, 370, 372, 373

Studenmare, Captain. Owner of the steamboat of which David Hogganbeck is the pilot.
366–368, 378, 380

Sylvester's John. Young Indian interested in Herman Basket's sister until Ikkemotubbe looks favorably upon her.
363, 365, 369, 370

LO!

Weddel (or *Vidal*), *Francis*. Chief of the tribe of Indians who live on
a large grant of land that Francis, one-half Indian, inherited from
his French father. His people pour into the nation's capital to be
present at the trial of Weddel's nephew, accused by the Indian
land agent of killing a white man who had bought the land and
established a tollgate at the only fording place of the river in the
tribal area. Weddel's nephew raced the white man for the tollgate
and the nephew's horse lost. Next day the tollgate keeper was
found with a split skull. Weddel insists that the President of
the U.S. grant his nephew a full ceremonial trial. This procedure
takes much time and trouble. At last the President appeases
Francis, and he and his people return home with the nephew a
free man. Only a short time later the President receives a letter
from Weddel telling him that a tollgate incident very similar to
the first one has occurred and requesting another trial for his
nephew. This time the President takes no chances but dispatches
troops to check the advance of the Indians on the capital.
383, 390–393, 396, 400, 402

AD ASTRA

Bland. American Southerner in the (British) Royal Flying Corps. He
is a handsome Rhodes Scholar. Women adore him, but men do not
like him.
407–409, 412, 414–418, 420, 421, 425–429

Comyn. Giant Irishman in the RFC. He is constantly looking for a
fight.
407, 409–411, 413–416, 419–421, 423–427

Franz. Brother of Monaghan's German to whom the latter wishes to
give his baronetcy. Franz finally becomes a colonel in the Kaiser's
army and is killed in Berlin by a German soldier.
418–420

Hume. Man who says Sartoris must have got the German who killed his brother.
> *414*

Monaghan. An American flyer in the RFC who takes into a French café a German flyer whose plane he has just brought down. He is getting the embarrassed German drunk against the latter's will, and the French patrons become outraged. Backed by his drunken fellow flyers, however, Monaghan remains impervious to the French sentiment. At length a fight develops—the outraged French people versus Monaghan and his friends—and the café is nearly wrecked, but Monaghan and his friends emerge from the wreckage with their German still safe.
> *410–412, 414–417, 420–427*

Sartoris. American Southerner in the RFC. Grieving over his twin brother killed in action, he flies alone in search of the killer.
> *407–410, 413, 414, 421, 423, 424, 428, 429*

VICTORY

Cunningham, Sergeant. Sergeant who tries to protect Alec Gray.
> *439–441*

Gray, (Captain) Alec. Young Scotsman from a line of shipbuilders who joins the army at a very early age for service in World War I. After brutally killing his sergeant major during an attack, Gray goes on to a life of military distinction, which he begins to prefer to a life of shipbuilding. After the war, as military heroes become outdated, he continues with his crisp, unbending officer role even after he becomes a beggar.
> *439–446, 448, 452–455, 458, 464*

Gray, Alec (old). Young Alec's grandfather. He is in favor of his grandson's joining the army.
> *441–443*

Gray, Annie. Wife of Matthew, Sr. She prefers her son Alec in mufti.
454

Gray, Elizabeth. Baby sister of young Alec; she is born after Alec joins
the army.
447, 448, 454, 456

Gray, Jessie. Young Alec's older sister, who marries while he is away.
444, 447, 448, 456

Gray, John Wesley. Young Alec's younger brother, Matthew's second
son.
442, 444, 447, 448, 454, 456

Gray, Matthew, Jr. Young Alec's youngest brother, third son of
Matthew, Sr.
442, 444, 447, 448, 454, 456

Gray, Matthew, Sr. Son of old Alec; the father of young Alec. Matthew
believes his son's first duty is to build ships.
441–443, 447, 452, 453, 455

Gray, Simon. Old Alec's brother.
442

McLan. Soldier under Captain Gray whom the Captain disciplines for
having a filthy rifle.
449

Walkley. A subaltern who met Captain Gray in a military hospital
during the war. After the war, Walkley, now a successful wheat
grower in Canada, sees the Captain selling matches on a London
street. When Walkley tries to speak to Alec he gets only a profane
answer in return.
463, 464

Whiteby. British officer who committed suicide after the war because
of "conditions."
457

CREVASSE

McKie. A subaltern who perishes with eleven enlisted men in a cave-in during World War I. Under the leadership of their captain and their sergeant, the remaining men, fourteen all told, manage to dig their way out of the closed-up cave just in time to save themselves from suffocating.

472

TURNABOUT

Albert. Military policeman.

478

Bogard, Captain H. S. American flight officer who takes young Hope on a dangerous flying mission, assigning him to one of the machine guns, where he performs admirably. Of the crew only Hope knows that one of the bombs has failed to leave the plane and is dragging dangerously. Hope, however, thinks that the others also know about the bomb; consequently he is deeply impressed with what seems to him their coolness under extreme danger. In return for Hope's aid, Bogard goes with Hope and Ronnie Smith on their torpedo boat and is thrilled and frightened by the danger involved. Afterward, when Bogard hears of the loss of the torpedo boat, he imitates torpedo technique by diving in his plane very close to a target before releasing his bombs. He is cited for extraordinary valor as a consequence.

480–509

Burt. Boatswain's mate on a torpedo boat X001 who perishes with the rest of the crew.

483, 508

Collier. American flyer who owns a mandolin.

491, 494

Harper. Bogard's gunner, whom Midshipman Hope, as guest flyer, replaces.
484, 509

Hope, Midshipman L. C. W. (Claude). A very young assistant commander of British torpedo boat X001. Having no place to sleep, he gets drunk each night and slumbers in the gutters of the nearby town. Intoxicated, he is taken by Bogard to the latter's quarters and goes on a flying mission as one of Bogard's gunners. Hope is so impressed by the dangers he thinks an aviator faces that he is apologetic when he takes Bogard on one of his highly dangerous torpedo runs into German waters. A short time later Hope perishes in action with his crew of four.
478, 480, 488, 508

Jerry. An American flight officer who underrates Hope because he misinterprets the midshipman's boyish talk.
483, 484

McGinnis, Lt. Darrell (Mac). American flight officer who, misinterpreting young Hope's light British talk, makes insinuating remarks about the young Englishman.
485–492, 494, 504, 509

Reeves. Able seaman in crew of torpedo boat X001. He perishes with his fellows.
483, 508

Smith, Midshipman R. Boyce (Ronnie). Commander of British torpedo boat X001; Ronnie and Hope play a game of their own design called "Beaver" even while they face the gravest of dangers. To honor Bogard the day he goes on the boat, Ronnie plans to go to Kiel, but at Bogard's suggestion he makes a shorter trip. Ronnie later perishes in action with his crew.
482–486, 491, 492, 494–508

Watts. Air gunner in Bogard's crew.
509

Wutherspoon, Jamie. One of Hope's acquaintances.
479

ALL THE DEAD PILOTS

Elnora. Negro servant of the Sartoris family.
529

Ffollansbye. Man attached to Sartoris' flying group.
513, 514, 518

Isom. Negro servant of the Sartoris family; he is mentioned in Johnny Sartoris' letter home.
529

Kaye, Major C. RAF officer who notifies Aunt Jenny [Sartoris] of Johnny Sartoris' death.
530

Kitchener (Kit). Nickname for Sartoris' London girl friend, so called because she has so many soldiers, including Spoomer.
514

Kyerling, R. RAF flyer who saw Johnny Sartoris die.
530

Sartoris, Johnny. Rash young American flyer in the RAF who risks life, limb, and reputation to avenge himself on Spoomer, his rival for the favors of Kit and later of 'Toinette. Sartoris finally is killed in action.
513–520, 522, 525–527, 529

* *Sartoris, Mrs. Virginia (Aunt Jenny).* Young Johnny Sartoris' great-aunt.
529

Spoomer. Nephew of the corps commander. Spoomer is, consequently, in high office. Being Johnny Sartoris' superior as well as his rival for the favors of 'Toinette, Spoomer is able to manipulate Johnny's assignment to his, Spoomer's, advantage. Through Johnny's trick-

ery Spoomer is removed from his command in France and recalled to England, where he becomes temporary colonel at ground school.
513–520, 522, 525–527

'Toinette. French girl in whom both Spoomer and Johnny Sartoris are interested.
523

[For the story "Wash" see the novel *Absalom, Absalom!*

HONOR

Harris. Owner of the flying circus where Rogers and Monaghan work.
559, 560

Jack. Man who tells Monaghan about Harris, who wants a wing-walker for his flying circus.
552, 553

John. Husband of one of the women for whom a car is being demonstrated.
563

Monaghan, Buck. Former war flyer who works as a wing-walker in an air circus. He has an affair with Mildred, the wife of Rogers, his pilot; and he and Mildred ask Rogers for a divorce. Meanwhile Rogers risks his life to save that of Monaghan, and Monaghan departs, alone. His last job, which he quits also, is that of car salesman.
554, 564

Reinhardt. Car dealer. He hires Monaghan as salesman.
563, 564

Rogers, Howard. Pilot with the air circus who risks his life to save Monaghan, the man he knows is having an affair with his wife.

When Monaghan leaves, the Rogerses become the happy parents of a boy and name Monaghan as his godfather.
553–555, 558–561, 563

Rogers, Mildred. Howard's wife, who falls in love with Buck Monaghan. After Buck leaves, however, she is happy with Howard and their new son.
556

Waldrip. An aviator who helped Monaghan learn wing-walking soon after the Armistice when they were both still in the army as test pilots.
552

West, Miss. Reinhardt's secretary, who is friendly to Monaghan.
551, 563, 564

White. Flyer acquaintance of Monaghan during World War I from whom Monaghan unwillingly won so much money that White committed suicide.
552

DR. MARTINO

Charley, Uncle. The porter at the summer resort.
585

Cranston, Lily. Proprietress of the summer resort where Louise King and Dr. Martino meet each year.
578, 579, 582, 584

Jarrod, Hubert. Wealthy Yale student in love with Louise King. With the unethical aid of Louise's mother, Hubert succeeds in breaking Dr. Martino's hold on Louise.
565–568, 570–573, 575, 576, 578–584

King, Mrs. Alvina. Louise's mother, who tricks Dr. Martino into releasing his hold on Louise.
567–569, 571–576, 578–582

King, Louise. Young girl caught under the spell of Dr. Martino, who has taught her much about courage. His philosophy, when applied to life, can be dangerous, however, as Hubert soon discovers.
565–577, 579–584

Martino, Dr. Jules. An old man with a weak heart. He has met Louise at Lily Cranston's resort every summer since Louise was a child, and has gained the courage, therefore the strength to live, through a spiritual affinity with Louise. Soon after he has been tricked into releasing his hold on Louise, he is found dead on his favorite bench.
571, 572, 574, 579, 584, 585

FOX HUNT

Allen. Wealthy Yale student, an Indian, in whom Mrs. Blair has long been interested. When Allen marries a show girl, Mrs. Blair gives herself to Gawtrey.
598, 601

Andrews. Blair's servant.
595

Blair, Harrison. Wealthy Englishman who marries a woman he does not love. A skilled horseman himself, he is so contemptuous of her because she cannot ride well that she turns to other men.
588–590, 592–603

Burke. Irish maid in Blair's home. She aids her friend Ernie.
597, 601–603

Callaghan. Riding instructor from whom Blair's wife takes lessons. Callaghan tells Blair that Mrs. Blair will never be a horsewoman.
596, 597, 600, 602, 603

Ernie. Valet-bodyguard to Blair. He helps Gawtrey to cuckold Blair.
594

Gawtrey, Steve. Man invited to Blair's home because, thanks to Ernie, Blair thinks Steve owns a fine horse that can be bought. Though Blair's wife loathes Steve, she lets him make love to her when she learns that Allen has married; thus Ernie's plan has worked out.
589, 599, 601–603

Mose, Unc. Old Negro man who helps take care of Blair's horses.
587

Van Dyming. Man mentioned by Ernie as being interested in buying Gawtrey's fine horse, a horse that does not exist.
600

PENNSYLVANIA STATION

Gihon, Danny. Young hoodlum who as one of his many crimes forges a note whereby he collects $130 from Mr. Pinckski which Danny's mother has paid on her coffin. Though he is too busy to attend his mother's funeral, Danny sends a $200 wreath.
610–612, 614, 615, 617–625

Gihon, Mrs. Margaret Noonan. Danny's mother, an old charwoman who buys her coffin at the rate of 50 cents a week. Though she cannot write, she says she wrote the note that Danny had forged to collect her coffin money. This act of Danny's hastens her death.
615, 622, 623

Pinckski. Man who sells a coffin to Mrs. Gihon at the rate of 50 cents a week.
612–618, 620, 622, 623

Zilich, Mrs. Sophie. Neighbor and friend of Mrs. Gihon.
617, 618, 620–624

ARTIST AT HOME

Blair, John. A poet, house guest of the Howes. After he falls in love with Anne Howe, he refuses to enter the house again, spending a night in the rain. After he has left, Howe sells a good poem of Blair's, but by then the unhappy poet is dead.
629, 642–645

Crain, Mrs. Wife of Amos.
631, 645, 646

Crain, Amos. Farmer neighbor of the Howes.
631, 632, 638, 640, 644

Howes, Anne. Roger's wife, who for a time thinks she may be in love with Blair. She soon realizes she is not and asks Roger to take her back.
628–630, 632, 636–645

Howes, Roger. A successful novelist who is resting on his laurels until Blair upsets the quiet of his home. The ensuing excitement inspires him to write a novel about the poet and Mrs. Howes. The novel is good, and the Howes renew their happiness in each other.
627–630, 632, 634–646

Pinkie. The Howes's Negro cook.
630, 632–634, 640, 641

THE BROOCH

Boyd. Howard's father. He leaves home six months after Howard's birth.
647

Boyd, Mrs. Cold, ruthless woman who, though paralyzed, dominates her son's life and wrecks his marriage.
651–653, 656, 657, 662

MY GRANDMOTHER MILLARD AND GENERAL BEDFORD FORREST AND THE BATTLE OF HARRYKIN CREEK

three months until his anger subsides. Then he organizes a cavalry troop for General Forrest's command and returns to the war.
684, 697

Snopes, Ab. Self-styled independent horse-captain with Colonel Sartoris. He steals horses wherever he can get them.
673–677, 679, 681–686, 688, 693

GOLDEN LAND

Ewing, Ira, Jr. California businessman. At fourteen, lacking the fortitude of his parents, he fled his bleak Nebraska home town. At forty-eight he is a wealthy realtor in Beverly Hills, California, drinking heavily to escape the life he now has: his wife and he are enemies, and their two children are tragic failures. Consequently, he comes closest to happiness when with his mistress, a wise woman who seems to love him sincerely. Also he takes comfort in the belief that he has made his widowed mother happy, having installed her in a good house in Glendale, all bills paid, where he visits her each day.
702, 707, 709–711, 715, 716, 718, 722–724

Ewing, Ira, Sr. Strong pioneer with the will to endure. He wrenched a living from the pitiless Nebraska soil and had a town named after him.
702, 704, 712, 724

Ewing, Samantha (April Lalear). Daughter of Ira, Jr. She is an extra in motion pictures, who in her campaign to become a star, has followed a sordid path and has just made the headlines as one of the three principals in a charge involving sexual orgies. (April Lalear is her professional name.)
705, 706, 708, 711, 713–715, 721, 722

Ewing, Mrs. Samantha. Widowed mother of Ira, Jr. Having been denied the solace of her grandchildren by a hostile daughter-in-law, Samantha lives an empty, albeit secure life, alone in the house

Ira, Jr., had formerly occupied with his wife and two children; and she secretly nurses a desire to return to Nebraska. When her son finally learns of this desire, it is incomprehensible to him that she should want to go back to stark Ewing, Nebraska. As he sees it, if she went back there, "the first month of winter would kill her." Consequently, Samantha, though all her bills are paid by Ira, cannot raise the few dollars she needs to take her "back home." She is trapped in Glendale, California, the Golden Land, where, she muses, "I will stay . . . and live forever."

> 707, 721

Ewing, Voyd. Effeminate son of Ira, Jr. He hates his father.

> 705–707, 709

Kazimura. Japanese gardener of Mrs. Samantha Ewing. By showing her the newspapers, he thwarts, consciously or not, Ira's efforts to keep his mother ignorant of the sordid details surrounding her granddaughter's attempts to become a movie star.

> 712

THERE WAS A QUEEN

Caspey. Elnora's husband, in prison for stealing.

> 727

* *Du Pre, Mrs. Virginia (Miss Jenny; Aunt Jenny).* Ninety-year-old sister of Colonel John Sartoris, she lives with Narcissa Sartoris and son. Shortly after hearing of Narcissa's rendezvous in Memphis, she is found dead in her wheel chair.

> 727–729, 732–734, 742, 743

Elnora. Cook for the Sartoris family. Though she does not know it, she is the daughter of Colonel John Sartoris by a Negro slave.

> 727–734, 743, 744

Isom. Elnora's son.

> 728, 731–734, 737, 743

Joby. Elnora's son, now living in high style on Beale Street in Memphis.
727

Saddie. Elnora's daughter, who takes care of Miss Jenny Du Pre.
728, 729, 731, 737, 743

Sartoris, Bayard (old). Son of Colonel John.
727, 735, 736, 739

Sartoris, Bayard (young). Husband of Narcissa. He was killed in an airplane crash shortly after their marriage.
727, 728, 730, 734–736, 739

Sartoris, Benbow (Bory). Son of Narcissa and young Bayard.
728, 729, 734, 740–742

Sartoris, John. Son of old Bayard.
727, 734

Sartoris, Colonel John. Famous Civil War officer and railroad builder. He was Miss Jenny Du Pre's brother.
727, 732–734

Sartoris, Johnny. Twin brother of young Bayard. He was killed in France in World War I.
728, 735

Sartoris, Narcissa Benbow. Widow of young Bayard and mother of Bory. She keeps a rendezvous in a Memphis hotel with a Jewish federal agent to recover certain letters which he legally has in his possession—obscene mash notes written to her years before by an anonymous admirer.
727–730, 732, 733, 735–737, 740, 743

Simon. Colonel John Sartoris' Negro servant, now deceased. He was the husband of Elnora's mother.
727

MOUNTAIN VICTORY

Hule. Young boy who tries to save Weddel's life. He is Vatch's brother.
764, 765, 772

Jubal. Weddel's Negro servant and companion.
764, 769, 771

Vatch. Mountain youth whose primitive hatred for Confederate soldiers drives him to ambush Weddel and Jubal. He accidentally kills Hule, his brother.
749–751, 756, 758–763, 766–770, 774, 777

Vidal, François. French émigré, general of Napoleon, father of Francis Weddel.
759

Weddel, Francis. Choctaw chief, one-half French, father of Saucier.
755, 759

Weddel, Major Saucier (Soshay). A Confederate major, one-quarter Indian, on the way to his Mississippi home after the Civil War. He and his body servant Jubal seek shelter with a mountain family. Though warned to leave at once, he remains until dawn because Jubal is too drunk to ride before that time. When the Major does depart he is ambushed and killed by Vatch despite efforts on the part of Hule and his sister to save him. The sister is in love with Saucier, and her brother Hule had hoped that Saucier would marry her.
746–754, 756–762, 764–777

BEYOND

Allison, Howard. The Judge's son, killed at the age of ten while riding his pony.
794, 796

Allison, Sophia. The Judge's tenderhearted mother. She died long ago.
790

Chlory. Judge Allison's Negro cook.
782, 783

Jake. Judge Allison's Negro gardener.
782, 783, 797

Mothershed. Man with whom Judge Allison talks in The Beyond.
785–788, 791, 796

* *Peabody, Lucius.* Doctor in attendance on Judge Allison. As the Judge is dying, he goes in spirit to The Beyond to find out about immortality.
781, 782

Pettigrew. Judge Allison's lawyer or executor.
796, 797

BLACK MUSIC

Carter. Architect for whom Midgleston worked.
809, 810

Harris, Elmer. Chief of Police on the Van Dyming case.
819

Midgleston, Mrs. Martha. Wilfred's wife, who, when Wilfred is said to be dead, becomes the recipient of Wilfred's insurance money, a large sum, and soon remarries.
804, 810, 819, 821

Midgleston, Wilfred. Architect's draughtsman who has a strange experience, probably under the influence of liquor, in which he believes himself to be a faun. Deluded, he chases the wealthy Mrs. Van Dyming and then disappears in a nearby wood. Believed dead,

Midgleston gets some attention in the newspapers, and he proudly sends the articles anonymously to his wife, thinking she will be pleased by the publicity. Since that time he has been living in total poverty in a Latin-American country.

799, 802, 806, 819, 820

Van Dyming, Carleton. A wealthy man who, to gratify his wife, agrees to finance the construction of various buildings, including a theatre in the ancient Grecian manner.

807–809, 816, 818, 819

Van Dyming, Mrs. Carleton (Mattie). Van Dyming's wife, born Mathilda Lumpkin. In the sylvan setting of the Carleton estate she is pursued by a nearly nude man armed with a knife (really a tin whistle) and by a bull.

807–809, 816–819

Widrington. Manager of the company that owns the house in whose attic Midgleston sleeps.

803

* *Widrington, Mrs.* The manager's wife. She gives Midgleston permission to sleep in the attic over the cantina.

803

THE LEG

Davy. Young American friend and Oxford classmate of George. Soon after George's death in World War I Davy has a leg amputated. In his ether dream and in subsequent dreams he begs George, whose apparition appears to him several times, to find his leg and make sure that it is dead. After Jotham Rust, Corinthia's brother, has attempted to kill Davy, the padre from Poperinghe gives Davy a picture found among Jotham's personal effects. It is a picture of Davy which was taken *outside* the hospital during the very time Davy was a patient *inside* the hospital talking to George's apparition. There is about it "a quality vicious and outrageous and unappalled"; it is inscribed "To Everbe Corinthia" followed by an unprintable phrase.

824, 826–828, 833, 834

George. British classmate of Davy at Oxford. George is very fond of Corinthia from the early days. He is killed within a year after the war begins.

823–827, 829, 830, 832–835, 841

Rust, Corinthia (Everbe). Daughter of Simon. She helps her father manage the boat lock on the Thames. Here she meets Davy and George, the latter boyishly enamored of her. Some time after, during World War I, just after George has been killed and Davy has had a leg amputated, Corinthia keeps nocturnal rendezvous with some being who has a singular laugh. On one occasion Corinthia disappears from home, reappearing some hours later, unconscious. When her senses return, she screams hysterically and soon dies, apparently of fear.

823–825, 828, 835–839, 841

Rust, Jotham. Brother of Corinthia. He notes her strange behavior and follows her when she, as if under a spell, makes one of her nocturnal trips to the nearby Thames. Jotham hears a weird laugh and notes that a punt he had seen seconds before has disappeared. When Corinthia dies in hysteria, Jotham deserts his regiment to locate the owner of the satanic laugh. At length he attempts to stab Davy while Davy is asleep, but trips over Davy's wooden leg, which leans by the bedside, and is captured before he can harm Davy. Found guilty of desertion in wartime and of attempted murder, Jotham is executed. Before his death he gives the padre from Poperinghe certain personal belongings which he charges the padre to destroy. Among these effects is a strange photograph of Davy (*see* Davy).

835–838, 840, 841

Rust, Simon. Father of Corinthia and Jotham. Simon's death, of which he has intimations, closely follows that of Corinthia.

824–826, 828, 835, 836, 838–840

Samuel (Sam'l). Man who helps Davy when George falls from the boat.
825

MISTRAL

Calvacanti. Family name of Giulio's aunt, keeper of a wineshop where Don and the narrator have some drinks.
870, 875

Don. An American youth who with his friend, the narrator, also a young American, finds himself in a tiny Italian village during the sad mistral season. The two youths are much concerned with the situation surrounding an old priest who is undergoing spiritual torture because of his physical interest in his ward, a wild young girl. The girl's lover, Giulio, had been drafted into the army unexpectedly, and the priest had arranged a betrothal between her and a rich man. The wedding is put off for three years and, when it is finally to take place just prior to Giulio's return, the rich man dies suddenly, apparently of poison.
843–875

Farinzale, Giulio. Young sweetheart of the priest's ward, Giulio finds himself unexpectedly drafted into the army. He returns to the village on the day Don and the narrator are there, however, and meets the young girl, who has apparently been awaiting him.
848, 849, 851

DIVORCE IN NAPLES

Carl. Eighteen-year-old messboy aboard a merchant ship. He loses his virginity in Naples and, knowing George will disapprove, he is hesitant about returning to the ship.
877–880, 882–890, 892

George. Greek cook aboard the merchantman. He feels responsible for Carl's virginity and is considerably upset when Carl, with whom

he maintains an attachment with homosexual overtones, loses it in Naples.
877–890, 892

Monckton. One of the crew aboard the merchantman.
877, 879, 881, 882, 886, 889, 890

CARCASSONNE

Luis. Operator of the cantina in whose dark attic lives a lonely pauper. (In "Black Music" the pauper's name is Wilfred Midgleston.) The pauper's bed is the floor and a strip of tarred roofing-paper; his companions are numerous rats. Despite these sordid surroundings this man's spirit is often free and ranges the skies, seeking to create.
897

* *Widdrington, Mrs.* Wife of the manager of the Standard Oil Company, owner of the cantina building. She believes that if a man is white and does not work, he is either a tramp or a poet. It is she who permits the pauper to use the attic; perhaps it is her belief that inspires him to want to create.
897, 898

BIG WOODS (1955)

(*Big Woods* contains four hunting stories, each introduced by a prelude, and an epilogue. Only two of these stories, "A Bear Hunt" and "Race at Morning," are included in the section that follows. The other two are found elsewhere in the Guide: for "The Bear" and "The Old People" see *Go Down, Moses*. [The prelude to "The Bear" is reprinted from pp. 101–105 of *Requiem for a Nun*; the prelude to "The Old People" is a revised part of "Red Leaves," from *Collected Stories*; the prelude to "A Bear Hunt" is a revised part of "A Justice," from *Collected Stories*; and the prelude to "Race at Morning" is a revised part of "Mississippi," from *Holiday*, April, 1954. The epilogue is a revised part of "Delta Autumn," from *Go Down, Moses*.])

A BEAR HUNT

Basket, John. Leader of the Indians who frighten Luke Hogganbeck into losing his hiccups.
> *155, 156, 158, 162*

Compson, General. A member of old Major de Spain's hunting club.
> *145*

de Spain, Major (old). Father of the present Major de Spain and host of the original hunting club. He and McCaslin Edmonds supported Boon Hogganbeck all of his life.
> *145, 147*

✳ *de Spain, Major* (young). Present host of the hunting camp. He is a banker who helps support the family of the improvident Lucius Hogganbeck.
> *145, 146, 147, 149, 161*

de Spain, Mrs. Wife of young Major de Spain.
> *145*

Edmonds, McCaslin. A member of old Major de Spain's hunting club. He helped de Spain support Boon Hogganbeck, father of Lucius.
145, 147

Ewell, Walter. A member of old Major de Spain's hunting club.
145

Fraser. One of young de Spain's hunting club.
158

Hogganbeck, Mrs. Wife of Lucius. She helps support her family by sewing.
146

Hogganbeck, Boon. Loyal man-Friday of old Major de Spain's hunting club and the father of Lucius.
145, 147

Hogganbeck, Lucius (Luke). Formerly one of the wild Provine gang, now tamed by the years. At Ratliff's suggestion he goes to a nearby Indian camp seeking relief for his hiccups. The Indians cure him by frightening him so badly that he beats Ratliff in retaliation. (During his youthful days he was called "The Butch.")
145–147, 149–153, 156, 159–164

McCaslin, Uncle Isaac. A member of old Major de Spain's hunting club. He is the only living member of that group and still hunts with young de Spain's club.
145, 152, 153, 158

Provine. Family name of the two brothers who once led a wild gang of which Luke Hogganbeck was an outstanding member.
146, 147

Ratliff. Ubiquitous sewing-machine agent. He is beaten by Luke Hogganbeck for advising him to go to the nearby Indians for relief from his hiccups. Ratliff is the narrator of this incident.
145, 147, 149, 157

RACE AT MORNING

NEW ORLEANS SKETCHES (1958)

FRANKIE AND JOHNNY

(The only one of the eleven short sketches originally published under the title "New Orleans" [*Double Dealer*, VII (January-February 1925), 102–107] which has named characters.)

Johnny. Young tough who protects the girl, Frankie, from a drunken bum and then falls tenderly in love with her.
  40, 41

Ryan. Policeman who described Johnny as a "young tough."
  40

MIRRORS OF CHARTRES STREET

Ed. Probably the name of the one-legged drunk. When the policeman arrests him, Ed speaks eloquently in his own defense.
  56

DAMON AND PYTHIAS UNLIMITED

Iowa. Apparently a friend of the narrator.
  61

McNamara. A consumptive youth at the New Orleans racetrack. He is introduced by Morowitz as his cousin, who will give tips on the races in return for a little donation to a jockey friend of theirs who is in the hospital. Because they fall to quarreling between themselves, they lose all chances of gaining at the stranger's expense.
  67

Morowitz. A self-appointed guide of gentlemanly pretenses despite his poor appearance. He takes the stranger in New Orleans to the racetrack and there, with the aid of McNamara, attempts to trick the visitor out of some money. Individual greed causes Morowitz and McNamara to quarrel as they vie for the stranger's favor and thus they lose all they stood to gain as a team.

    63

HOME

General, the. One of the friends to whom Jean-Baptiste has promised aid in a crime.

    74, 77, 78

Jean-Baptiste. An immigrant. He struggles within himself as to whether or not he will keep his word to certain friends and aid them in a crime. Hearing a familiar melody of his childhood played on a musical saw by a street musician, he decides to stay within the law even though he remains poor. Pete and the General will not find him waiting when they come for him.

    73, 75, 77, 79

Pete. A friend of Jean-Baptiste. Pete and others are about to perpetrate a crime with the special aid of Jean-Baptiste.

    74, 76–78

Tony the Wop. One of the men about to perpetrate a crime with Jean-Baptiste.

    74, 76, 78

JEALOUSY

Antonio (Tono). Italian restaurant owner violently jealous of his pretty young wife. He accidentally shoots to death a young waiter with whom he has recently quarreled.

    83, 84

CHEEST

Potter, Jack. A jockey. He steals his girl-friend's garter to wear for good luck in his next race. He wins over the favored horse, and his boss asks for a contract with his girl so she can provide garters for all of his riders.

94

OUT OF NAZARETH

Spratling. An artist. Impressed by the features of a seventeen-year-old boy, he attempts to hire him as a model. The boy, homeless, jobless, has, nevertheless, the independence of youthful illusion and believes in the freedom of innocent vagabondage; consequently he will not promise to keep an appointment with Spratling, even though the latter is willing to pay him well.

101, 102, 104, 105, 110

THE KINGDOM OF GOD

Jake. Man mentioned by the idiot's brother as owner of a place where the idiot could not be left that day. The brother of the idiot and his partner are arrested for delivering whisky because the partner shakes the poor idiot, and the latter's brother attacks the partner, thus attracting the attention of two policemen, who subsequently discover two sacks of illicit whisky in the partners' truck.

114

THE ROSARY

Harris. Man who hates two things: his neighbor Juan Venturia and a song called "The Rosary." Harris dies of pneumonia and by his death robs Juan of his greatest joy, that of plaguing Harris.

123–128

Venturia, Juan. A shopkeeper who lives for his hatred of his neighbor Harris. Knowing how Harris loathes "The Rosary," Venturia plays under Harris' window a horrible rendition of "The Rosary" on a saxophone that he has just bought for that purpose. Perhaps Harris has the last laugh, however, for he has just died of pneumonia; and only he would have been able to recognize Juan's solo as being "The Rosary."
123–128

THE COBBLER

There are no named characters in this sketch. It is the story of an ancient cobbler who, when he was young, lost his sweetheart to a wealthy man. Now he cannot remember details very well.

CHANCE

There are no named characters in this sketch. It is the story of a pretentious beggar who wins $1,000 and soon loses it through his foolishness.

SUNSET

Bob (Mist' Bob). Employer and landlord, probably, of a Negro who tries to go to Africa. After paying $4 to a white man for a boat ride, the Negro is put off at a place that he is told is Africa. Fearful of the new country, he shoots what he thinks is a lion. In the chase that follows, he, thinking he is beset by wild African natives, kills two other men, one a Negro. At last he is killed by his pursuers.
149, 155, 157

Wallace, Captain. Leader of a detachment of soldiers. They track the Negro killer down and shoot him.
147

THE KID LEARNS

Gray, Johnny. A young mobster. A girl causes him to cross the Wop, his more experienced rival, before he is ready. This circumstance results in Johnny's death.
161–164, 166, 167

Mary. The girl Johnny rescues from the Wop.
167

Otto. Johnny's friend. He advises Johnny to wait until he is more experienced before trying the Wop's power.
161, 162, 164, 165

Ryan. A policeman who has known Johnny a long time. It is to Ryan's house that Johnny takes Mary after he has rescued her from the Wop.
165

Ryan, Mrs. Ryan's wife.
165, 166

Wop, the. A reigning mobster. When he attempts to force his attentions on Mary, Johnny interferes.
162–165

THE LIAR

Ek. A great yarn-spinner. One of his intended lies turns out to be the truth in that it describes the actions of a murderer so well that the murderer, who is one of Ek's audience, shoots Ek and flees.
173–177, 181, 183, 184

Gibson, Will. Owner of the store where the loafers gather to hear Ek's stories.
171, 173, 174, 177, 181, 183, 184

Haley, Lem. Owner of some big dogs that were used to tree Ek when, in his youth, Ek ran wild because his father tried to make him wear shoes.
176

Harmon, Mrs. Owner of the house through which Mitchell's scared horse ran.
173

Lafe. One of the loafers at Gibson's store.
176, 177, 183

Mitchell. Resident of a country town that bears his name. Once, some hill people who had just seen their first train were so frightened that they tore into Mitchell's horse and buggy and caused the horse to run away.
172

Rogers, Ken. Sheriff in the town of Mitchell.
175

Simpson. Family name of some boys who make whisky.
174

Starnes, Mrs. Hill woman who is leaving her husband to go with another man.
177

Starnes, Joe. A farmer in the hill country. He surprises his wife and her lover together. The men then fight and Joe is knocked unconscious. At this time his opponent completes his original plan: to have Joe bitten by a rattlesnake.
177–179

Tim. Sheriff's deputy.
177, 178, 180, 181

EPISODE

Joe. Aged, blind beggar. He and his old wife pose for an artist friend of the narrator, who is a writer. After the artist has completed his picture of the old blind beggar and his wife, he and the writer see that the woman's face has exactly the same expression as the Mona Lisa.
  8–9

COUNTRY MICE

Gilman. Airplane owner and pilot. He and his twin brother, the deputy, and their father, a country Justice of the Peace, not only foil the efforts of three bootleggers to deliver whisky to New Haven but make a large sum of money as well.
  205–207

Gus. Brother of the narrator. Both are bootleggers who are outwitted by a country Justice of the Peace and his two sons.
  198, 201, 204–207

Joe. A partner in the bootlegging venture. He and his associates regard Gilman and his family as "hicks" until they find themselves completely outmaneuvered.
  201, 202, 205–207

YO HO AND TWO BOTTLES OF RUM

Ayers, Freddie. Mate aboard the *Diana,* a steamer sailing Eastern waters which is officered by British and manned by Chinese. Mr. Ayers, a violent man, accidentally kills Yo Ho, a Chinese messboy, with a blow intended for the boatswain, whose skull is harder than that of Yo Ho. The mate remains untouched by his deed until the Chinese insist that Yo Ho be buried on land. The mate's blustering

does not alter their stand; consequently the ship spends several days making land while the corpse rapidly decomposes in the hot weather near the equator. Mr. Ayers begins to repent his deed. On land at last, Ayers and the other white men who accompany the burial party drink the whisky that was to be put in the grave with Yo Ho and resolve to get more liquor by killing other Chinese. Instantly the Chinese disappear and so does the corpse. The white men return to the beach, frightened, there to find the crewmen waiting and the cart that had contained the body of Yo Ho empty. The Oriental has triumphed over the "superior" white man.
213–223

Bucky. A name uttered by the drunken chief engineer. It is his nickname for Ayers or for one of the other officers.
221

Yo Ho. Chinese messboy aboard the *Diana*. He is accidentally killed by Mr. Ayers, the mate.
214–220

Appendix

CHARACTERS HANDLED
INCONSISTENTLY

Armstid. The Armstid of *As I Lay Dying* and *Light in August* is quite different from the Henry Armstid of the Snopes trilogy. To begin with, the wife of Armstid in *As I Lay Dying* is named Lula; in *The Hamlet* (and in *Light in August*) she is named Martha. The Armstid of the Snopes trilogy is a bitter man, greedy and ruthless, who finally goes mad seeking buried money on the worthless land Flem Snopes tricks him and his two partners into buying. In the other novels Armstid is a kindly and helpful man. Further, since *The Hamlet* is set some thirty years earlier than *Light in August*, the Henry Armstid of the former novel, confined, as he was, to an asylum, can hardly be identified with the later Armstid.

Beauchamp, James Thucydus (*Tennie's Jim*). In "The Fire and the Hearth" Jim runs away from home "before he became of age." In "The Bear" he "*Vanished sometime on night of his twenty-first birthday.*"

Beauchamp, Tomey's Turl. The contemporary character of this name in *The Town* should not be confused with the older Tomey's Turl, a McCaslin slave.

Benbow, Horace. Although Horace as a character is treated consistently wherever he appears, it is obvious that he is an early sketch of Gavin Stevens. Both have similar educational backgrounds and World War I experiences. Both took a Snopes to Europe to serve in the YMCA. Benbow disappears after *Sanctuary* (except for mention of the family name), and Stevens, a more complex character, emerges beginning with *Light in August*.

Compson, Benjy. In the Appendix to *The Sound and the Fury*, which Faulkner prepared for the Viking Press *Portable Faulkner*, Benjy is disposed of by Jason Compson, who sends him to the insane asylum in 1933 when their mother, Caroline Bascomb Compson, dies. In *The Mansion,* however, Mrs. Compson is revivified, and her persistent whining forces Jason to take Benjy home from the asylum. Consequently, some time later, Benjy, who has always loved fire, sets fire to the Compson house and perishes in the blaze.

Compson, Mrs. Caroline Bascomb. In the Appendix to *The Sound and the Fury* Mrs. Compson dies in 1933; but according to accounts in *The Mansion* she lives longer, and forces Jason to bring Benjy home from the asylum.

Compson, Quentin [*Maclachan*]. In *The Mansion* it is he who receives the original land grant from Mohataha. In the Appendix to *The Sound and the Fury* Jason Lycurgus Compson procures the land.

Cook, Celia. The girl who scratched her name on a window in *The Unvanquished* is named Cecilia Farmer in *Requiem for a Nun.*

de Spain (sometimes De Spain). Although this family is described with fair consistency, a de Spain said to be the son of old Major de Spain appears in the story "A Bear Hunt." He is clearly not Manfred de Spain (who is a bachelor), though he may be consistent with still another de Spain, the central character in the short story "Shall Not Perish."

Doom. See Ikkemotubbe.

Du Pre, Mrs. Virginia. The sister of Colonel John Sartoris, she is called by a variety of different names in the works. The most serious variations occur in "All the Dead Pilots," in which she is called Virginia Sartoris (her maiden name), and in *Requiem for a Nun,* in which she is called Mrs. Depre. Further, in *The Town* she is called old Bayard's sister, though she is his aunt.

Edmonds, Carothers (*Roth*). Though he is the son of Zachary Edmonds, in *The Town* he is called the son of McCaslin Edmonds, who is, elsewhere, his grandfather.

Edmonds, McCaslin (Cass). In "The Fire and the Hearth," from *Go Down, Moses,* Cass wrests the McCaslin land away from Ike McCaslin. In "The Bear" Ike relinquishes it to Cass, who accepts it unwillingly. Further, in "The Fire and the Hearth" Ike is paid $50 monthly. In "The Bear" the sum is $30 monthly.

Farmer, Cecilia. See Cook, Celia.

Fathers, Sam (originally Had-Two-Fathers). In "A Justice" Sam Fathers is the son of Crawfishford, the Indian who visits the Negro slave woman, later Sam's mother, while her husband works in the fields. In *Go Down, Moses* Sam is the son of the Chickasaw chieftain Ikkemotubbe, and derives from his father the stately dignity of his character.

Had-Two-Fathers. See Fathers, Sam.

Hampton. The sheriff who is called Hope in *Intruder in the Dust* and Hubert (Hub) in *The Town* and elsewhere.

Houston. This Frenchman's Bend farmer is called Jack in *The Hamlet* and *The Mansion,* and Zack in *The Town.* In *The Hamlet* he marries Lucy Pate. In *The Town* his wife is named Letty Bookwright Houston.

Ikkemotubbe (Doom). Usually the nephew of the Chickasaw chieftain Issetibbeha. He becomes chieftain after Issetibbeha's sudden death and the abdication of Issetibbeha's son Moketubbe. In an early story, "Red Leaves," the relationships among the Indians are quite different from the relationships that are fairly consistent thereafter. In "Red Leaves" Ikkemotubbe is Issetibbeha's father and Moketubbe's grandfather. In "The Bear" he is said to be the son of Issetibbeha.

Issetibbeha. See Ikkemotubbe.

Joby. He is called Simon Strother's grandfather in *Sartoris.* In *The Unvanquished* he is Simon's father.

MacCallum. Name of a family introduced in *Sartoris.* Often spelled McCallum in later works.

MacGowan, Skeet (*s*). The lecherous drugstore clerk in *As I Lay Dying* has his name spelled McGowan in later works.

MacKenzie, Shrevlin (*Shreve*). This Canadian, Quentin Compson's roommate at Harvard named in the Appendix to *The Sound and the Fury,* is named Shreve McCannon in *Absalom, Absalom!*

Moketubbe. See Ikkemotubbe.

Peabody, Dr. The country doctor of this name in *As I Lay Dying, Sartoris,* and other works cannot be the same Dr. Peabody who is already an adult in the historical interchapters of *Requiem for a Nun* set in the 1830's, unless his age is ignored.

Quick. In *As I Lay Dying* there are two Lon (Solon?) Quicks, father and son. Later, in *The Hamlet,* there is an Uncle Ben Quick, who raises goats, and a Lon Quick who owns a sawmill. But in *Knight's Gambit* Ben Quick owns a sawmill and has a son, Isham, whose description tallies with Lon Quick of *The Hamlet.*

Redlaw. In *Sartoris* Redlaw, Colonel John Sartoris' partner, is the man who murders the Colonel. In *The Unvanquished* and elsewhere he is called Redmond.

Redmond. See Redlaw.

Sartoris, Mrs. Virginia. See Du Pre.

Simon. See Joby.

Snopes, Byron. In *The Town* Byron obtains a medical discharge by taping a plug of tobacco under his armpit to speed up his heartbeat. In *Sartoris* Montgomery Ward Snopes evades the draft by using the same technique.

Snopes, Montgomery Ward. In *Sartoris* Monty goes abroad to serve in the YMCA with Horace Benbow. In *The Town* he goes with Gavin Stevens.

Stevens, Gavin. See Benbow, Horace.

Stevens, Gowan. He is called Gavin Stevens' cousin in *The Town.* In *Requiem for a Nun* he is Gavin's nephew.

Strother, Simon. See Joby.

Suratt. The itinerant sewing-machine salesman in *Sartoris* and *As I Lay Dying* is named Suratt. In later works, this character is named Ratliff.

Widrington. This name in "Black Music" is spelled Widdrington in "Carcassonne."

Zsettlani, Piotr (Pierre Bouc). In *A Fable* Zsettlani is clearly a St. Peter figure. He denies the Corporal (Christ) and later tries to

rejoin him and the other apostles. The Judas figure in the novel is Polcheck—the man who betrays the others. At the end of the novel, however, a man appears at the house of the Marys who is identified only with the question "You are Zsettlani?" This stranger, never clearly identified, tries to pay for his food; the price, thirty coins, is mentioned. The general suggestion is that the visitor is a Judas figure. However, the mention of Zsettlani and the absence of any mention of Polcheck works a disturbing confusion, not easily resolved.

Genealogical Charts

THE McCASLIN-EDMONDS-BEAUCHAMP FAMILY

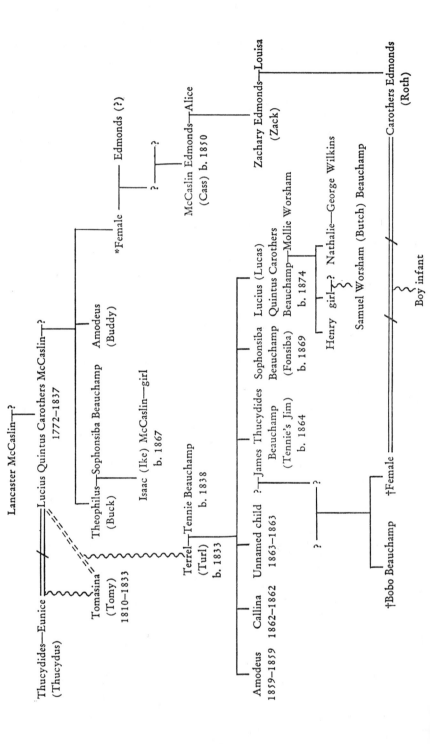

≠ denotes an illicit relationship.

==== denotes an incestuous relationship.

∿∿∿ denotes the issue of an illicit or incestuous relationship.

* It is not clear whether this McCaslin married an Edmonds, or whether she had a daughter who did so.

† Grandchildren of Tennie's Jim.

[Ned William McCaslin (b. 1860) is said to be the son of a slave daughter of Lucius Quintus Carothers McCaslin.]

See also Thomas J. Wertenbaker, Jr., "Faulkner's Point of View and the Chronicle of Ike McCaslin," *College English*, XXIV (1962), 169–178.

THE SARTORIS FAMILY

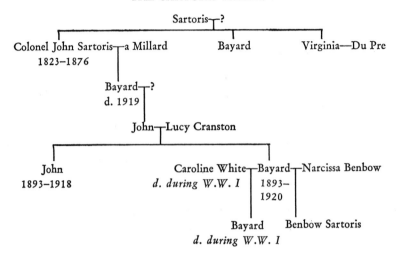

Sartoris—?

Colonel John Sartoris—a Millard   Bayard   Virginia—Du Pre
1823–1876

Bayard—?
d. 1919

John—Lucy Cranston

John   Caroline White—Bayard—Narcissa Benbow
1893–1918   d. during W.W. I   1893–
                                            1920

                        Bayard   Benbow Sartoris
                      d. during W.W. I

THE BURDEN FAMILY

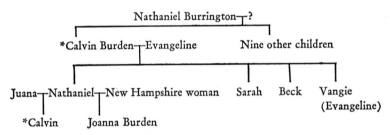

Nathaniel Burrington—?

*Calvin Burden—Evangeline   Nine other children

Juana—Nathaniel—New Hampshire woman   Sarah Beck Vangie
                                                     (Evangeline)
*Calvin   Joanna Burden

* Killed by Colonel John Sartoris for attempting to introduce Negro voting in Jefferson.

Master Index of Characters

MASTER INDEX OF CHARACTERS

Callicoat, David
  "A Justice" 270
Callie, "Aunt"
  Reivers 206
Calvacanti
  "Mistral" 293
Canova, Signor
  Knight's Gambit 133
Carl
  "Divorce in Naples" 293
Carruthers, Miss
  Light in August 70
Carter
  "Black Music" 290
Caspey see Strother, Caspey
  "There Was a Queen" 287
Casse-tête
  Fable 149
Cayley, Miss
  Knight's Gambit 134
Cayley, Hence
  Knight's Gambit 134
Chance, Vic
  Pylon 78
Charley
  Light in August 70
Charley
  Reivers 206
Charley, Uncle
  "Dr. Martino" 280
Charlie
  Sound & F 29
Chlory
  "Beyond" 290
Christian, Mrs.
  "Uncle Willy" 265
Christian, Walter
  Town 158
Christian, Uncle Willy
  Town 159
  Mansion 180
  Reivers 206
  "Uncle Willy" 265
Christmas, Joe see McEachern, Joe
  Light in August 70
Church, Mrs.
  "That Will Be Fine" 266

Cinthy
  Light in August 71
Clapp, Walter
  Reivers 206
Clay, Sis Beulah
  Sound & F 29
Clefus
  Town 159
Clytemnestra
  Absalom 86
Cofer
  Wild Palms 103
Colbert, David
  "A Courtship" 271
Coldfield
  Sound & F (appendix) 41
  Requiem 142
Coldfield, Goodhue
  Absalom 86
Coldfield, Rosa
  Absalom 87
Coleman, Mrs.
  Soldier's Pay 3
Collier
  "Turnabout" 276
Collyer
  Fable 149
Compson
  Requiem 142
Compson, General ix
  Sound & F (appendix) 40
  Absalom 88
  Unvanquished 95
  Intruder 124
  Requiem 142
  Town 159
  Reivers 206
  "Old People" 242
  "Bear" 246
  "Delta Autumn" 250
  "My Grandmother Millard" 284
  "Bear Hunt" 295
Compson, Mrs.
  Unvanquished 95
Compson, Mrs.
  Town 159
  "My Grandmother Millard" 284

Freeman, Mrs.
Hamlet 111
Frony
Sound & F 32
Sound & F (appendix) 49
"That Evening Sun" 269
Frost, Mark
Mosquitoes 11

Gabe
Reivers 208
Gambrell, C. L.
Knight's Gambit 135
Gant, Mrs.
"Miss Zilphia Gant" 234
Gant, Jim
"Miss Zilphia Gant" 234
Gant, Zilphia
"Miss Zilphia Gant" 234
Gargne
Fable 150
Gargne, Mme.
Fable 150
Garraway
Town 161
Gary, Dr.
Soldier's Pay 4
Gatewood, Jabbo
Town 161
Gatewood, Uncle Noon
Town 161
Gauldres, Capt.
Knight's Gambit 135
Gawtrey, Steve
"Fox Hunt" 282
Gene
Sanctuary 60
General, the
"Home" 299
George
Hamlet 111
George
"That Will Be Fine" 267
George
"The Leg" 292
George
"Divorce in Naples" 293

Georgie
"That Will Be Fine" 267
Gibson, Dilsey *see* Dilsey
Sound & F 32
Gibson, Roskus *see* Roskus
Sound & F 33
Gibson, T. P. *see also* T. P.
Sound & F 33
Gibson, Versh
Sound & F 33
Gibson, Will
"The Liar" 302
Gihon
Mansion 182
Gihon, Danny
"Penn. Station" 282
Gihon, Mrs. Margaret Noonan
"Penn. Station" 282
Gillespie
As I Lay Dying 53
Gillespie
Wild Palms 104
Gillespie, Mack
As I Lay Dying 54
Gilligan, Joe
Soldier's Pay 5
Gillman
Light in August 71
Gilman
"Country Mice" 304
Ginotta
Mosquitoes 11
Ginotta, Mrs.
Mosquitoes 11
Ginotta, Joe
Mosquitoes 11
Ginotta, Pete
Mosquitoes 11
Ginsfarb
"Death Drag" 264
Gombault, Uncle Pete
Requiem 142
Town 161
"Tall Men" 258
Goodwin, Lee
Sanctuary 60